'Internal coaching is a key component for any organisation serious about creating a coaching culture. In this fully updated second edition, the authors share insights from research and practice, to set a new standard for those involved with internal coach communities. Well written, informative and an essential addition to your bookshelf.'

Professor Jonathan Passmore, *Henley Business School and Senior Vice President, EZRA Coaching, LHH*

'This indispensable guide delves into the intricacies, challenges, and rewards of internal coaching. It is a true practitioner's handbook, offering invaluable insights, experiences and practical how-to guides. Use this book to plan your approach, engage with stakeholders, develop and sustain your internal coaches for organisational impact. If you are contemplating internal coaching within your organisation, this book is an absolute necessity.'

Judith Barton, *Founder and Director of Coaching and Mentoring, British School of Coaching*

'This 2nd Edition is an invaluable guide for all internal coaches and sponsors of internal coaching services. It brings to life what it is like to be an internal coach with all its rewards, pitfalls and ethical dilemmas. The authors provide an extended range of useful examples and templates, brought up to date for 2025, on how organisations are now approaching the challenge of setting up, supporting and harnessing the power of internal coaching. Essential reading.'

John Leary-Joyce, *CEO, Academy of Executive Coaching*

'Being an Internal Coach can sometimes feel like a lonely place. This book allows you to feel as though you are part of something big; a movement that is having an enormous impact. Looking for multiple perspectives, it is a fantastic guide to all aspects of internal coaching. A must-read for a community that is changing the face of coaching from within the commercial world.'

Clare Walker, *Coaching and Mentoring Lead, Vodafone*

'This fabulous book is an invaluable resource for anyone involved in internal coaching. It offers comprehensive insights into the evolving landscape of internal coaching, addressing both the challenges and opportunities faced by coaches and organisations alike. The practical examples, case studies, and evidence-based approaches make it a must-read for experienced coaches, leaders and those new to the field. Don't run an internal network without it!'

Mike Taylor, *Talent Development, Co-op Group*

'This book is a gift to anyone involved in the complicated and rewarding world of internal coaching. It offers practical, relevant and researched solutions throughout to overcome some of the murkier areas of challenge for internal coaches with updated case studies to unpack the changing landscape of coaching as a practice. It zooms directly into the inner world of the internal coach - how we coach, who we coach and explores and unpicks the foundations of what organisations, teams, coaches, clients and stakeholders all gain from coaching. I love the new additions that highlight the challenges we face to become wiser, more diverse, more ethical, more mindful, more conscious and aware on the path to better serve our clients. I cannot recommend this text highly enough to celebrate and shine light onto the value and contribution that internal coaches make to their organisations and systems. It is also unafraid to illuminate the darkness, shadows and dilemmas faced by them in doing so. Every page you turn has a new, relevant and well-considered offering.'

Cath Brown, *Director of Cath Brown Consultancy Ltd*

'This book is packed full of all things an internal coach needs to know and do to perform at their best and I am delighted to endorse it as an all-encompassing resource. I will be recommending it to all our coaches at the University of Liverpool and members of the EMCC's Internal Coaching Special Interest Group.'

Tracy Ellis, *Lead Coach, University of Liverpool and Lead, Internal Coaching SIG, EMCC UK*

'Internal coaching is one of the most helpful development opportunities that organisations offer. All it touches will reap huge benefits but to make this happen, and do it successfully, is not without its challenges. This book provides a wonderful synthesis of learning from many organisations – there is no need to start from scratch if you are looking to embed coaching in your organisation.'

Amisha Wilde, *Head of Coaching, Network Rail*

'If you're a leader who is passionate about building a coaching culture or you're an internal coach who wants a guide for their work - this book is a must for you. It guides you through building a coaching culture that fits your organisation. It cleverly leads you through the trickier scenarios and ethical considerations that go right to the heart of the work of an internal coach. Brilliant insights that I wish someone had shared with me years ago!'

Catherine Boddington, *Founder, Internal Coach Network*

'The term 'inside story' is an extremely apt way of describing what this book can offer the reader. It normalises the complexities and real challenges associated with internal coaching, whether related to power, diversity, ethics or collaboration.

An excellent array of case studies offers the reader permission to find their own individual approach to internal coaching. I have no doubt that the sharing of this book within any organisation can promote meaningful reflection and purposeful conversations, all in service of people coming together to design, offer and celebrate internal coaching.'

Steven Johnstone, *Director of Learning Solutions, BPP*

'Reading this book is like having a friend who completely understands the challenges we face and offers really insightful ideas. Whether you are building a coaching culture, or you are an internal coach, it's an essential read for the Internal Coaching world, that offers guidance and expands thinking.'

Beth Krucien, *Organisational Development Manager, Veolia*

Praise for the First Edition:

'Finally, a book dedicated to the internal coach. Finally, a handbook for coaches that puts ethics before everything else. It gives me great pleasure to recommend this accessible and inspirational book for everyone engaged in helping conversations inside organisations.'

Erik de Haan, *Director of Centre for Coaching, Ashridge, and Professor of Organisation Development and Coaching, VU University, Amsterdam*

'Highly practical, engaging, and long overdue. This book is an important contribution to a growing area of coaching. The combination of experience, research, practice and theory present in this book make it a must for organisations and practitioners thinking about, or currently running, internal coaching programmes. While targeted towards internal coaching, the wide variety of case examples, insightful commentary, and a willingness to approach difficult issues make this book an important resource for all coaches.'

Dr Michael Cavanagh, *Coaching Psychology Unit, University of Sydney*

'*Internal Coaching* is essential reading for any lead coaches and supervisors looking to protect and build on their organisation's investment in coaching, engage and support internal coaches, and assure ethical and accountable practice. I'm sure many will wish they had had this resource when they first embarked on their journey with coaching.'

Katherine Long, *Director of Development and Supervision, OCM*

Internal Coaching

Internal Coaching: The Inside Story provides a window into the world of internal coaching: the challenges and rewards for the coaches themselves and the ways in which organisations can ensure that they can get the best value for money from their investment in them.

Internal coaching is booming yet there has been surprisingly little written about the unique nature of the internal coaching role. Drawing on the stories of hundreds of internal coaches, coach sponsors, lead coaches, supervisors of internal coaches and coach trainers, this book gives internal coaches a voice. Building on the success of the first edition, this brand-new edition offers an accessibly written mine of information for practitioners and academic researchers alike, incorporating many real-life examples of different practice, provided by internal coaches themselves, plus references to over 180 sources of relevant research.

Whether you're an experienced coach, a leader building a coaching culture within your organisation, or someone just beginning to explore this fascinating field, this book is here to support and inspire you.

Katharine St John-Brooks was a leadership coach for 20 years after a career in the Department for Business & Trade advising Government ministers. The first edition of *Internal Coaching: The Inside Story* was published in 2014 and was followed by chapters on internal coaching in the *Complete Handbook of Coaching* (2018, 2024), *Coaching Supervision: Advancing Practice, Changing Landscapes* (2019) and a contribution to the *Ethical Coaches' Handbook* (2023). Katharine holds an MSc in Organisational Behaviour and an MA in Professional Development (Coaching) and is a fellow of the Institute of Consulting. She founded and has chaired EMCC UK's Third Sector Coaching and Mentoring Forum since 2017 and co-hosted two series of podcasts for the EMCC UK on supervision for internal coaches. She has completed a thriller based on a coach's uneasy relationship with her new client – a recently appointed government minister – and has started writing the second in the series. A long-time humanist, she trained as a non-religious pastoral care volunteer, working in a local hospice, in 2025. Katharine lives in London with her husband, Vivian Bazalgette.

Julia Duncan is a professional and pragmatic coaching supervisor and coach, dedicated to supporting new coaches, coaching practitioners and coaching clients to pursue their aspirations and goals. She is a Fellow of the CIPD and a qualified ILM L7 Coaching Supervisor and ILM L5 Coach. Passionate about professional and personal growth, Julia has trained over 500 internal coaches and provides supervision to internal coaches from all sectors. Her wealth of experience is gained from working internationally in HR and OD leadership roles in the private sector and she is owner of The Development Partnership, a thriving leadership development and coaching business. Julia lives in Southwestern France with husband Chris and Border terrier Bertie and she is a keen acapella singer, cook and gardener.

The Professional Coaching Series

This series brings together leading exponents and researchers in the coaching field to provide a definitive set of core texts important to the development of the profession. It aims to meet two needs - a professional series that provides the core texts that are theoretically and experimentally grounded, and a practice series covering forms of coaching based in evidence. Together they provide a complementary framework to introduce, promote and enhance the development of the coaching profession.

Titles in the series:

The Evidence-Based Practitioner Coach: Understanding the Integrated Experiential Learning Process
By Lloyd Chapman

An Integral Approach to Transformative Leadership: Dancing Through the Storm
By Dorrian Aiken

A Guide to Formulation in Coaching
By David A. Lane, Sarah Corrie and Louise C. Kovács

Coaching Strategies for Corporate Innovation: A Systemic Approach to Coaching Teams and Leaders
Ivan Yong, Sam Lee

Internal Coaching: The Inside Story, 2nd Edition
By Katharine St John-Brooks and Julia Duncan

For further information about this series please visit https://www.routledge.com/The-Professional-Coaching-Series/book-series/KARNPROFC

Internal Coaching
The Inside Story

Second Edition

Katharine St John-Brooks and Julia Duncan

Routledge
Taylor & Francis Group

LONDON AND NEW YORK

Designed cover image: Getty Images

First published 2026
by Routledge
4 Park Square, Milton Park, Abingdon, Oxon OX14 4RN

and by Routledge
605 Third Avenue, New York, NY 10158

Routledge is an imprint of the Taylor & Francis Group, an informa business

British Library Cataloguing-in-Publication Data
A catalogue record for this book is available from the British Library

Library of Congress Cataloging-in-Publication Data
Names: St John-Brooks, Katharine author | Duncan, Julia author
Title: Internal coaching : the inside story / Katharine St John-Brooks
and Julia Duncan.
Description: Second edition. | Abingdon, Oxon ; New York, NY : Routledge,
2026. | Series: Professional coaching series | Previous edition: 2014. |
Includes bibliographical references and index.
Identifiers: LCCN 2025021980 (print) | LCCN 2025021981 (ebook) |
ISBN 9781032858050 hardback | ISBN 9781032858036 paperback |
ISBN 9781003519911 ebook
Subjects: LCSH: Executive coaching | Mentoring | Self-actualization (Psychology)
Classification: LCC HD30.4 .S7184 2026 (print) | LCC HD30.4 (ebook) |
DDC 658.4/07124--dc23/eng/20250916
LC record available at https://lccn.loc.gov/2025021980
LC ebook record available at https://lccn.loc.gov/2025021981

ISBN: 978-1-032-85805-0 (hbk)
ISBN: 978-1-032-85803-6 (pbk)
ISBN: 978-1-003-51991-1 (ebk)

DOI: 10.4324/9781003519911

Typeset in Times New Roman
by KnowledgeWorks Global Ltd.

Contents

Acknowledgements

First of all, a special shout out to our husbands! Chris Duncan has had the patience of a saint helping us with the internal coach survey, the graphics, the QR code and endless technical challenges, while Vivian Bazalgette has read and reviewed every word of the text. Any comma issues – please refer them to him.

The personal stories and organisational case studies in this book stem from the myriad conversations we have had with dedicated coaching professionals. You know who you are! So many people have been so generous with their time in talking to us about their experiences. Thank you all. We are particularly grateful to the following:

Karice Baker Quow, Alison Bain, Brajesh Bajpai, Janet Barker, Judith Barton, Tracy Barton, Fiona Beighton, Hermione Blake, James Blyth, Hazel Brinkworth, Catherine Boddington, Adele Bradley, Cath Brown, Alison Carter, Nick Ceasar, Katherine Chowdry, Ngozi Lyn Cole, Cheryl Cooper, Elizabeth Crosse, Serena Cunningham, Julie Danskin, Samantha Darby, Dr. Bijna Kotak Dasani, Jane Deans, Simon Dennis, Susan Dixon, Ilka Dunne, Liz Dunphy, David Eaton, Kate Elliott, Tracy Ellis, Sue Fairbrother, Jude Fairweather, Debra French, Leslie Goldenberg, Jeremy Gomm, Samantha Goodfield, Gwen Jefferson, Sarah Jessett, Steven Johnstone, Paul Haynes, Catriona Hudson, Nicola Hudson, Sam Isaacson, Manoj Kerai, Beth Krucien, Gamal Lewis, Jeremy Lewis, Lise Lewis, Amanda Maclean, Christian McGrath, Jennifer Mclelland, Beth McManus, Julia Menaul, Jason Miller, Louise Miller, Liam Moore, Hazel Murgatroyd, Sue Noble, Clare Norman, Mia O'Gorman, Lawrence Parsons, Giovanna Pisano, Amanda Robinson, Hazel Russo, Joanne Scott, Neelam Sharma, Ken Smith, Baz Stokes, Morwenna Stewart, Mike Taylor, Luca Turconi, Eve Turner, Trayton Vance, Clare Walker, Anne Welsh, Jonathan Whitham, Amisha Wilde, Sandra Wilson, Damion Wonfor, Kelly Woods and Ciaran Wrynne.

Thank you too to our editors at Routledge: Katie Randall, Sophie Ganesh and Manon Berset, and to Prabhu Chinnasamy in the production team.

Permissions

We would like to thank the publishers, organisations and individuals who granted permission to reference, adapt or reprint the following cited material:

Genius Within for permission to use their Neurotypes graphic, which was developed from the work of Doyle (2024).

Jessica Kingsley Publishers for permission to quote extracts from Carroll and Shaw's *Ethical Maturity in the Helping Professions* (2013).

Ken Smith for permission to quote an extract from the Listener (www.kensmith-coaching.co.uk).

Professional Coaching Publications, Inc. for abridged case study taken from Carter, Wolfe and Kerrin (2005).

The personal stories and case studies that we have used in this book are genuine and are drawn from the stories of people whom we know personally, or with whom we have worked professionally. On occasion, to protect confidentiality, we have changed names and certain stories are a blend of several people's experiences.

Series editor foreword by Professor David A. Lane

A rich and expanded resource for everyone involved in Internal Coaching

It is a delight to welcome the second edition of this important and definitive book on Internal Coaching. When it first appeared, internal coaching was becoming an important area of practice yet a comprehensive look at the field was missing from the literature. Hence, it became a foundational guide. The second edition has over 40 new case studies and personal stories, a whole new chapter on the relationship between the internal coach and their client, new or expanded sections on EDI, power in internal coaching relationships, coaching with technology and how to sustain a coaching pool. It also draws on new research.

The past decade has seen a considerable advance in our understanding of the power of internal coaching. The emerging challenges to us all and to the organisations in which we work have resulted in a more complex landscape for our practice and a deepening role for the internal coach. The second edition reaches into these challenges through exploring developments in the field and providing detailed case studies to help shape future practice.

The book will be of value to all who use, sponsor or research internal coaching, whatever level of experience you have. Internal coaching has definitely moved from being in the shadows to growing popularity. There was little initially to underpin the field and the first edition did much to support its growth as a practice. We now have the benefit of more research and case examples and the authors access the experience of hundreds of practitioners to enlighten and share practice.

While drawing on research the aim of the book is practical, posing questions for our readers to encourage reflection and engagement with a range of ideas. The authors are clear that they are not advocating one strategy or approach as best practice, emphasising that what works in one setting may not be appropriate in another.

The second edition retains many of the topics from the first edition, where they remain relevant, while reflecting on the changes in the workplace since then. We have faced the impact of Covid and the challenges that brought to both work practices and mental health. However, the authors also address changing attitudes to work and the role of team coaching and new technologies in the coaching space.

In creating the second edition, the authors surveyed 137 internal coaches to gain a sense of the areas which matter to them now and used this to supplement the original research from 2010. This ensured that the book covers the topics of relevance to the field today. The book addresses the experience of being an internal coach, and the ethical and practice dilemmas that they encounter. It also covers in depth the role of those who sponsor, organise or manage internal coaching and the processes for setting up an effective internal coaching resource.

The new material in the book, that as Series Editor I particularly valued, includes:

- The new case studies and personal stories (over 40) from internal coaches which give a real sense of their practice.
- A range of useful templates (many made accessible via a QR code) to assist in the establishment of internal coaching within organisations.
- Consideration of growing areas such as EDI, wellness, the shift to virtual coaching, team coaching and coaching with technology.

The authors hope that this book empowers you to make a lasting, positive impact, not only within your organisation but also in the lives of those that you – or the people you manage – coach.

It is clear that they have achieved their aim and consequently I am proud to see this as the latest contribution to the Professional Coaching Series.

Professor David A. Lane
Professional Development Foundation

Chapter 1

Introduction

Internal coaching has come a long way in the past decade, emerging from the shadows to play a vital part in supporting employees' personal and professional development. Many things have changed in the internal coaching landscape since the first edition was published in 2014, not least the massive changes that the Covid-19 pandemic has triggered in organisations. The need for fresh insights, shared experiences and evidence-based approaches has never been greater.

The second edition of *Internal Coaching: The Inside Story* offers many examples of practice from those shaping the future of internal coaching. Whether you're an experienced coach, a leader cultivating coaching within your organisation or someone just beginning to explore the field, this book is here to support and inspire you on that journey.

When I wrote the first edition, the practice of in-house or 'internal' coaching – where one employee within an organisation has a formal role coaching another employee outside their own team – was experiencing a surge in popularity. Over a decade before, Frisch had described it as "flying under the radar" of mainstream coaching (Frisch, 2001). While that was no longer the case, there was little referenced research to explain how it all worked so I sought to fill that gap.

The aim of the second edition is unchanged: to make a difference by sharing the experiences of hundreds of internal coaches, coach leads, coach supervisors, employers, researchers and coach training organisations with a view to:

1 Shedding light on what it is like to be an internal coach – thus providing insights and ideas for existing internal coaches and people thinking of training to be one.
2 Sharing practice to enable organisations with an internal coaching resource – plus those aspiring to have one – to reflect on how it can best be done effectively in their own context (and the pitfalls to avoid).

DOI: 10.4324/9781003519911-1

I recently heard a phrase that really resonated with me, which was to "Pinch with Pride". That is exactly what I have been doing. If I heard about a new or interesting practice, I would pinch it at once for this book. The whole idea is for readers to learn by reading about what other people are doing and deciding whether it can be adapted to work in their organisation too. This is what the book has always been all about. We're not claiming best practice for anything we include – because what works well in one organisation might not in another, for reasons of culture or sector or the size of the employer – but we *are* sharing things that some people have found worked for them. Then readers can decide if they are ideas worth pinching!

As with the first edition, the approach is intensely practical. If someone's experience or the results of a piece of research could be of interest and assistance to practitioners, then I've put it in. Practitioners' interests are very much to the fore. What I'm seeking to do is to pose a series of questions for coaches and organisations to think about and then to provide plentiful examples of how different organisations have tried to address those issues. My dream now, as then, is that every few pages a reader will think: "That's interesting, we should think about whether that idea could work for us".

So, what's new in the second edition? While many of the topics covered in the first edition are just as relevant in 2025 as they were in 2014, much has changed in the workplace since then. It's not just bombshells like the impact of the Covid pandemic on working patterns and employees' mental health but also attitudes to work have seen a lot of changes as the baby boomers retire, giving way to the Gen Xers, millennials and Gen Zers with different priorities and concerns around work-life balance, self-esteem, self-confidence, resilience, EDI and wellbeing. Also, approaches like team coaching have gained in popularity, and the impact of technology in the coaching space has developed hugely, plus, nowadays, there is no such thing as a non-busy job. All these changes need to be reflected in the new edition.

To support me in responding to the changed agenda, I have a co-author for the second edition. Julia Duncan has been training, coaching and supervising internal coaches since 2007 and we have been working together since 2015. We put together a survey in 2024 – which was completed by 137 internal coaches – to understand the issues that matter to internal coaches in the 2020s and have used that to validate the content that we wanted to cover and to supplement the coach experiences that were part of my original research in 2010.

New material in the second edition includes:

- Results from the 2024 internal coach survey.
- Over 40 new case studies and personal stories from internal coaches.
- Research and first-hand experiences relating to growing areas such as EDI, wellness, the shift to virtual coaching, team coaching and coaching with technology.
- Useful templates, guides and examples (many made accessible via a QR code).

Access to all QR code documents is clearly marked in relevant chapters of the book. There is also a unique URL to take you to the documents.

The QR code for accessing these additional resources is here. These resources are not included in the body of the book and aim to offer you more detailed guidance or provide a useful template that you can download as a Word document to support your coaching practice.

The URL below will also link you to the online material.

Figure 1.1 QR code and URL link

https://dplearningzone.the-dp.co.uk/2025/03/21/internal-coaching-the-inside-story-2nd-edition/

How to get the most out of this book

In Part I (Chapters 2–5), we focus on the experience of being an internal coach. It is designed primarily for internal coaches or individuals deciding whether to train to be one. It should also be of value to those of you who are thinking of setting up an internal coaching resource – giving a taste of what it is actually like.

In most ways, the internal coaches in my original research operated no differently from their external coach colleagues in terms of the approaches they used or the skills and techniques they deployed. Some had postgraduate qualifications and many had years of experience. However, it was also clear that they encountered more ethical issues as a consequence of coaching internally.

The idea that internal coaches are likely to have to deal with more ethical dilemmas than external coaches equates to the notion that the role of the external coach is 'cleaner' than that of the internal coach: that is, the management of confidentiality, boundaries and conflicts of interest is likely to be more challenging for internal coaches than for most external coaches. When I first published my research about ethical dilemmas (St John-Brooks, 2010), it came as no surprise to experienced internal coaches but it was an eye-opener to some coaching sponsors who had not previously appreciated the complexity of the world in which internal coaches operate.

Key issues, peculiar to internal coaches, are how to handle the intricate network of relationships that they have within their organisation and the pressures that come from being part of the same system as their clients. The interactions that Julia and I have had with hundreds of practitioners over the past 10–15 years suggest that, while this by no means hamstrings internal coaches' activities, it does mean that they need to be constantly alert to the challenges, contract with their clients very tightly and be alive to the possibility of ethical dilemmas arising.

Part II (Chapters 6–11) is aimed principally at people, generally in human re-sources (HR), learning and development (L&D) or organisational development (OD) functions, who already have or are seriously thinking about setting up an internal coaching resource within their organisation. It draws on and shares the experiences of numerous organisations, many of whom have now deployed internal coaches for well over a decade. The aim is to offer ideas along the whole spectrum of running an effective internal coaching service from setting the strategy; selecting, training, and matching the coaches to clients; through the marketing of the coaching service within the organisation and establishing the necessary framework to support the coaches properly; to the options for provid-ing supervision and continuing professional development (CPD) and evalua-tion of the effectiveness of the coaching. As such, Part II is also very relevant to coaching champions, coaching supervisors, coaching researchers and coach trainers.

There is still an overwhelming need for guidance on the process of setting up an internal coaching resource. For example, are you clear about the purpose and positioning of your coaching service? Is there buy-in from the board, senior man-agers and influential stakeholders? Has the coaching strategy been properly worked through and aligned with the business strategy? Will the coaches get the support they need – in particular, continuing professional development and supervision? Are there fully developed policies and guidance on such issues as how to deal with coaching relationships that are not working, how session records are kept or what happens if a client keeps cancelling sessions? Is there a code of ethics? And how will you evaluate the impact and benefit from your coaching service to evidence a clear return on investment?

It is possible that some organisations regard internal coaching as a quick, cheap fix to fill the gap when external coaching is perceived to be too expensive. When this happens, internal coaches are trained but then left swinging in the wind with-out support, isolated and feeling vulnerable. This book makes the case for chang-ing that by providing guidance on what organisations need to consider in order to set up and manage a successful internal coaching service that values the internal coaches and gives them the support they deserve.

Summary

If you are an internal coach or coach lead, we hope that this book will leave you feeling fully affirmed in all that you do and inspired to do even more. As coaches, we hope you will feel more able to identify ethical dilemmas, the implications for your practice and how to resolve them, and also more knowledgeable about what the options are for your further professional development. If you are thinking about becoming an internal coach, we hope you will have a clearer idea about what it involves, both the challenges and the huge rewards. If you are running an internal coaching pool, we hope the book will provide you with a benchmark of how other organisations are approaching this in terms of working to a clear coaching strategy, having robust policies, providing a good training and development programme for the coaches, and evaluating impact and success. And if you are thinking about setting up a pool of internal coaches, we hope you will gain a strong sense of what your choices are.

Above all, may this book empower you to make a lasting, positive impact, not only within your organisation but also in the lives of those that you – or the people you manage – coach. Know that your efforts are shaping a more productive and rewarding future for everyone involved in the coaching experience.

Katharine St John-Brooks
November 2025

Part I

What Internal Coaches Need to Know

Part I is designed for those of you who are:

a   Deciding whether to volunteer to become an internal coach.
b   Already working as an internal coach.
c   Thinking of setting up a cohort of internal coaches.
d   Conducting research into the practice of internal coaching.

Our aim is to give those of you who are not internal coaches a real feel for what it is actually like, plus to give those of you who are already experienced an opportunity to benchmark your practice against other practitioners and what has emerged from the research.

Chapter 2

The role of the internal coach

What this chapter is about

This chapter looks at how internal coaching is changing, highlighting the move towards more diverse coaching pools and how the scope of coaching assignments is broadening to encompass more personal and existential topics. While a few organisations employ full-time coaches, most train employees to coach on top of their primary roles (so-called 'job-plus' coaches).

This chapter explores:

- What internal coaching is like
- The rewards and challenges of internal coaching
- Who internal coaches are
- What internal coaches do and don't do

Who are internal coaches?

The prevailing model of internal coaching in Europe is a pool of trained coaches who coach on top of their 'day job'. It used to be said that internal coaches were mostly white, middle-aged, middle-class, neurotypical women but nowadays EDI (equality, diversity and inclusion) is gaining traction and almost all organisations aspire to having a wide variety of coaches in their pool. However, many still struggle to achieve the diversity they want. Sometimes, employees can feel unconfident about putting themselves forward to train as coaches, so it is important that organisations do some talent spotting and tap potential coaches on the shoulder. If you're interested, do find out more. Many organisations now encourage their coaches to emphasise in their written profiles whether they have personal experience of, say, neurodiversity or working with clients from under-represented groups. When you're thinking of what you can offer to clients, do take a look at the guidance in Chapter 8.

Karice's story illustrates the power of being an internal coach with experience of what it is like to be a minoritised person.

DOI: 10.4324/9781003519911-3

Karice's story

More than meets the eye: embracing my whole self

As a black woman with albinism, my own experiences are intersectional and have, from the outset, had an impact on my coaching approach. Over the years, I have had to contend with discrimination and bias based on race, gender and disability. Because my albinism is the most visible, much of the discrimination, low-key bullying and negative judgements have been based on the way I look. So, for me, my albinism was always at the forefront of everything I did – it became more prominent in my life than it needed to be. If asked to introduce myself, I would try to pre-empt people's responses by saying: "Hi, I'm Karice and I'm an albino". In effect, I internalised all these feelings and created my own personal barriers to growth.

One of the sad things about experiencing discrimination is that it robs you of your full identity. People have made pre-judgements about my intelligence and ability to fit in, and this has affected how they interact with me. I became hyper-focused on that one thing about me that caused such a stir in people instead of embracing *all* of the things that made me, me. I wasn't, and am still not, just an albino. I am a million other things and, once I embraced this, I became a happier and more confident person.

So how do my experiences inform my approach to my role as an internal coach? Well, coaching is about seeing the entirety of the person in front of you. Coaching clients are more than the issues they bring and the goals they want to achieve. By exploring the person's whole self, you're helping them to learn things about themselves – their strengths, weaknesses, values ... all of which can help them to be their authentic selves on their coaching journey.

As a coach, you won't be familiar with every aspect of your client, particularly if they hold back from disclosing significant things about themselves during the chemistry meeting. You may not, unlike me, have experience of what it's like to be a minoritised person, or a person living with a disability, but the key is to ask! You should be willing to learn from your clients because no one knows them better than they do themselves. Be willing to show some vulnerability by using phrases such as "I'm sorry, I'm not familiar with albinism, what is it?" or "You mentioned you have ADHD. I have a general idea of what that is, but can you let me know how it presents for you?"

It's okay to feel nervous at first – your client will be generous if you make unintentional mistakes. Ultimately, the coaching relationship is about seeing the whole person and that is what I have learned and try to bring to my role as an internal coach.

In addition to ethnicity, neurodiversity, gender, age and so forth, many organisations also try to ensure variety in terms of coaches' work experience, such as how senior you are and what part of the organisation you work in. While some organisations look to HR, organisation development (OD), and learning and development (L&D) practitioners when seeking internal coaches – the rationale being that they will often have relevant experience and there is a high likelihood that they will use their enhanced skills in their day jobs – others prefer to identify employees from all parts of the organisation or even positively avoid selecting HR specialists for coach training, partly because of their concern about the increased scope for role conflict.

Sometimes, individuals thinking of training to become internal coaches are concerned that they may appear too young to have credibility with clients. Part of this may be a hangover from the idea of the mentor – someone who has 'been there, done that' with the grey hairs to prove it. Coaching and mentoring are not the same thing (though coaches and mentors use many of the same skills). Much more important than age or seniority are the relevant skills and experience that a coach brings to the party and the degree to which they project warmth and confidence in their role as a coach.

What are internal coaches there to do?

The role of the internal coach has changed and flexed over the years to accommodate changes in the working environment, and many coaches have remarked on the massive impact that the Covid-19 pandemic has had on employees. One said:

> "Career coaching is still the number one request in our organisation but since the pandemic a lot of the conversation is around 'Finding their why' i.e. questions like 'Why am I here? Is this where I should be and what I should be doing?' There are also lots of concerns around work-life balance – particularly for millennials – and a big rise in clients experiencing general anxiety. My coaching colleagues and I have all noticed a trend, post Covid, towards holistic coaching because that's what the clients want and need. In the past, when we trained as coaches, we'd be told not to stray outside work-related issues but not any more".

Many organisations have a coaching strategy and this shapes the kind of coaching that they expect their internal coaches to deliver. So, for example, the focus could be on leadership development (for the talent pool), personal development (to support employees on management programmes), transition coaching (for recent recruits, returners after a career break or employees who have been promoted into new roles) or improving employee engagement (linked to organisational values and purpose). Other organisations take a broader approach and simply offer coaching as a strand of their L&D menu, open to all employees.

In Katharine and Julia's research, conducted in early 2024 with 137 internal coaches – especially for this second edition – the two most common topics reported, by quite a margin, were career development and 'building confidence and self-esteem'. It does not take a big imaginative leap to identify a causal link with the impact of the Covid-19 pandemic. As highlighted above, it was reported that many employees were using coaching as an opportunity to do a considerable amount of existential self-questioning: wondering whether their lives – not just their jobs or careers – were in the right shape. And remote working (both during the pandemic and subsequently), with its loss of social interaction, seems to have had a marked negative impact on employees' confidence, feelings of self-worth and social anxiety. Other prevalent topics were leadership development, working on challenging relationships, resilience (see also Rees et al., 2015) and wellbeing. Coaching to support women through menopause is also rising in prominence.

It is worth pausing, for a moment, on the change in the nature of post-pandemic coaching conversations and how this may be part of a longer-term trend. Grant (2017) argued that there have been three generations of workplace coaching so far: the first in the 1990s focusing on performance management; the second in the 2000s focusing on talent development, maximising employees' potential and driving change; the third in 2010 and beyond focusing on shifting mindsets and 'quality conversations' that are not necessarily goal-focused. It is important in third-generation coaching to coach holistically. So, while still seeking to enhance performance,

> "the other dimension that is equally important is the well-being dimension. Indeed … focusing solely on performance can lead to distress, disengagement and burn out – unintended outcomes all too familiar to contemporary organisations". (p. 44)

One way and another, internal coaches have been noticing that coaching conversations, over the past ten years or more, have increasingly involved working on a variety of personal issues related broadly to wellbeing (Jarosz, 2021). They may initially present in the guise of career development, burn-out, work-life balance challenges, overwhelm, generalised anxiety or in all sorts of other ways. The pandemic seems to have accelerated this trend. It is important that you, as a coach, feel equipped for these conversations, through training and/or CPD, to support and enhance the overall wellbeing of your clients. This may involve raising client awareness of techniques such as stress management. Quotations from coaching clients in Hicks et al.'s (2012) research into the impact of coaching on employee wellbeing, engagement and job satisfaction included:

- "Made me feel better equipped to handle whatever comes my way".
- "Made me more aware that if I'm in trouble then I can usually think of a solution".
- "Made me more aware that I could solve difficult problems if I tried hard enough". (p. 4)

There have been other changes in the internal coaching landscape too, in recent years, such as the increase in three-way contracting (with line manager involvement); an expectation that coaches contribute to organisational learning by sharing themes emerging in their client sessions and the growth in demand for team coaching.

Team coaching is a whole different ball game. Graves (2021) pointed out that it involves four different roles:

Mentor/expert: Sharing knowledge to add perspective.

Teacher/trainer: Demonstrating skills (listening, asking questions) and sharing, e.g., models to explain what might be going on in the team.

Facilitator: Designing the session, holding the space, keeping some structure.

Referee: Managing the process, helping the team make choices, pointing out when individuals are going off-topic.

Fulfilling these roles may not be a big jump for coaches with a background in L&D, who may already be experienced group facilitators with an understanding of team dynamics. For other coaches, team coaching may involve a whole new skill set with different approaches and techniques to manage a much more complex coaching environment. There are benefits to team coaching in pairs but the coaches themselves are sometimes reluctant because they may be worried about being judged by the other coach, and there is a whole extra layer of process: preparing together, co-ordinating during the session, holding wrap-up sessions. It is tempting for the coach to say: "it's fine, I'll fly solo". The organisation may be reluctant too because of the opportunity costs, but there is a lot to be said for sharing the load.

What are internal coaches not there to do?

Internal coaches are not employed to be counsellors, therapists, trainers or consultants. Chapter 4 explores in some depth the issue of maintaining boundaries and, in particular, what ethical dilemmas can arise when grappling with those boundaries. The key for individual internal coaches is to get some clarity from your employers about their expectations of you in the following areas.

Coaching vs mentoring: Does your organisation expect you to offer pure coaching (maybe it also has a separate mentoring scheme) or to operate along the whole coaching-mentoring spectrum? How do you manage the coaching/mentoring/ expert roles? What if your client is struggling with something that you could explain to them in no time or they specifically ask you what you would do in their shoes? An experienced coach might feel that you would be achieving more in terms of building the client's capability if you persevered with getting them to work out the answer for themselves, but Julia has noticed a shift over the past ten years towards coaches operating along the whole continuum from directive to non-directive (the 'coaching dance').

Professional competence: An inexperienced internal coach may feel uncomfortable saying they do not have the expertise to explore a particular issue with a client, perhaps fearing that their credibility could suffer, but you are there to coach not, say, to be a financial adviser or marriage counsellor. Your organisation should provide you with a referral route if your client clearly needs some training or professional help with their mental health or issues around substance misuse, personal finances, bereavement or family relationships.

Work life vs personal life: The world has moved on over the past fifteen years and it is much more common now for organisations to be comfortable with their internal coaches taking a holistic view of the client's situation. If they want to discuss a personal issue that is taking up their head-space then that's generally fine, on the grounds that it may be having an impact on their performance at work. But there are still some organisations that think of 'performance coaching' in narrower terms and would raise their eyebrows at funding sessions where, for example, the session was spent discussing the emotional impact of a brother's cancer diagnosis or a daughter's anorexia. Your client's general wellbeing may be the most important thing to you, as their coach, but it is worth being clear about your organisation's stance.

Distinction between the roles of coach and line manager: Managers sometimes suggest that a direct report gets a coach because they don't want to have difficult conversations with them themselves. Others are very clear that they are in alliance with the coach to support their team member's development. If your organisation encourages three-way contracting – including the line manager/sponsor – at the beginning of a coaching relationship, you should have the opportunity to explore who does what and ensure that you are not usurping the line manager's role (and that they are not ducking their responsibilities).

What is internal coaching like?

How much coaching do internal coaches do?

Most internal coaches coach on top of their 'day job'. Your line manager would normally need formally to authorise you to spend time training to be a coach, holding sessions with clients, receiving supervision and attending continuing professional development (CPD) sessions (if offered). Sometimes coaching will be recognised as a formal part of your role – particularly if you work in HR, L&D or OD – but often there will be no formal recognition of your coaching in performance management terms. Internal coaches' line managers may not necessarily know, or be concerned about, how many clients you have as long as the day job gets done. Often, however, there will be a maximum commitment agreed, for example one day a month or a maximum of two clients concurrently. It is the coach's responsibility to manage that.

Data extracted especially for this book on 14 March 2025, from the Coaching Hub (www.coaching-focus.com/coaching-hub), a coach management platform run by Coaching Focus Group, showed that the 1763 internal coaches, from around 83 organisations, who used the system were coaching, on average, 1.2 clients each. Data from the same source showed that the average length of a coaching session was around one hour and the average number of sessions was around five. Also, interestingly, 35% of the coaches on the system had no current clients. That is concerning as a break in delivering coaching can have all sorts of repercussions such as the coaches feeling deskilled and losing confidence, and a negative impact on the return on investment.

How is internal coaching delivered?

Post-pandemic, the world has shifted in terms of how coaching sessions are delivered. In Katharine and Julia's research with 137 internal coaches in January 2024, around 80% of the coaches met their clients virtually and 20% face-to-face (despite 60% of them saying that they preferred coaching face-to-face). This is almost the exact opposite of the situation a decade earlier (there is also a small amount of telephone coaching taking place). This will, of course, mainly be because virtual meetings have become the working norm. They offer the advantage of accessibility, convenience and no travel time and anyway, in 2024, many employees still worked part or all of the week from home.

But is something lost by coaching virtually? Ken Smith (https://kensmithcoaching.co.uk), a coach and supervisor of many years' standing, believes that there's something about the energy fields in a room and witnessing people's somatic experience which is not as accessible to a coach or supervisor if they're not in the same physical space (see 'Patrick's story' illustrating this in Chapter 8). Plus, the opportunities for creativity and improvisation are much reduced. He said:

> "I was with a supervisee once, working in a cafe near her workplace, and she gathered together on our table a number of salt and pepper shakers to represent and work through the connections between the different conflicting roles she had. She was totally absorbed in the process, which I would not have been able to facilitate as effectively if we were on Zoom".

Ken also uses David Grove's Clean Space approach (Lawley & Tompkins, 2000) where the coach invites the client to find different physical spaces to represent different aspects of their thinking – difficult to do virtually. In Chapter 3, the pros and cons of virtual coaching are explored further.

What support do internal coaches receive?

The spectrum of support offered to internal coaches by their employers is very wide indeed. Katharine's research (St John-Brooks, 2010) included one coach who said:

> "They have funded my attendance at Academy of Executive Coaching Masterclasses, NLP diploma, Gestalt workshops"

while another said:

> "There is no provision for internal coaches, but I have my own supervision arrangements and my own CPD, which I fund myself as it is a disgrace that none is provided".

In Katharine and Julia's 2024 research, there was still a very wide spectrum with some coaches greatly appreciating the broad range of CPD being offered by their organisations while others specifically mentioned the lack of investment in it. However, it is fair to say that provision has definitely improved. The same goes for supervision. While 20% of respondents still said that they were not offered supervision, most of the rest had access to either group supervision or one-to-one supervision and sometimes both. For much more about the benefits of supervision, and alternative approaches where an organisation may have no budget, see Chapter 10.

Opportunities for internal coaches to access development events have expanded considerably in recent years. The coaching professional bodies, e.g., Association for Coaching, European Mentoring and Coaching Council and International Coaching Federation often put on virtual CPD events and even group supervision that both members and non-members can attend (non-members sometimes have to pay a fee), and there is growth in the number of networks or communities of practice across the UK offering CPD and supervision to their members.

Internal coaches can tap into a whole range of resources and approaches to support their coaching practice. The following graphic gives some examples that coaches can access either through their employer, or by setting up their own support networks with fellow coaches.

Figure 2.1 Support available to coaches.

What are the rewards and challenges of being an internal coach?

The experience of being an internal coach will differ depending on a wide variety of factors: what is the status and reputation of internal coaching within your organisation? What are the challenges for the organisation as a whole? What's morale like? How big is the coaching pool? How senior are its champions? What support are you offered? How many clients are you expected to have? How comprehensive was your training? How experienced a coach are you? What's your background? How heavily loaded is your day job? All these factors and many others can make a significant difference to how the role feels and your ability and capacity to perform it. But while the nature of the role can vary considerably from person to person and organisation to organisation, internal coaches agree about many of the rewards and challenges associated with doing the job.

The rewards

The rewards tend to fall into four main categories: making a contribution, being part of something bigger, personal growth/learning and enhanced organisational awareness.

Making a contribution

Coaches gain considerable fulfilment from seeing the results that they help clients achieve.

Making a difference: There are few things that match the buzz of a client's having a 'light bulb' moment. But even something as small as asking a client who has been wrestling with some issue: "Do you have to do this by yourself? Is there a colleague who could support you to think it through?" and the client pausing then saying "I've just realised that Y could help. I wonder why I didn't think of her before …" can be deeply satisfying.

Seeing clients grow: Many internal coaches talk about finding coaching a privilege. To be invited into a colleague's life, to share their hopes and fears and play a role in helping them to become more effective at what they do (or happier in their work or more comfortable in their relationship with a colleague) is a special experience. As one internal coach working in a media company said, "It's hugely rewarding to feel that you have fundamentally improved someone's enjoyment of their professional life".

Giving something back: Managers who decide to train as coaches late in their careers are often motivated by wanting to give something back. In a large Indian production company, senior general managers were trained as coaches. They said that one of their motivators was "to give back something to the organisation" before they retired (Mukherjee, 2012, p. 80).

Here are two stories that illustrate the rewards of being an internal coach.

Baz's story

The rewards of internal coaching

I'd wanted to be a helicopter pilot since I was seven, so I joined the Royal Air Force as soon as I could. Nearly twenty years later, I'm still flying helicopters but now I'm the most experienced Puma helicopter pilot in the RAF – training pilots and pilot instructors.

There came a point, in 2017, when I was training older pilots and I realised that the role was as much about leadership as it was about the technical stuff. The 'expert' part of flying a helicopter was not what my students struggled with, the obstacles were more to do with what was going on inside their heads. So I trained as a systemic and team coach at Henley Business School then became an internal coach – coaching one-to-one then later as a team coach – on top of my day job.

The return on investment was always clear – I was mainly coaching advanced pilots and air traffic controllers who had had tens of thousands of pounds invested in their training. Keeping them in the military was self-evidently of value.

But why do I really do it? Some of the reasons are connected with the skills I've learned, e.g., deep listening. It was tempting to ask students questions to which I knew the answer but now I ask them genuine questions and really listen to the replies. They may be different from what I'd have come up with but just as good.

It is very fulfilling to see air crew starting to believe in themselves and trusting their decisions. I've retained some or they have realised that being air crew is not for them but have still stayed in the military.

I've also found considerable satisfaction in working as a coach with senior teams. It gives me the opportunity to have a greater impact – to support officers who have responsibility for hundreds of people (and, by extension, to support their families) – and I'm learning all the time. It's great to see individuals in a team spark off each other, and also to drop in those extra nuggets that I've learned from the day job. I love finding areas of connection and taking the opportunity to feed in a new perspective or discovery from outside the 'normal' realm of military leadership. Seeing how the team engage with it can be fascinating.

And the challenges? Well, it can be frustrating when I see a team going off-track. It's difficult to resist the temptation to 'shape' the direction. And in team coaching it's a slower burn, you don't get the same 'aha' moments as you do in one-to-one coaching. Also, the practicalities of bringing a team together regularly can be a nightmare – operational requirements take team members away which messes with the dynamics. This can be more of a challenge for an internal coach than an external one where the costs are explicit.

But the personal and team growth that coaching unlocks makes overcoming the challenges so worth it!

Manoj's story

Hindu stories and the rewards of sharing these with clients

I've explored mindfulness, breathing techniques, yoga, and meditation – all of which have deep roots in Hindu scriptures – and wondered if these ancient teachings might offer coaching benefits too so I decided to explore them with my clients.

One client struggled with confidence, comparing themselves to a colleague they felt was 'better' at everything. After three sessions, I asked if they were jealous and they admitted that they were. So, I shared a story about Narada and Tumburu.

Tumburu was a gifted singer, always praised by God. Narada, feeling envious, tried to outshine him but never received the same praise. Determined, Narada practised for years but when he performed again God still preferred Tumburu's voice. Finally, Narada asked Tumburu to be his mentor. With his guidance, Narada improved and, when he sang again, God was pleased at last.

This story holds powerful lessons. Jealousy drains energy and creates negativity. But what if, instead of resenting someone's skills, we learned from them? By turning envy into admiration and mentorship, we not only grow but let go of unnecessary rivalry. Actions done without jealousy come from a purer intent which helps us to achieve things in a better way.

My client took this approach and asked their colleague for guidance. The relationship improved, and rather than feeling inferior, they gained valuable skills. This client was also able to achieve big wins in their role, just by channelling their new mentor's guidance.

Then I worked with a client overwhelmed by negative thoughts. I introduced them to a verse from the Bhagavad Gita:

> "For the person who has conquered the mind, the mind is the best of friends; but for one who has failed to do so, his mind will remain the greatest enemy".

(Chapter 6, Verse 6)

Using this, we did a thought-mapping exercise. Over 24 hours, they tracked their thoughts, categorising them as positive or negative. Then we grouped the thoughts into useful thoughts (driving change) or useless thoughts (weighing them down). If a thought was negative but useful, we worked with it. If it was negative and useless, we reframed it or let it go. So much of our energy is spent dwelling on things that don't serve us. By freeing up mental space, my client could shift focus to what truly mattered. This clarity allowed them to set and achieve goals they had struggled with for years.

I'm excited to keep exploring Hindu scriptures for more wisdom to bring into my coaching. Ancient teachings have so much to offer.

Being part of something bigger

When an organisation brings its coaches together regularly in a community of practice there can be a real sense of a joint endeavour for the benefit of the whole organisation – not just for each individual client.

Being part of a community of coaches: Internal coaches enjoy getting to know their fellow coaches from all parts of the organisation and forming new relationships, creating and developing a sense of belonging. One said: "Several have become friends, and we lean on each other a lot when the going gets tough! As well as supporting each other in our coaching work ... it has spilled over into supporting each other more generally at work too".

Feeling valued by the organisation: Coaches appreciate the fact that their potential has been recognised and that their employer has invested in them: "Knowing that the business has input into my training and development to become a coach - that's the personal reward I take from the coaching programme".

Knowing you are delivering something important: When coaches are kept informed about the strategic purpose of the coaching and how it is supporting the business, there can be a strong flavour of "we're all in this together to make the organisation work more effectively".

Personal growth/learning

Some of the many benefits of training as a coach are expanding our skillset, raising our levels of self-awareness, improving our effectiveness as a manager/leader in the day job and enriching our lives and careers.

Becoming a better leader/manager: Many coaches feel they have enhanced their leadership skills in their day job by deploying a coaching approach with staff and peers, such as listening more effectively and focusing more on developing their staff. One said: "I could get frustrated with not knowing how to get the best out of someone and I think coaching enables me to".

Expanding your horizons: Some coaches say how they have learned a lot about strategy, project management and dealing with complex issues through coaching leaders who were grappling with issues that they had not yet encountered themselves.

Gaining confidence in your abilities: Hearing about how other managers in the business see their role and cope with the challenges can help coaches to benchmark their own capabilities: "Coaching my peers and sometimes my seniors has boosted my own confidence as I now realise that they struggle with difficulties and doubts just as much as I do".

Expanding your career choices: Training to be a coach can open your eyes to different ways of working and being and even lead to a whole new career path.

Kate's story illustrates the personal growth she experienced as a result of training to be an internal coach.

Kate's story

Conquering imposter syndrome and finding a new career

In 2016, Kate was working in recruitment in a multinational company. She was good at it but was also plagued by imposter syndrome. Outwardly confident, she had a fiercely critical inner voice. In meetings with senior people, it would tell her: "Don't say that, they'll think you're silly". She still contributed, but usually building on something that someone else had said.

However, her empathetic style was noticed and in 2019 she was headhunted into development as a business partner. Her line manager was inspirational and knew a lot about coaching. She used a coaching approach with her and gave her the opportunity to have a coach herself. Kate fell in love with coaching.

In 2021, Kate moved into Organisational Development in a role introducing culture change and trained to be an internal coach. Soon she started noticing differences in herself: she listened much better and her critical voice had quietened down. She realised that it was just a voice, and she didn't have to listen to it. What it was saying was not a 'fact'. She started speaking up in meetings, feeling increasingly comfortable with not knowing it all.

As her confidence continued to grow, she became involved in creating a vision for the internal coaching pool and then in creating a pilot programme. When the lead coach left in 2024, Kate applied for the role and was appointed, on promotion. She quickly became relaxed in her new management role and said: "I understand my own value now. I've changed my mindset, and I'm no longer frightened of looking silly".

Within five years, Kate's career had completely changed. She believes the sky's the limit and feels a strong need to connect with people and to connect them with each other, so she loves bringing the internal coaches in the pool together and looks forward to making coaching more and more central to what the company is all about.

Enhanced organisational awareness

Through your role as a coach, you'll meet other internal coaches – during your training then at CPD events and during group supervision – and also clients who work in parts of the organisation that you may have previously been unfamiliar with. This can have positive knock-on effects.

Understanding the organisation better: It is common for employees to know little about certain parts of their organisation – you may not know anyone working there and may not really understand what those departments do. Working with clients, and sometimes meeting their line managers too, can assist in breaking down silos, identify common interests and contribute to doing your job better. One coach said: "I find it rewarding to meet different people from around the business and learn more about what they do and how their department works. This has helped me to learn about my company".

Expanding internal networks: By becoming part of a coaching community, coaches meet other coaches and extend their personal network into new parts of their organisation. One said: "You get to meet people from other disciplines that you wouldn't normally, and it can sometimes help in my day job".

Understanding the internal politics better: Hearing about others' approaches to issues can be an eye-opener to the coach and reframe how they think about an issue. One said: "I have always felt that 'internal politics' were not for me but I have learned a lot from my clients about the importance of convincing the movers and shakers if things are to get done. Formal channels are only one way of influencing an outcome, often not the most important one".

The next story is a powerful testament to how training to be an internal coach can change lives.

Jen's story

Breaking barriers: a journey of resilience and empowerment in policing

My journey to becoming an internal coach began with being coached myself at a pivotal point in my policing career. I am now an ILM Level 5 professional coaching practitioner, dedicated to coaching the next generation of ethical and authentic police leaders. I am fortunate to be in a position of authority to help others achieve their aspirations and foster a culture where women can confidently pursue their careers in law enforcement, breaking down barriers along the way.

At a low point in my career, being coached ignited a fire within me, transforming me from merely surviving to thriving. My goal now is to instil self-belief in women and encourage perseverance despite systemic barriers. I am an advocate for equal rights in policing, proving that femininity and professional success can co-exist.

As a female police officer, I have faced both challenges and rewards over nearly 30 years of service. Currently, I serve as a Detective Superintendent for major crime, leading serious youth and gang violence investigations. My passion for empowering women led me to establish the first Girls' Independent Advisory Group for the police in Birmingham. Coaching has been essential for my personal growth and resilience.

My path to success has been fraught with challenges, including battles for respect, exclusion, and bullying. Returning from maternity leave, I struggled with shift work while caring for a young child. I faced discrimination in job opportunities and fought against an elite 'Boys' Club' promotion system. Despite excelling in exams, promotions were often given to male colleagues before I had even been interviewed. These experiences tested my resolve, but I remained determined to succeed in this male-dominated field.

A turning point came when I joined the College of Policing's 'Coach to Grow' programme. My coach helped me organise my thoughts, stay focused, and maintain a forward-looking perspective. Coaching helped me to develop self-awareness, cope with difficult relationships, and reframe challenges into opportunities for growth. It was instrumental in helping me to navigate failed promotion boards, isolation, and being labelled a 'troublemaker' for challenging the status quo. I learned to embrace my drive as a strength and became proud of questioning outdated policing hierarchies.

If I can help others through coaching to be brave, develop their confidence and resilience strategies in a world where women in policing are valued for who they are, then my goals as a coach will be fulfilled.

The challenges

The key challenges experienced by internal coaches fall into five main categories: balancing the roles, being part of the same system, practical issues, coping with emotions and handling ethical dilemmas.

Balancing the roles

Fulfilling your responsibilities to both your day job and your role as a coach can be demanding.

Time pressures: You may decide to train as a coach at a time when your day job is containable within normal working hours and then hit a busy spell or take on additional responsibilities that put you under a lot of pressure. At such times, your line manager may have misgivings about the time you have to give to your coaching role so you may have to handle that issue too.

Guilt: Internal coaches report feeling guilty and talk about the challenge of fitting everything in, reminiscent in tone to working parents trying to combine work and childcare. Even when the actual coaching sessions are easily accommodated, internal coaches can feel bad about carving out time from the day job for preparation, reflection after a session, CPD or supervision – without which the coach's performance (and therefore the experience for the client) is likely to suffer.

Switching 'head space': Many internal coaches are also managers and spend the time when they are not coaching making decisions, organising work, delivering projects. As a manager you are often a multitasking 'doer' whereas as a coach you listen, avoid being directive and give your undivided attention to the client. One said: "It's difficult trying not to tell the client what to do and how to do it!" It can also be hard to change gear to attentive listening mode – even for experienced coaches – when you have just torn yourself away from a demanding meeting and know that there will be countless pressing issues competing for your attention when the client session is over. Another said: "It is hard to switch off before going into a coaching session. In an ideal world you'd have a bit of time out to calm the mind ahead of a session but that's not always feasible. The client, too, may have other things on their mind when they are talking to you". The move to end-to-end virtual meetings can exacerbate this issue. Taking the client through a mindfulness exercise at the start of a session can help both of you.

Being part of the same system

Internal coaches often talk about the difficulties thrown up by working in the same organisation as the client.

Maintaining objectivity: It can be challenging to stay independent. The following were both said by internal coaches: "It can be hard to disassociate your own experiences and your own feelings towards the business situation that a client is describing, as you help them work through their challenges and remain neutral" and: "The issues that affect all staff also affect us. It can be more difficult to step back and take an independent view about an issue that causes concern for you, too, as an employee".

Knowing the same people: When lead coaches are responsible for matching coaches and clients, they normally try to ensure that the coach and client work in different parts of the organisation. However, many organisations now use automated coach management systems, where the clients choose from a list of coach profiles, so it becomes your role as coach, during any chemistry meeting, to check out if you may know your client's colleagues. As one coach put it: "When coaching someone who is talking about someone you know, it's hard to not let your own views about them get in the way".

Providing an appropriate level of challenge: Coaches need to strike a balance between supporting the client and holding them to account. Clients do value being challenged. There may be no-one else – particularly if they are senior – prepared to do that. Yedreshteyn (2008) points out that "… clients want coaches to follow up, challenge them, and hold them accountable for meeting their goals. Coaches suspected this when they said they wished they had challenged their clients more, as that is exactly what their clients wanted" (p. 86). This can feel uncomfortable for inexperienced coaches but holding your clients to account could be crucial to their achieving sustainable change.

Practical issues

It can be useful to anticipate some of the everyday issues that may arise.

Dealing with cancellations: Internal coaches can find themselves with clients who keep cancelling or postponing sessions. In some organisational cultures this can be quite prevalent. By and large, external coaches charge for cancelled sessions which discourages cancellations but the same leverage is not available to internal coaches (unless there is some system of cross-charging). Cancellations can lead to a loss of momentum in the coaching and loss of confidence for the coach. With clear contracting and organisational support for your taking a robust approach with your client, this problem can generally be overcome.

Not having enough clients: Coach supervisors report that internal coaches often refer to not having enough, or any, clients. There can be many reasons for this: perhaps the scheme has not been marketed effectively; or a highly pressurised period could mean that fewer people feel that they have time to be coached; or a particular coach may have specialist skills that are temporarily not called for by clients. This can be a challenging time for a coach who may feel deskilled and demotivated as a result. Coaches experiencing this often find that engaging in group supervision allows them to listen, understand and learn from the experience of others to keep their practice alive and maintain their skills.

Finding an appropriate venue offering privacy: With only one-fifth (or fewer) of coaching sessions taking place face-to-face, and meeting rooms in office buildings being under less pressure now that many people work from home for at least part of the week, finding a suitable place to meet has become less of an issue than it was a decade ago. In fact, one of the benefits of virtual coaching is having the flexibility and choice by both coach and client to choose their own safe space for confidential conversations.

Using technology: What technology can you use? should you use? are you licenced to use? Many coaches are looking to enhance their practice assisted by technology and it can offer big benefits. But at a simple level, virtual sessions can sometimes be spoiled by technology that is not working well. See Chapter 8 for a lot more on the pros and cons of coaching with technology.

Coping with emotions

In a well-managed scheme, internal coaches have access to a dedicated supervisor or to a mentor in the shape of the lead coach. Some schemes, however, are poorly resourced or may still be in their infancy so the coaches may have to cope with difficult feelings alone.

Feelings of isolation: While you are training, most internal coaches have considerable support. You will be part of a cohort of trainee coaches and will have regular help from the training provider. The lucky ones will then join their organisation's coaching community, meeting regularly for supervision, sharing experiences and attending CPD events. But some coaches find that once they finish the training, they are pretty much left to themselves. In these circumstances, you would do well to be proactive, keep in touch with the other coaches, and practise a little self-help – while putting pressure on your employer to facilitate regular gatherings of the coaches to exchange experiences and offer each other support.

Aftermath of client sessions: You may have unprocessed feelings after sessions, for example if the client has become distressed, and it can have an impact on your mood or even your confidence. If you don't have access to supervision, see if you can buddy up with another coach. Journalling can also be an excellent way to offload and process any anxieties you may have picked up.

Feeling undervalued: Internal coaches can feel that they are not valued as highly as external coaches even though the service delivered may be as good. One coach said: "The organisation does not recognise internal excellence but appears to see external coaches as more professional". Your line manager may know little, if anything, about the coaching work that you are doing but, ideally, the person heading up your internal coaching scheme will give you feedback and support. Many internal coaches have to be content with the direct feedback that they receive from their clients during or after sessions.

Handling ethical dilemmas

Part and parcel of being an internal coach is addressing actual or potential dilemmas – whether it is coping with a powerful figure who is pressurising you to break confidentiality; dealing with role conflicts or deciding how to handle a client situation involving disciplinary issues. These can be made easier to manage by tight contracting with the client from the outset, experience, and using supervision or peer support but can still represent a challenge, particularly for inexperienced coaches and coaches who work in central services such as HR, OD or L&D.

Recognising and resolving ethical dilemmas is such an important issue for internal coaches that Chapters 4 and 5 are devoted to addressing the topic in much more depth.

Summary

The role of the internal coach is a rich and varied one and can be hugely rewarding. It will look and feel quite different depending on how an organisation's scheme is set up and how well-resourced it is. This chapter has taken you through a number of factors that have an impact on what the role of an internal coach can be like and has outlined some of the key rewards and challenges that internal coaches have themselves identified. Having a clear understanding of what your organisation's expectations are - and the support that would be available to you - should help you to decide if you want to make the commitment to become an internal coach or, if you are already an internal coach, how you might improve how your internal coaching service currently operates.

Table 2.1 Questions to reflect on

Who are internal coaches? What do they do and what don't they do?

- Do you have the appropriate knowledge, skills and experience to do the job well?
- What can you bring to coaching that will benefit the organisation?
- What type of coaching are you most interested/not interested in delivering?
- Who are you prepared to coach and at what level in the organisation are you most comfortable coaching?

How much coaching is the internal coach expected to deliver?

- Is there clarity on how many clients you would be expected to have at any one time?
- Do you have the support of your line manager to make enough time for your coaching role?
- What long-term career aspirations do you need to take into account, when considering whether to train to be an internal coach?

What support will be provided?

- What range of CPD and networking activities do you regard as a "must have" to support your coaching role and ongoing practice?
- To what extent are you prepared to invest in your own development and growth?

What are the benefits of being an internal coach?

- What is your motivation for being an internal coach?
- What personal benefits are you looking to achieve?

What are the challenges in being an internal coach?

- What challenges most concern you about the role of an internal coach?
- What support can you expect to receive to resolve these challenges?
- How confident do you feel that you have the resilience required for the role?

Chapter 3

Building relationships

What this chapter is about

Coaching is a transformative process that extends beyond techniques and methodologies. At its core, it is built upon the strength of the relationship between coach and client. Research (de Haan, 2008; Whitmore, 1992) consistently highlights the quality of the coaching relationship as the most significant predictor of coaching success. This connection helps clients to feel understood, challenged and empowered to achieve their goals. As the coaching field evolves, it becomes increasingly clear that the relational aspect of coaching is the fundamental driver of meaningful change. For the relationship to be truly successful, coaches need to deploy their interpersonal skills, empathy and ability to create a non-judgmental environment (Starr, 2011). This chapter has a heavily practical bias, offering insights into how trust, authenticity and collaboration shape successful coaching outcomes.

This chapter explores:

- The uniqueness of the relationship between an internal coach and their client
- The relational challenges
- Building a trusting and transparent coaching relationship

  - Beginnings (one-to-one and team contracting; awareness of unconscious bias)
  - Middles (building trust; progress between sessions)
  - Endings (consolidating the learning, celebrating achievements)

- Building effective relationships when working with neurodiverse clients and those experiencing intersectionality

The uniqueness of the relationship between an internal coach and their client

The fact that you were selected for training as an internal coach probably means that building relationships and being interested in helping people to be their best authentic selves is already one of your strengths. You should take great pride in undertaking such a significant role in your organisation.

Julia has trained over 500 managers and leaders to be internal coaches in their organisations. The process requires the trainees to request feedback from their clients throughout the training. One of the questions is, "Describe the experience

DOI: 10.4324/9781003519911-4

of being coached by your coach?" Resoundingly, the positive feedback described aspects of the relationship. Here is a selection of client comments.

Client feedback describing the coaching relationship

Created a safe and trusted environment for both of us to talk openly and honestly

Showed empathy, understanding, never judged me, offered genuine support and facilitated out of me things I never thought possible at the outset

I shared stuff I'd not shared with anyone before, through their trust and understanding

Creation of a trusted environment was the best thing as building trust is one of my lines in the sand to get anything out of me, so well done!

You visibly listened, full of presence and interest in me as a person

Enabled me to be honest in our discussions. My coach has clearly established values that encouraged my openness

Managed to enable me to dig deep in generating ideas and helped me to create several 'light bulb moments'

I felt supported, as my coach was on the journey with me saying: "I know you can do this" and helping me to rephrase my self-belief to: "I WILL do this and conquer my fears"

Sessions were clearly in an ultra-safe space, trusted, empathetic environments

---

Internal coaches have a number of special roles. They include being a resourceful source of organisational knowledge, being a thinking partner and advocating for a coaching culture.

Internal coach as a source of knowledge: Having direct experience and knowledge of the organisation means that you are likely to understand the organisational context, its culture and its internal challenges and opportunities, helping you to engage with clients in an especially meaningful way. You can leverage your understanding of the organisation's resources, systems, and power structures to challenge their thoughts and choices. The trusting relationship that coaches have with their clients is unique, quite different and distinctive from peer or line manager relationships, as it provides a protected space for deep reflection and honest review.

Internal coach as thinking partner: Some organisations choose to use some of their coaches, in a targeted way, to work as 'thinking partners' with, for example, managers who are managing organisational change programmes. You have the advantage of being familiar with the organisation's history, operations and people and can use your coaching skills to help them navigate the choppy waters of organisational change, such as restructures, mergers or leadership transitions.

Advocate for a coaching culture: Internal coaches can support their clients to use a
wider variety of leadership styles and cultivate a coaching culture. You can role-
model, challenge or offer feedback to your clients, not only on their thinking and
actions but on how they come across. You can comment on the impact they have
on you in coaching sessions. This open and honest dialogue between the internal
coach and their client, through a shared understanding about how they both work
within the organisational system, can help to build a broader coaching culture.

The relational challenges

Chapter 2 explored five key challenges that internal coaches face: balancing the roles,
being part of the same system, practical issues, coping with emotions and handling
ethical dilemmas. Here we take a deeper look at some of the relational challenges.

Holding dual roles: Internal coaches rarely have the privilege of being a full-
time coach, so you are likely to have a day job as well as your coaching
role. This duality can create complexity and should be managed with care
to ensure that your knowledge of the workplace and the people that you and
your client both know do not subtly or unconsciously shape the dynamics of
the coaching relationship. Neutrality and objectivity are harder to achieve
when operating as an internal coach, where your personal views, perspectives and opinions can get in the way. It's critical to maintain a neutral
perspective and avoid colluding with the client's views on the organisation.
Pre-existing relationships: Internal coaches may have pre-existing relationships
with their client's colleagues, which can be beneficial in terms of understanding the broader context. However, it can also create tension if the client feels
their relationship with the coach is influenced by these other connections or if
the coach has a positive relationship with individuals that the client has difficulty with. Ideally, be open and explore this subject at the contracting stage.
Engaging with stakeholders: Knowing and engaging directly with stakeholders,
such as the client's line manager or an organisational sponsor, can be regarded
either as a benefit or a barrier to the coaching process. Many key stakeholders
are keen to support the development of the client or team, so it can be beneficial,
prior to the agreement of a coaching programme, to have a three-way contracting
meeting to set expectations. You need to be clear from the outset that your key responsibility is to the client (or clients), not to other stakeholders. Any information
that stakeholders might request can be supplied only with your client's consent.
Without formal three-way contracting and clarity about how the coaching relationship will work, dilemmas can arise which make the coach vulnerable. This is
where having the right coaching systems, processes and communications about
how the coaching service works is essential to protect the interests of the coach
and ensure that senior management and stakeholders are signed up.
Power differentials: These can throw up considerable ethical challenges and are
explored in depth in Chapter 4. So how can power differentials affect the coaching from a relational perspective? The different kinds of power that may be at
play – such as expert power, positional power or personal power – can influence

either the coach's or the client's confidence and ability to be their authentic selves and take good decisions. Encouraging your client to engage in a candid conversation about the impact that power differentials outside the coaching relationship are having on them may be the first time that they have had the opportunity or courage to talk about them. Your aim will be to empower your client to develop their understanding of their own worth, power and choices.

The coaching journey process

One way of thinking about the coaching relationship journey is to consider the process you may follow. This starts from the initial contact, through the coaching interactions, to the final review and evaluation giving both you and your client an opportunity to reflect on the whole experience.

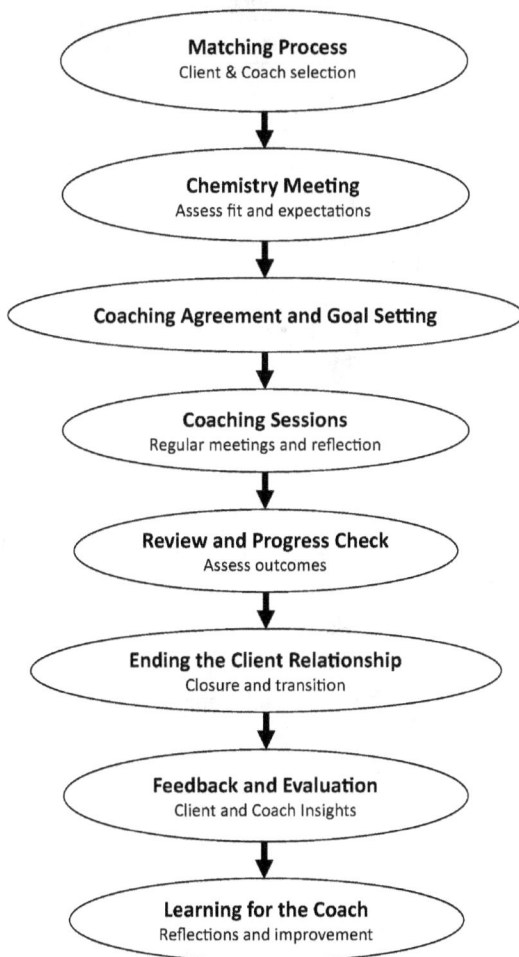

```
         Matching Process
       Client & Coach selection
                 │
                 ▼
         Chemistry Meeting
       Assess fit and expectations
                 │
                 ▼
   Coaching Agreement and Goal Setting
                 │
                 ▼
         Coaching Sessions
     Regular meetings and reflection
                 │
                 ▼
     Review and Progress Check
          Assess outcomes
                 │
                 ▼
    Ending the Client Relationship
        Closure and transition
                 │
                 ▼
       Feedback and Evaluation
       Client and Coach Insights
                 │
                 ▼
        Learning for the Coach
     Reflections and improvement
```

Figure 3.1 The coaching journey process.

Building a trusting and transparent coaching relationship

The internal coach-client relationship follows a natural flow with a clear beginning, middle and end. In the opening phase, the coach and client clarify objectives and expectations and set the foundations for a productive partnership. The middle phase is where the core coaching work gets done, building a productive and trusting relationship, engaging in honest conversations and reflective discussions, identifying challenges and developing actionable strategies. This stage is a dynamic process where the pace can change and may entail adaptations as new challenges emerge. The ending phase focuses on consolidating the learning, celebrating progress and ensuring that the client has the confidence and tools to continue their development independently.

Beginnings	Middles	Endings
Coach develops foundations to:	*Coach enables client awareness & responsibility to:*	*Coach and client explore how the relationship has worked:*
• Set and agree mutual expectations	• Develop trust and transparency	• Confirm achievements
• Define ways of working	• Build self-awareness	• Realise shift in growth
• Identify learning needs and learning styles	• Build self-understanding	• Affirm benefits of change
• Agree goals/objectives	• Build self-esteem and self-worth	• Agree ongoing commitment to sustain change
• Identify techniques and approaches best suiting the client	• Encourage confidence to change	• Provide feedback to each other on what has worked well and areas for improvement: behaviourally and emotionally
• Agree mutual coaching environment	• Develop accountability and desire to improve	
• Explore the importance of confidentiality both ways	• Explore motivational drivers to make change happen	• Coach to pass baton for future support by others
• Define what feedback is necessary with client sponsor	• Develop personal reflections learning and insight	• Agree what can be shared with sponsor and organisation on any generic themes for organisational learning
• Mutually agree contract terms (including 3-way)	• Coach provides in the moment feedback and session close feedback	
	• Client provides feedback to coach on how the process is working and any areas for improvement	

Figure 3.2 Three phases of the coaching relationship.

Beginnings

The first session is all about setting the scene, agreeing goals and expectations, and beginning to build mutual respect and trust, allowing you and your client to co-create a safe and productive partnership. The aim is for you to be a true thinking partner, where the client holds the power to make change and move forward, secure in the knowledge that you are committed to their success.

Barton (2024) talks about three aspects of preparing for the first, and subsequent, sessions: preparation of the space, preparation of the client and preparation of yourself.

The space: Pre-pandemic, the physical space was important, thinking about possible distractions and how neutral to make it. When working with neurodivergent clients (see more on this at the end of the chapter) the coaching environment could be even more important. Now that most coaching is online, there are considerations like someone sitting in their kitchen or their bedroom, with their partner or flatmate working on another laptop nearby. We need to be able to offer a confidential, psychologically safe service. What can you do to promote that? And how welcome do you make someone feel, whether it is physically or online? How would you describe that welcome? What does your environment look like when you are working online? How do you maintain that space? The aim is to get the client feeling comfortable and at ease, to get the rapport going as soon as possible.

The client: The faster we can get the client in the zone, the sooner they can start the proper work and be prepared to go deep. What does the client need to know? How quickly? What do they need from you to feel confident in the space?

The coach: How ready are you to coach? Each session is precious. The client will be entrusting you with important personal material. So, how do you look after yourself? Did you sleep well the night before? Do you need to ground yourself? How are you going to be ready to do your best work?

Contracting

One-to-one contracting: Contracting is the backbone of any effective coaching relationship. It ensures that the internal coach and client have a mutual understanding of how the coaching will operate: the boundaries, approach, outcomes and expectations.

Lane and Corrie's (2006) 'Purpose, Perspectives, Process' model identifies three aspects of contracting.

1 To contract with the client.
2 To agree and define the coaching journey process.
3 To guide your coaching conversation.

You and your client need to discuss the overall aim of coaching (*purpose*) and what each of you brings to the relationship *(perspectives)*. Then you will discuss and contract how the coaching will take place: timing, boundaries, possible tools and techniques to be used and the way the client prefers to work (*process*). You will also discuss the outcomes that your client hopes to achieve from the coaching and any results that may need to be visible to the organisation, including feelings and behaviours that the client would like to work on.

As a rule, coaches start the coaching conversation with *perspectives*: "Where are you now?" "What's happening with you?" "What's informing your thinking?" "What are your reflections on your current concrete experience?" then move on to identify *purpose*: "What do you want to talk about?" "What are your needs for today?" "What key outcomes do you want to achieve?" Once the coach has identified what needs to be worked on, then you can agree on the *process,* including what frameworks, tools or techniques are relevant. At the end of the session, a summary of any actions, learning and outcomes that have resulted from that contracting conversation can be agreed and recorded.

When things go wrong it can often be traced back to poor practice on the part of the internal coach, such as not setting proper boundaries in the contracting session at the outset (Ting & Scisco, 2006). Contracting and relationship building are crucial.

Three-way contracting: Many organisations like their coaches to facilitate a three-way contracting meeting involving the coach, the client and the sponsor (usually the line manager). The aim is to get joint ownership of the coaching process and goals, including defining how confidentiality and any ethical issues that may arise will be handled. It also ensures involvement by the sponsor in supporting the client's development, both during the coaching programme and after it is completed. Often, the three-way meeting will be repeated at the end of the assignment to wrap it up. Research by Gettman et al. (2019) explored contracting and its impact on the coaching relationship with some useful comments from practitioners illustrating the value of a three-way conversation.

"It raises key issues that are often not explicitly discussed. It increases honesty and clarity of objectives… I often think the 3 or 4-way meeting … is the most valuable moment in the coaching programme … These meetings also make the coach more aware of the organisational context".

(Male coach, 10+ years, European with an education background)

"My experience is that it is important to clarify what will be shared and not shared between sponsor and coach. Even so, some managers try to get more information. The contract then helps to state what can be shared and what not.

So, contracting can release some of these challenges but then helps to overcome them since an agreement has been signed in advance".

(Female coach, 2–4 years, Europe, with a media background)

The contracting meeting can be a very positive experience if the manager is supportive, but clients don't necessarily like the thought of them – some saying that they prefer to recruit a coach from the pool without their line manager's involvement and scrutiny. But a three-way meeting is an excellent opportunity for you to observe the relationship at close quarters, ensure that everybody is on the same page and for you to check that the outcome of the coaching is aligned with what was agreed with the sponsor (though there may often be additional, personal, goals added in).

In Julia's experience, internal coaches can fear these three-way meetings. They require facilitation skills and there may be power differentials at play as the coach will often be junior to the client's sponsor. So, if your organisation wants you to run them, make sure that they provide you with appropriate training. It can help to make it go well if, when setting the meeting up, you make clear the purpose of the meeting, its benefits and the role of all parties involved. Your role will be to guide the client and sponsor through the process.

A typical meeting may look like the following:

Opening 30 minutes: The coach and client (without the sponsor) provisionally contract about the purpose, goals and logistics of the relationship. This provides an opportunity to start to get to know the client and their priorities.

Next 20–30 minutes: The coach and client are joined by the sponsor to agree some overall key goals for the coaching assignment. The focus here should remain on the client, who should have complete control over what they wish to reveal. You will facilitate the session and ensure that the sponsor and client are clear about your role in the coaching process and have an opportunity to raise any questions they may have. It is crucial that you emphasise that the coaching process is founded on full confidentiality (subject to any caveats that they agree).

The remaining part of the first session: The sponsor leaves the session, and the coach and client begin the process of building their relationship.

An alternative model is for the sponsor to join in just for the final 10–15 minutes of the opening meeting.

Occasionally, a client may express reservations about the involvement of their sponsor, particularly if it is their line manager and they have a difficult relationship. You may need to make a judgement call as to whether a three-way conversation will add more than it subtracts. Sometimes, it might be better to begin working with the client and explore with them any actions they might take to rebuild that relationship. It is good practice to encourage your clients to have regular conversations with their sponsor about the focus and progress of the sessions and what continuing support they need.

Sarah's story

The importance of three-way contracting

Sarah is an internal coach in a large corporation. She has been working with Emma, a mid-level manager, for a few months. Emma has been struggling with her leadership role, particularly around balancing her team's dynamics and her relationship with her manager, Peter (who is also a stakeholder in the coaching process).

Emma feels caught between pressure from Peter to improve her team's performance and her own desire to create a supportive, open environment for her team members. Emma has confided in Sarah about the stress she's feeling, mentioning that Peter often gives vague, sometimes contradictory feedback, making it difficult for her to implement any clear strategies. She also feels that Peter's expectations are unrealistic, and she worries that if she pushes back, she could jeopardise her position within the company.

One day during a coaching session, Emma brings up her growing frustration with Peter's demands and her lack of clarity on the coaching goals, revealing that she feels she's being set up for failure. She asks Sarah for advice on how to manage Peter's expectations without risking her job. Sarah listens intently but is now faced with an ethical dilemma.

As an internal coach, Sarah knows that her role is to support Emma's development while remaining neutral and keeping in mind the company's interests. However, she is also aware that Emma's concerns about Peter's leadership and expectations might need to be addressed in a larger organisational context. If Sarah were to help Emma by coaching her to push back against Peter directly, it could potentially undermine the relationship between Emma and Peter and create a rift that could harm Emma's standing in the organisation.

Sarah needs to decide if she should continue coaching Emma within the bounds of her role, focusing solely on Emma's personal leadership skills and emotional resilience. Or should she bring the issues Emma has raised about Peter into the open, either with him directly or through other organisational channels?

After much thought, Sarah realises that the ethical dilemma lies in maintaining the balance between being a confidential resource for Emma and fulfilling her duty to the organisation as an internal coach. She decides to arrange a three-way meeting with Emma and Peter to discuss their expectations and clarify the coaching goals, bringing transparency to the situation and ensuring all parties are aligned.

Summary of lessons learned

1 *Three-way contracting is key:* This story underscores the importance of three-way contracting at the start of the coaching process rather than midway through the programme. Sarah initially worked only with Emma, but she learned that it's crucial to get all relevant parties aligned at the outset. Three-way contracting can help avoid misunderstandings, clarify roles and make expectations clear from the start.

2 *Confidentiality vs Organisational interests:* As an internal coach, Sarah needed to navigate the delicate balance between confidentiality and fulfilling her role within the organisation. Try to consider how the coaching process may have an impact not just on the client but also the larger organisation.

3 *Honesty and transparency:* Sarah learned that rather than working in isolation, addressing issues openly with other stakeholders helps to ensure that coaching leads to sustainable changes. Bringing Peter into the conversation meant that Emma's concerns were heard and that the coaching process had a clear direction, benefiting both Emma and the organisation.

4 *Empathy and professional boundaries:* Sarah was able to show empathy for her client's struggles while maintaining professional boundaries, staying neutral and focused on her development goals.

Team coaching contracting

Team contracting is a more complex process that still aims to establish clear expectations, roles, and goals, fostering trust and a shared commitment to the coaching process. The contracting session also seeks to start the process of building the relationship between the coach and the team and facilitate open dialogue between all team members, allowing them to voice any concerns. Contracting identifies and helps to clarify the roles and responsibilities within the team coaching process to avoid misunderstandings later.

It helps if goals are as specific and measurable as possible but, as it is such a dynamic process, there needs to be an understanding and expectation among team members that there may need to be flexibility within the contract, to allow adjustments to the goals if new needs or challenges emerge. Finally, team contracting helps to encourage the team's ownership over the process to increase engagement and buy-in.

The following is one approach to team contracting.

Initial discussion with key stakeholders: This is to set the stage for the team coaching engagement. The coach meets with key stakeholders (such as the team leader, HR or other managers) to gather insights about the team's current challenges and desired outcomes. This helps the coach to understand the context and think about how to tailor the coaching approach.

First meeting with the team: This contracting meeting has a number of functions:

Team dynamics: It will give you, as the coach, an insight into the relationship between the team leader and the team and any visible tensions between team members.

Clarifying the purpose and goals: You will need to engage the team in a discussion about the purpose of the coaching, including identifying the team's goals, both as a group and as individual members. You can help the team to articulate specific, measurable outcomes and agree what success looks like.

Defining roles, responsibilities, and boundaries: You will seek some clarity around expectations, explaining what the team can expect from you, e.g., facilitation, feedback and resource, plus what their roles and responsibilities will be, including the commitment expected from each team member and from the team leader.

Setting ground rules and norms This is key to creating a safe and productive environment for the coaching. You and the team will co-create ground rules and behaviours that may include guidelines for respectful communication, confidentiality, trust-building, participation and feedback.

Confidentiality and trust: The bedrock of any coaching relationship is to establish a safe space for open dialogue and, given the complexity and dynamics of team relationships, you will need to be absolutely clear about the confidentiality boundaries of the coaching engagement, e.g., what information will remain private (within the coaching sessions) and what can be shared outside the sessions, e.g., with team leaders or stakeholders.

Establishing feedback and evaluation mechanisms: As in any coaching relationship, there needs to be a process agreed for ongoing reflection and assessment of progress. You should agree with the team on how progress will be monitored and evaluated. This might include regular check-ins to measure the progress made and effectiveness of the coaching. The team may also provide feedback to the coach to ensure that the process is meeting their needs to allow for necessary adjustments during the coaching engagement.

Unconscious bias

Being aware of unconscious biases: Another aspect of beginnings, in both one-to-one and team coaching assignments, is to examine our unconscious biases. First impressions – made within the first few moments of meeting a new client – will always influence our unconscious biases but, of course, the problem can be our lack of awareness that it is happening. For example, we may think better of someone because we believe that we're alike or less of someone because that person is different from us – they might be of a different race, religion, gender or age. We want to give our clients the best possible experience and build the best possible relationship with them, so it is important that we assess what may be going on for us.

The ACAS (2017) definition of unconscious bias is:

"How a person thinks can depend on their life experiences. Sometimes they have beliefs and views about other people that might not be right or reasonable".

There are many forms of unconscious bias within the workplace, e.g., cultural bias, confirmation bias, horn effect, halo effect, gender bias, attribution bias, beauty bias, conformity bias, affinity bias and contrast effect. Within the context of coaching, we need to understand the impact that unconscious bias – by ourselves or the client – can have on the process. If we have an acute curiosity about the client and their experiences, then our personal preferences and biases should not restrict us from taking an objective and open approach to the coaching.

We can reduce the impact of unconscious biases on our coaching relationship in several ways.

- Regularly reflect on our thoughts, assumptions and reactions to different clients.
- Notice patterns in our expectations, judgments or assumptions based on a client's background, appearance or communication style.
- Catch ourselves making a quick judgment about a client's capabilities or motivations, pause and ask ourselves, "What evidence do I have for this belief? Could there be another perspective?"
- Stay present with in-depth listening and repeating back what we have heard so as to help the client spot any biases in the information repeated back to them.
- Ask for feedback from the client. This may reveal if any unconscious biases have leaked.
- Keep a journal to track our reflections and any recurring biases so that they can be corrected.

Just as coaches may harbour tendencies towards unconscious bias, so the client may also display unconscious bias behaviours. As a coach you can challenge any that you pick up by helping the client to identify from where the biases stem, treating them with curiosity and an open mind and putting an emphasis on evidence and facts as opposed to impressions and gut feelings.

Transparency about biases is more than just honesty. It is about keeping lines of communication open, clear and consistent. This openness builds a sense of security and confidence, allowing for potential vulnerabilities to be shared from both sides in the belief that trust and mutual understanding create an environment for possibilities and change.

Middles

The middle phase of the coaching relationship is when the real work gets done, supporting the growth and development of the client (or clients in team coaching assignments).

During this stage, you play a vital role in fostering heightened awareness and personal responsibility. Through tailored strategies and insightful conversations, you can empower the client(s) to deepen self-understanding, enhance self-esteem and self-worth, embrace change and strive for continuous improvement. Together, you and your client(s) explore their motivational drivers and engage in reflective practices to spark meaningful transformations. Constant feedback from both the coach and client(s) ensures the coaching process remains effective and responsive to their evolving needs.

One of the most important things during this middle phase is to build an increasing sense of trust by partnering with clients in a thought-provoking and creative process that inspires them to maximise their personal and professional potential.

What do we mean by trust?

Zeus and Skiffington (2002) say:

> "Trust is an emotional skill; it is something we choose and a personal investment for which we take responsibility. By trusting, the coach and coachee are responsible for making a commitment, and choosing goals and a course of action".

Brené Brown (2017) has spent two decades studying courage, vulnerability, shame, empathy and, crucially, trust. She developed her model BRAVING to define the main pillars of trust. This is particularly relevant to building a close coaching relationship when you are working within the same organisational system as your client. Brown borrows a definition from leadership and wellbeing coach, Charles Feltman (2008), who says:

> "Trust is choosing to make something important to you vulnerable to the actions of someone else".

Trust is not built in grand gestures but in the small moments when people treat with care something that is important to you.

Brown's acronym BRAVING stands for boundaries, reliability, accountability, the vault, integrity, non-judgment and generosity. Understanding that these are components of trust and how they work can help us really understand how we do or don't trust others. When we trust, we are braving a connection with someone.

The seven BRAVING elements from a coaching perspective

Boundaries

You respect my boundaries, and when you're not clear about what's okay and not okay, you raise it or ask. You're also both at liberty and willing to say no. In the coaching relationship, you need to understand and clarify what stays within the boundaries of the coaching relationship and what is not part of coaching. For example, you realise that there is a wellbeing issue for your client that requires the intervention of another professional. You help them to recognise for themselves that they need to pursue that alternative form of expert help, outside the coaching relationship.

Reliability

You do what you say you'll do. In a coaching relationship, this means both you and your client stay aware of your capacity, limitations and your work demands, to ensure that neither of you overpromises but you deliver on your commitments and maintain a balance between competing priorities.

Accountability

You own any mistakes, apologise and make amends. In the coaching relationship, the client is responsible for their own growth, learning outcomes and actions. Your accountability, as an internal coach, is to be responsible for taking a systematic approach to the client's goals and session processes; to be empathetic to their needs and struggles; to be motivational; to have unconditional positive regard for them; to inspire their positive self-belief and always to be professional and ethical in your conduct.

Vault

You don't share information or experiences that are not yours to share. This is all about the importance of confidentiality in the coaching relationship – what must stay inside the room and what cannot. It is why formal contracting before coaching commences is such a critical factor in the foundation of a strong coaching relationship and so essential for internal coaches, particularly where there may be multiple stakeholders and powerplay.

Integrity

You choose courage over comfort. You choose what is right over what is fun, fast, or easy. And you choose to practise your values rather than simply professing them. In the coaching relationship this when you, as the internal coach, are honest, transparent and can share your own vulnerability with the client. It makes it easier for the client to be open, honest, and vulnerable too. It will also be a good basis for discussing any ethical dilemmas that may arise. A good exercise, early on, is for you to share some stories about what integrity means to you and why it is important. Giving honest feedback is a great example. It may not feel comfortable, but you are being truthful about your client's behaviour, progress or self-perception in the service of helping them to determine if they want to change and how best to do so.

Non-judgement

I can ask for what I need and you can ask for what you need. We can talk about how we feel without judgement. In the coaching relationship, being non-judgemental means how you allow yourself to 'be with' the client, inside their thinking and experience, rather than being stuck in your own reactions to it. Our role is to facilitate the thinking and self-insight of our client, to reflect back what we have seen and heard. We ask questions to gain clarification and to open up possibilities. We listen and observe to pick up the full spectrum of communication – verbal and non-verbal – that reveals the reality behind the words.

Generosity

You extend the most generous interpretation possible to the intentions, words and actions of others. This is all about having unconditional positive regard for your client. Everyone's human and the coaching relationship can be tested at times, for example when the client does not follow through on commitments or cancels sessions. For you, this is where generosity needs to kick in. As an internal coach you will have an appreciation of the organisational pressures, internal politics and work environment. Generosity is being considerate, kind and willing to forgive and explore the reasons behind the client's actions or behaviour so that, together, you can agree a way forward. It is also an important reminder for you to be generous to yourself, reflect on why you coach and give yourself permission to be kind and caring about your own situation, capabilities and self-worth.

Team coaching relationships

Building effective team coaching relationships involves all the same factors covered above but with the additional complexity of having multiple parties involved. Experience as a team facilitator is a key requirement when accepting a commission to provide team coaching as it requires a sophisticated understanding of team dynamics. So, let us consider some of the factors necessary to ensure that the relational process provided by internal team coaches, throughout the assignment, is effective.

Alignment with organisational and team goals: As a team coach you will have established the team's coaching purpose and how it aligns with broader organisational objectives during the contracting phase. This helps to ensure that the coaching supports the organisation as well as taking forward the specific goals that the team wants to achieve during the process, e.g., improved communication, better decision-making and enhanced collaboration.

Building trust and psychological safety: It is your role as a team coach to build close relations with both the team leader and team members and to ensure that sessions feel like a safe space where they can share ideas, concerns, and feedback without fear of judgment. This can be trickier in a virtual setting, so ask what has worked well before when they have had team meetings and discussions online. There may be times when there is resistance to change, which will require you to think on your feet and make 'in the moment' choices about how to ensure that team members feel that they can express their concerns honestly. Questions at the start of the process can help, such as:

"How shall we ensure that every voice is heard in this team?"
"What do you need from each other to build trust?"
"How do we handle conflict in a way that strengthens our relationships?"
"How can we support each other in times of challenge or stress?"
"What is one thing we could do differently to enhance our collaboration?"

Promoting confidentiality and transparency: Internal team coaches need to ensure that team members understand the confidentiality of the process and build that trust that enables sensitive discussions during the coaching process to be respected when delicate issues arise. You can set expectations that disagreements are normal and productive and reframe any negativity into constructive dialogue. Useful questions include:

"It's okay to have different opinions. How can we move forward in a way that benefits the whole team?"
"Let's focus on the issue, not the person. What's the key takeaway here?"
"I can hear there are strong feelings on this topic. Let's take a step back - what's most important for us to resolve?"

Encouraging open dialogue: This is essential if the team is to grow and develop. As a team coach you will need a mix of actions, facilitation techniques and carefully chosen language. Setting ground rules during the contracting phase should encourage respectful exchanges. Statements like "No idea is a bad idea" or "Let's encourage curiosity over judgement in the ideas we bring" fosters a mindset of exploration rather than criticism. Useful prompts include:

"This is a space where all voices matter; you don't need to have the perfect answer, just your honest perspective".
"I want to invite all perspectives, especially those we haven't heard yet. Who would like to share?"
"How did this discussion feel for everyone? What can we do to make these conversations even more open?"

"What's one thing we can commit to as a team to improve our communication?"
"I appreciate everyone's honesty today. Let's keep this level of openness going".

Recognising and celebrating achievements: This really helps to build team morale. Here are some useful questions:

"What challenges did we overcome together to reach this point?"
"What risks did we take that paid off?"
"How did we support each other in achieving this goal?"
"How do we celebrate our successes together?"

A team coach's approach to building relationships is fundamental to the team's success, as it fosters trust, psychological safety and open communication. By modelling active listening, facilitating honest dialogue and recognising contributions, the team coach can create an environment where the team members feel valued and heard. The stronger the relationships within the team, the more likely that the team will work productively toward a shared goal. Ultimately, your ability to nurture authentic connections will help set the foundation for long-term team effectiveness and better collective performance.

Helping the client(s) make progress between sessions

Coaches often talk about how the real work for the client happens between, rather than during, coaching sessions – though of course, as coaches, we relish those moments when a client has an 'Aha' moment in our presence! There are ways that we can support both individual clients and teams to make progress between sessions.

Set clear goals and actions: Part of the coach's role is to ensure that the client has a realistic goal for each session and maintains focus on how that fits in with their overall purpose. Ensuring that they depart, at the end of each session, with agreed action points and asking questions like "What will success look like for you between now and next time?" can help the client(s) stay on track.

Build self-awareness and understanding: You can help a lot by offering observational feedback on how you are experiencing them in what they say (or don't say), the emotions they may display or how they behave during a session. Honest feedback about any differences you are noticing as the coaching progresses can be a powerful motivator for them to work hard between sessions. Questions such as "I notice when you said X that you seem to be thinking differently" or "I am observing when you talk about Y that you seem to have really moved on" is a great way to offer feedback that promotes reflection and self-awareness.

Invite client feedback: Every client or team is unique and feedback helps you to tailor your language, approach and level of challenge and support to fit their specific needs, preferences and goals. Client feedback helps us as coaches to understand what is working and what isn't, allowing us to refine our techniques, communication style and overall coaching methods to meet the needs of our clients more effectively. So, ask your client(s) if there is more – or something different – that you could be doing to help them to make progress back in the day job.

Progress and results: Your sessions offer a great opportunity to celebrate success. As mentioned before, giving feedback on the pace and degree to which progress is being made (no matter how small the steps may be) can be very encouraging. Shifts like an increase in confidence or collaboration may be more evident to the coach than to the client(s). And the coach is likely to be the only person who is fully aware of the effort and commitment that has been invested to shift their values, thinking, perspective, behaviours or actions in a more positive direction.

Endings

The 'Endings' phase of the coaching relationship is a critical and reflective stage, where both the coach and the client(s) assess the progress made and prepare for continued success beyond the coaching partnership. It is worth mentioning though, in one-to-one coaching assignments, that sometimes the clients don't want the relationship to end. In a tightly managed scheme, the number of sessions is set in advance with little flexibility. However, in other schemes, monitoring of the coaches' activities can be pretty hands-off and they are free to extend the assignment if the client wishes. While this is always flattering, you need to be alert to the possibility that you are creating a dependency that does not enhance their resourcefulness.

In the endings phase, the focus in both one-to-one and team coaching assignments is on celebrating achievements and recognising the positive changes that have been made. It is an opportunity for both parties to affirm the impact of the work done, secure a commitment from the client(s) to sustaining any changes, and provide constructive feedback on what worked well and where improvements can still be made. The coach can facilitate a smooth ending by identifying ways that the client(s) can carry forward their growth afterwards, while also considering how the insights gained might contribute to broader departmental or organisational learning.

Ensuring a smooth and productive transition involves a number of elements.

- *Reviewing achievements* by reflecting on the goals set at the beginning of the coaching relationship, recognising accomplishments and acknowledging progress made.
- *Acknowledgement of growth* by discussing the personal and professional growth experienced, noting any shifts in behaviour, mindset or skills.
- *Commitment to sustainable change* by ensuring that individual clients have the tools and appropriate support to continue applying independently what they have learned. This may involve developing a plan for maintaining progress with their line manager or a mentor. In the case of team coaching, the

final session needs to include a discussion of how any new behaviours will be reinforced.

- *Feedback exchange* by both the coach and client(s) to harvest what worked well and areas for improvement.
- *Sharing of insights* by agreeing on what aspects of the coaching process can be shared with the client's sponsor or the lead coach (particularly any generic themes that might be relevant for broader team or organisational learning).
- *Closure* through acknowledging the emotional aspects of what has taken place and providing a sense of resolution, making sure that the client feels empowered and ready to move forward.
- *Celebrating together* by recognising the client's journey, reinforcing their sense of achievement and confidence as you both move forward.

The emotional impact of endings: Ending a coaching relationship can evoke a range of emotional responses from both the coach and the client, influenced by the depth of the connection made. For the client, there may be feelings of loss as the coach has become a trusted guide and source of support. This sense of loss can sometimes create fear, where the client may feel uncertain about navigating challenges without the coach's continued presence. On the coach's side too, there may be a sense of attachment and emotional investment, especially if they have witnessed significant growth in the client. Coaches may feel a bittersweet sense of pride in their client's progress but also a natural sadness that the partnership is ending. Both parties may experience a moment of vulnerability, as the closure of the relationship requires both to confront the reality of moving forward without the regular dynamic they have shared. Navigating these emotions is a crucial part of the coaching process, as it ensures the client feels empowered to maintain the changes they have made while acknowledging the coach's role in their development.

Building effective relationships when working with neurodiverse clients and those experiencing intersectionality

Working with neurodiverse clients

Neurodiversity is the concept that all humans vary in terms of their neurocognitive ability. We all have both talents and things we struggle with. However, for some people the variation between those strengths and challenges is more pronounced, which can bring advantages but can also be disabling. Internal coaches can help to identify and reinforce the client's strengths, explore their challenges and help them to develop coping mechanisms that empower them to navigate their challenges independently. However, people who are neurodivergent will often have grown up with the idea that they should fit in so are often highly skilled with strategies aimed at 'masking' their differences. It may not be immediately obvious to the coach, therefore, that their client sees the world in a different way. There are certain behaviours that might provide a clue such as hair twisting (known as 'stimming' or self-stimulatory behaviour, helping to calm and self-regulate the person when they're feeling stressed or overwhelmed), which we can look out for.

It is important that the coach sees the client for who they are. The client may feel shame at being different and may have spent a lot of their working lives 'withholding' what they really feel, so being affirmed by the coach can make a lot of difference.

Coaching neurodivergent clients require a thoughtful and individualised relational approach. Internal coaches need to be clear and explicit in their communications and be conscious of avoiding ambiguous language. Being led by the clients, who know how they work best, will always be an internal coach's most helpful guide, thus establishing a firm platform for a trusting relationship by demonstrating empathy, active listening and promoting a safe space where they feel comfortable in expressing themselves.

If meeting face-to-face, internal coaches should be mindful of any sensory sensitivities that neurodivergent individuals may have and consider factors such as lighting, noise levels, and seating arrangements to create a comfortable coaching environment. Asking the client what kind of environment works best for them is always a good place to start.

To give the coaching relationship the best chance of flourishing, you need to be open to being flexible in your coaching methods and scheduling, as some neurodivergent clients may be easily overwhelmed and benefit from breaks or adjustments to your coaching approach. Getting feedback early on how the relationship is working for the client is essential. Feedback could include things like shortening each session to accommodate energy and concentration levels and ensure the best use of time for both of you.

Use your skills as an internal coach – being adaptable, patient and willing to understand your client's perspective – to help them to develop their own ways of learning. You may also encourage them to have the confidence to share what they learn with their colleagues, thus allowing their peer relationships to thrive too.

When gathering stories and case studies for this book, Julia and Katharine had the privilege of meeting with many internal coaches and hearing about their experiences. One of these wonderful coaches is Morwenna. She is herself non-neurotypical and specialises in coaching neurodivergent clients. Here are her thoughts and opinions on how neurodiversity may show up in the workplace.

Morwenna's view of being non-neurotypical and cognitively unique

The most important thing about people with neurodivergent minds is that we tend to be specialists and have quite a tricky narrative. Sometimes we'll slip into "we're deficits and we're broken" or "we're brilliant at some skills and we're superheroes", so we have to try to keep a balance. But having said that, many of us do have some quite intense sorts of skills. We talk about something called 'spiky profile abilities', which means that most neurotypical skills are on a graph of highs and lows. With the spiky profile, neurodivergent abilities have much higher highs and much lower lows, so there is a much more intense pattern of activity. This can mean that you'll have people who are brilliant at certain things but will really struggle at other things, which can be quite confusing.

In the workplace, we expect people to be able to cope with administrative tasks like organising their diaries, but neurodiverse people can really struggle with some things that you might find surprising. They may have struggled, throughout their careers, with functions like time management and scheduling. Or they may seek a coach because of a problem with work relationships. They may never have quite known why they found them a challenge. It's often when people hit a crisis that they will come to coaching, or maybe they have a new manager and the cracks start to show. The person's manager or peers won't understand, or they may misinterpret the person's approach.

Our intention as internal coaches is normally to focus on a positive outcome such as a client choosing to stay in their role and helping them thrive. But there are times when the best outcome for a neurodivergent client – and for their organisation – is for that person to realise that they are not in the right job, or not in the right place. Perhaps they need to be doing something else as it's not a good fit for them: the role, their manager, or the organisation is asking more than they can deliver.

Coaching a neurodivergent person to help them to 'fit in', is not necessarily the right outcome. It is common for neurodivergent clients to realise, through coaching, that their organisation is the wrong place for them and they're in the wrong job, which is asking the wrong things of them. So sometimes, as a coach, it is appropriate to be respectful of this realisation and support them to find an alternative role where they are valued for who they are and what they offer. This is also huge learning for organisations, who may need to review their thinking on how to retain their best talent, with all their differing gifts and expertise.

Morwenna is a specialist in supporting neurodivergent clients but she recognises that even within neurodiversity, internal coaches can have their own areas of expertise. Her niche is autism and ADHD – both her special interest and where she has personal experience. There are multiple niche areas. For example, there are nine (or more) different types of dyslexia. It's a complex area and no internal coach can be an expert in all of them. The key is to focus on the person and initiate an open and honest conversation with them about what they need. The aim is to establish whether or not the internal coach's knowledge, skills, approach and competence will be enough to provide the right type of development to support the client.

To give a sense of the complexity of and range of neurotypes, this graphic shows how many there can potentially be.

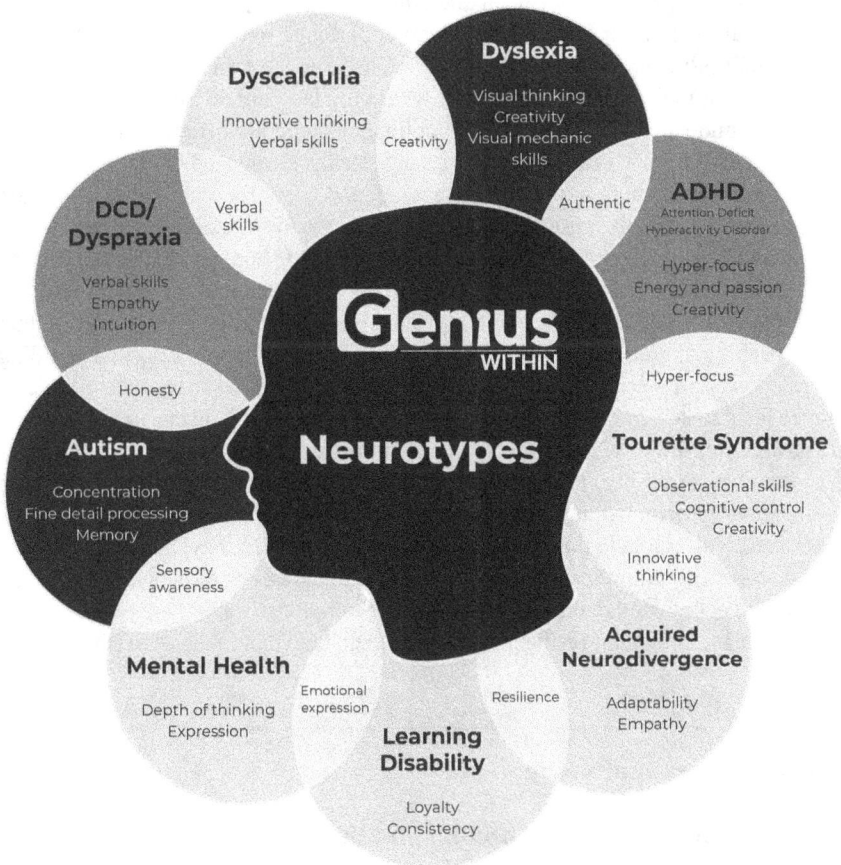

Figure 3.3 Genius Within: Neurotypes.

Graphic by kind permission of Genius Within. Taken from Doyle (2024). Neurotypes Venn Diagram: Based on the DANDA Chart work of Mary Colley.

Working with those experiencing intersectionality

Intersectionality refers to the interconnectedness of social categories such as race, gender, class, sexuality and ability – all of which shape an individual's identities and experiences and, when combined, can create unique modes of discrimination or privilege. The term intersectionality emphasises that these identities do not exist independently of one another but interconnect to shape individuals' experiences within social structures (Crenshaw, 1989).

As coaches we need to understand the impact that some of the factors of intersectionality can have on people from different backgrounds, as many of these aspects are unseen or unacknowledged or even talked about by organisations.

Intersectionality correlates with many things, including being subject to micro-aggressions and discrimination, under-representation, different values and different cultural backgrounds and social and cultural vulnerabilities.

People affected by intersectionality can experience poor treatment and narcissistic behaviour from management and/or peers. The latter may be conventionally intelligent but make assumptions about what they see, and do not take the time or interest to understand fully those work colleagues who are different from them.

An empathetic coach can support those that are disadvantaged or treated inappropriately through creating a trusting space where the client feels psychologically safe and able to talk about their true selves so they can begin the process of recognising that they are worthy of recognition, success, progression and happiness in the workplace.

If you work with an employee experiencing intersectionality, you should approach the nature of the intersectionality sensitively and thoughtfully to ensure that your coaching approach is inclusive and considerate. You should prioritise building the relationship by creating a safe, open and non-judgmental space where the employee feels seen, heard and valued for their unique identity. You can actively listen, acknowledging how various aspects of the employee's identity (such as race, gender, sexuality, disability) may intersect to have an impact on their experiences and challenges. By demonstrating cultural competence and being sensitive to these intersections, you can help the client to explore their strengths, navigate systemic barriers and identify tailored strategies for their personal and professional growth. It's essential to acknowledge the complexity of the individual's experience and support them while building their resilience and courage to help them feel more empowered.

Bijna's personal story

Overcoming intersectionality in the workplace

As a British-born, Indian-origin female with African roots, and often the 'youngest' in the room, Bijna received judgement, labels and poor treatment explicitly because of her appearance in the workplace. For example, at one investment bank she was addressed (on the first day of a new role) as 'a child' by direct reports older than her but junior in designation.

As she gained seniority, she exercised her voice to create and advocate for Diversity, Equity and Inclusion policies, but the early years left imprints on her of how the next cohort of hires should *not* be treated.

Intersectionality can have a significant impact on the confidence, competence and performance of individuals at work, and may cause people to:

- Self-sabotage and feel that they are not worthy of praise, reward or promotion.
- Lack personal self-worth and so fail to appreciate their strengths and capabilities.
- Experience impostor syndrome.

If not addressed, this can lead to a downward spiral where the individual can become depressed, unwell, underperform and withdraw from engagement with work colleagues, family and friends.

For example, Bijna experienced anxiety in the first year of her career as she was suffering from a new diagnosis of severe polycystic ovary syndrome and a line manager told her if she did not 'learn to walk to the printer faster' she would risk losing her job. He implied people of Asian origin have a slower pace, basing his understanding on Asian culture instead of being open to the idea she might be internalising a gender-specific medical issue. Bijna did not have the confidence or psychological safety to discuss this with anyone in the firm so internalised it which led to constant anxiety over the following year.

From Bijna's story, we can recognise that intersectionality can have a significant impact on the confidence, competence and performance of individuals at work.

This is where the unique role of the coach comes into its own to support people feeling psychologically unsafe. Coaches who understand the factors involved in diversity and intersectionality can be proactive in building an open and trusting relationship through detailed contracting and managing the sensitivities of third-party interventions by sponsors or line managers. It is your role to build a sound foundation of trust where the client feels psychologically safe. Ask, don't assume. Building trust is particularly important where they may not trust their colleagues.

The barriers that the client may place on themselves can lead to self-limiting beliefs regarding their career, growth, potential and happiness. These need to be sensitively explored in order to help the client to better understand their world and the issues that present themselves, then come to terms with them and make decisions about what they want to do.

How might you sensitively start the conversation to help build awareness in your client? Here are some openers:

"How would you describe your personal value system?"
"Do you feel you have multiple identities?"
"What do you see as your own social identity and what do you regard as your 'true' personal identity?"
"How willing are you to speak up when challenged?"
"How aware are you of your own behaviours?"
"What needs to happen to help you to feel psychologically safe at work and to be honest with colleagues about things that affect you?"

Your role as a coach may be to help your client to find their true identity so that they can show up as their best selves. In essence, your clients may need to learn to love themselves, be brave and have the courage to speak up and challenge unjust comments, behaviours, actions or treatment toward them.

Terri's story offers a more encouraging example.

Terri's story

Championing diversity – A journey of growth

Terri was invited to work with an employee, Maria, who identified as a Latina woman, a first-generation immigrant and a parent. She talked about the challenges that she believed she faced in advancing within the organisation. She felt overlooked for leadership opportunities.

Terri started by acknowledging Maria's unique experiences. She recognised that Maria's challenge of not being identified as someone suitable for promotion might stem from gender bias, racial/ethnic stereotypes or assumptions about her caregiving responsibilities (or all three). Instead of addressing these identities in isolation, Terri explored with Maria how those aspects overlapped and affected her experience at work. Terri also realised that she must remain self-aware, really listen and continually reflect on her own biases. It was important that she avoid stereotyping Maria or making assumptions about her ambitions and priorities.

Terri knew that she must invest in creating a judgement-free, supportive environment and developing an open and trusting relationship with Maria so that she felt comfortable sharing her experiences. At first, Maria found it hard to articulate them but gradually she revealed the micro-aggressions and biases that she had been subjected to over many years. She felt that she had been excluded from the informal networks that facilitate promotions – possibly due to cultural differences or unconscious bias.

Terri helped Maria to identify systemic barriers and how they might be having an impact on her career prospects, then together they developed some tailored strategies. One was working with Maria to develop her assertiveness, while still respecting her cultural values, and assisting her to navigate workplace dynamics to create stronger networks. Terri also built Maria's awareness of her own unconscious biases and encouraged her to identify allies and advocates in her wider team who understood the value of her multifaceted identity and could help her.

Terri encouraged Maria to explore how the organisation's existing systems might support her better. It turned out that there was a mentoring programme that she could apply to join and flexible working arrangements that she could have been taking greater advantage of to support her caregiving responsibilities.

By adopting an intersectional approach, Terri successfully empowered Maria to address her challenges effectively and 18 months later Maria gained the promotion she was after.

Summary

In this chapter, we have shone a light on how the relationship between an internal coach and their client is the cornerstone of successful coaching. We have explored how we can nurture and build the relationship to achieve an empathetic, respectful and non-judgmental environment that fosters trust, rapport and psychological safety. By acting as 'thinking partners', coaches and clients are able to co-create a unique and special bond that enables deep self-reflection, self-discovery and the achievement of desired outcomes that benefit both the coach, the client and the organisation.

We have acknowledged that internal coaching relationships face unique challenges, including role duality, the sensitivities of pre-existing relationships, the management of stakeholder expectations and the careful navigation of power differentials. However, engaging in robust contracting helps build and foster a firm foundation for the relationship to thrive, both for individuals and for teams.

All coaches need to be aware of potential unconscious biases that may occur, and this chapter has provided some insights into how to develop effective and individualised relationships with neurodiverse clients and those experiencing the challenges of intersectionality. Ultimately, the success, impact and return on investment in coaching starts by the coach ensuring that there is a trusting and supportive relationship. If this is secure, then everything else falls into place to make it a rewarding and productive journey for both coach and client.

Table 3.1 Questions to reflect on

The unique and challenging role of being an internal coach

- How do you describe your role and approach as an internal coach to clearly showcase your worth and value to the organisation?
- What support systems can you tap into to ensure you are an active part of the coaching community in your organisation to support your practice?

Beginnings – middles – endings

- Do you have clarity about the different ways that you can contract with clients for one-to-one, three-way and team assignments to ensure that all parties understand its importance?
- What is your approach to building a mutually safe, open and trusting relationship?
- What can you do to raise awareness of your own and your client's potential unconscious biases?
- What procedural and emotional practices do you need to consider to end the coaching relationship in a way that sustains and maintains growth and learning?

Team coaching relationships

- What is different about team coaching that you need to be aware of before accepting any team coaching commissions?
- What potential challenges may you face in team coaching and what are the potential strategies you can utilise if these arise?

Working with neurodiverse clients and those experiencing intersectionality

- How can you build trust and psychological safety that helps individuals be proud of who they are, what they offer and be their authentic selves?
- How can you recognise what your client needs to determine if you are the right coach to provide them with the support they need from the coaching process?

Chapter 4

Recognising ethical dilemmas

What this chapter is about

What would you do if you smelled alcohol on your client's breath at ten o'clock in the morning? Or your client launched into a rant about a 'difficult' colleague who is actually a close friend of yours? An understanding of coaching ethics is fundamental to being a coach. As Albert Camus said: "A man without ethics is a wild beast loosed upon this world".

This chapter explores:

- What ethical dilemmas are and why they are important
- The four most common varieties to arise:

    - Boundaries: recognising them and how to avoid crossing them
    - Confidentiality: what are the limits and where are the strains?
    - Bias: managing bias, discrimination and intersectionality
    - Power: dealing with power differentials both inside and outside the coaching relationship.

- Ethical dilemmas for team coaches

Why two chapters about ethical dilemmas?

It is, of course, important that all coaches, both internal and external, practise ethically, i.e., decently, morally and honourably but that doesn't mean it's easy or that ethical dilemmas won't arise. Maria Biquet's (2021) survey in partnership with EMCC Global, carried out with 353 coaches from 46 countries, found that nearly three-quarters of them had experienced between one and four dilemmas in the preceding 12 months. Add into that the fact that internal coaches are likely to encounter dilemmas more often than external coaches do (St John-Brooks, 2010) as a consequence of working in the same system as the client, which in turn throws up more complexities around boundaries, confidentiality and power, and you have a heady brew.

Over the past decade, a focus on coaches' ethical responsibilities has grown and an understanding of them has moved more centre stage in training programmes. In 2021,

DOI: 10.4324/9781003519911-5

Wendy-Ann Smith founded the Coaching Ethics Forum (CEF) which hosts a Global Ethics Conference, publishes the Journal of Coaching Ethics, and the magazine Ethical Edge Insights, and launched the Champions of Courage Awards. Wendy-Ann published The Ethical Coaches Handbook (2023) and Ethical Case Studies for Coach Development and Practice (2024) to advance ethical conversations in coaching.

What exactly are 'ethical dilemmas'?

An ethical (or moral) dilemma arises when a coach finds themself in a situation where they need to make a choice of action and none of the available alternatives seems satisfactory from an ethical perspective. When this happens in the moment, during a coaching conversation, you could find yourself at a loss as to what to say or do.

There is something about the word ethical that can make some people switch off or turn away. As Judit Varkonyi-Sepp put it in her report on the eighth annual conference of the British Psychological Society's special group in coaching psychology (Varkonyi-Sepp, 2013):

> "The word 'ethics' might send shivers down one's spine thinking about this as an abstract, boring, legislation-filled dry topic, but it is not … Ethics is everywhere in what we do and it was a light bulb moment to recognise how very practical it is". (p. 108)

This thought was echoed by Hawkins and Turner (2020) when they wrote:

> "ethics is all around – it is in every conversation, it is part of the fabric of our societies, of being human, of everyday choices". (p. 167)

So, what sorts of dilemmas might you, as an internal coach, find yourself faced with? Here is a random selection of common examples:

- Your client wants you to coach them to prepare for an interview outside the organisation that they have not told their line manager/sponsor about.
- From your 'day job' you have information about the client that is relevant to their performance but they don't know that you have it and do not refer to it so you feel that you cannot raise it either.
- You are under pressure from your client's line manager to provide information about how they are 'getting on'.
- You are selected to be a team coach for a team that needs to build more cohesive relationships as they are not performing well. You have a personal dislike of one or more team members that you suspect could influence your coaching of this team.
- You learn from your client that they are being badly bullied but they don't want you to tell anyone.
- A conflict of interest between your day job and your role as a coach only becomes apparent after you have taken a particular client on.

- HR is instituting disciplinary proceedings with your client and is demanding some input from you.
- Your client is planning to do something that would be unacceptable to the organisation if they knew.
- Your organisation does not practise what it preaches on EDI. Your client is experiencing intersectionality issues, and their career progression is being hampered by their disability, religion and gender but they don't want to raise it.

In practice, dilemmas often do not fit into neat categories but for convenience we are going to group the dilemmas into four key areas: boundaries, confidentiality, bias and dealing with power differentials.

Boundaries

In the responses to our survey of 137 coaches, carried out in preparation for this second edition, to a question about ethical dilemmas, two key themes cited were blurred boundaries and conflicting interests between the client and their sponsor/management.

Maintaining boundaries in coaching is about paying attention to where the limits to your role as a coach are and not going beyond them. Given the many interconnecting relationships that internal coaches need to navigate in their organisations, recognising and holding the boundaries can be complicated. You may find yourself under pressure to blur them so you should give considerable thought and care to boundary management.

Professional competence

We need to be clear with ourselves and our coaching clients about what we are competent to coach them on and what we are not. At the contracting stage of the coaching relationship (covered in detail in Chapter 3), you would normally remind the client of what you are not there to do, e.g., act as a consultant, therapist or be their mentor. In the moment, you may feel uncomfortable saying that you do not have the expertise to deal with a particular issue when it comes up, either fearing that your credibility could suffer or maybe simply because you want to help the client with their challenge. One formulation that you could use with clients at the contracting stage is: "if the conversation moves into territory where I feel that I am not competent to coach you, say, difficulties with a partner, or finances, or mental health then I will tell you and we can discuss alternative sources of support".

Competence may be about professional boundaries but could equally well concern psychological limits. For example, we know of coaches who say that they cannot coach well if the client wants to discuss issues around shame. Bullying is another subject that some coaches choose not to coach people on because they have experienced it themselves and feel they cannot stay dispassionate. The key is for us to be honest with the client if an issue is broached where we feel we cannot add value and to make alternative arrangements for them.

This is underpinned by two paragraphs in the Global Code of Ethics (2021):

- Para 2.26 Members will encourage the client or sponsor to terminate the coaching, mentoring, or supervision engagement if it is believed that the client would be better served by a different form of professional help.
- Para 4.1 Members will operate within the limit of their professional competence. Members should refer the client to a more experienced or suitably qualified practising member where appropriate.

The boundary between coaching support and therapeutic support can be fuzzy. When does a highly stressed executive become someone with clinical depression who needs medical help? Does a client have to be experiencing panic attacks for anxiety to be classified as a mental health issue? We are not expected to 'diagnose' the client but simply to notice our responses to their levels of stress and invite them to consider whether they might need to access other professional support.

In conversation with a number of internal coaches, the following points were made.

- A boundary would be crossed if coaches attempted to deal with a potential mental health issue simply as part of the coaching. Most would encourage the client to seek professional help, starting with their GP.
- A sensible strategy might be to seek early advice from your supervisor or lead coach as you should not be the sole person to hold this knowledge, thus making you vulnerable for any actions that you or your client may take. You could also familiarise yourself with your organisation's employee assistance programme (often a source of counselling support) and any other referral options.
- It might be desirable to discuss with the client suspending the coaching until they are on a more even keel, though keeping continuity of support from the coach, in parallel with any other arrangements, is also an option.

An inexperienced coach might feel wary of broaching the subject of seeking professional help or not know what to do if the client brushed off the suggestion. They might be concerned that the coaching relationship would suffer if they persisted. But it is important to be brave. One internal coach in a medical establishment referred to a complicated dilemma they had in relation to a severely depressed client:

"I supported my client in seeking help from a colleague – another health professional – who was better placed to support them, as their depression was outside my area of professional competence. However, I faced an ethical dilemma on hearing that they did not attend the appointment – particularly as my client led me to believe that they had. The client did not know that I had this information as the health professional told me, without my asking, which put me in a difficult position in relation to our contractual arrangements".

There are, of course, other types of issues that may require the coach to suggest to the client that they seek help from another professional. The most commonly cited are problems with drugs or alcohol, personal finances, bereavement and marital or other family relationship difficulties.

Deciding where to refer a client will be more straightforward for some coaches than others. Two comments were: "I lack information on who to refer clients to with needs greater than coaching", and "I need to build up a more comprehensive list of support organisations".

Some coaches work in companies where employees can access a free, externally sourced counselling service which makes referrals straightforward. Other organisations have an employee assistance programme, a wellbeing service or similar welfare arrangements. However, there can sometimes be issues around confidentiality. For example, the client's line manager might be made aware that they had accessed those services, which could discourage the client from taking that route. An additional problem can be that the confidential service provided is either not trusted or has a poor reputation.

If you find yourself being asked for guidance on where to go for help outside the organisation, seek advice on referral routes, taking care to maintain the client's anonymity. And if a client tells you that they have accessed an external source of counselling, it is good practice to make a note in your records to that effect.

Ellie's story

Breaking confidentiality for a client's mental health issue

I was working as a lead coach when a Director asked me to support Jake, one of his senior leaders. Jake had management problems and he was not meeting performance targets. The Director indicated that if he didn't see improvements soon, then he would need to replace him. I agreed to help but got the impression that the Director expected me to collude with him to help manage Jake out of the business. I felt a divided loyalty between my client (Jake) and my employer (represented by the Director, who was quite a powerful figure) and was aware of potential risks around confidentiality and to my professional reputation. As the relationship between the Director and Jake had broken down, my initial aim was to help both parties be honest with me with a view to helping them rebuild trust.

In my initial coaching session with Jake, it emerged that he struggled with empathy for customers and he disclosed that he was suffering from anxiety. He knew that some of his team were experiencing stress too which made things worse and affected his ability to make rational decisions. Jake revealed that he wasn't sleeping, was constantly anxious and felt unwell. I had a duty of care to help him get professional support, but he was resistant. He worried that revealing his mental health issues would harm his career. I was concerned about breaching confidentiality and sought a discussion with my supervisor. Eventually, Jake agreed to my intervention and, in the end, said he was relieved that I had taken action on his behalf. He took the advice of the healthcare professionals and went on sick leave.

The eventual outcome was positive: Jake recovered and, on his return, moved to a role with less pressure in a different department. I carried on talking to the Director who acknowledged that he should have paid more attention to his relationship with Jake, who might then have been more open about what he was coping with and the stress levels in his team. He had learnt more about the importance of wellbeing in the office and, to my relief, I had managed to maintain a level of trust with both him and Jake.

What did I learn?

1 Not to let the power differential with a senior leader push me into colluding with his plan. I contracted tightly which protected both me and Jake – and I managed to maintain the reputation of the internal coaching service.
2 I was explicit about how confidentiality worked, built trust with both of them and was clear about what I could and could not say.
3 I consulted my coach supervisor, trusted my intuition, and was guided by the Global Code of Ethics and my moral compass.
4 I remembered that I was representing my organisation and needed to comply with the organisation's legal, health and safety and well-being practices.

But I was also aware that it could so easily have gone wrong and was grateful for the experience.

Role blurring

Conflict of interest

Managing the boundary between an internal coach's coaching role and their 'day job' is one of the most common challenges encountered by internal coaches. Yedreshteyn (2008) pointed out that:

"boundary maintenance may be less of a concern if the coach does not interact with the same group of people as his or her client does".

If the internal coaching scheme involves a managed matching process between coach and client, then the matcher will normally try to avoid the possibility of the coach's and client's networks overlapping too much. But where the process involves the client selecting potential coaches from a register, then it is your responsibility as the coach to check out, in the 'chemistry meeting' (an initial meeting where the coach and potential client decide if they can work well together) whether the two of you work in sufficiently different areas to minimise the risk of role conflict. This is more difficult to achieve if the coach or client is very senior, as the pyramid in most organisations narrows significantly towards the top.

If a coach works in the centre of the organisation, for example, HR, OD or L&D the potential for role conflict rises. These comments from internal coaches working in HR illustrate the types of role conflict issues that can occur.

- "Some conflict of interest when I have been coaching internal clients through to partnership as I am also involved in the sign-off process for them becoming a partner".
- "I have had to declare that as a result of potential confidentiality issues I was unable to take part in a personnel selection process".
- "I have been involved in coaching individuals around their performance and then been asked to provide HR support in a grievance procedure involving the same individual".
- "Where a line manager wanted advice about one of her members of staff that she was having problems with, and did not know that I was that individual's coach (as the person had self-referred)".

One HR director described a vivid example of a mistake he made. He found himself in a conversation with his coaching client's line manager that shifted into a discussion about the client's potential. He was surprised into being asked for a view that was then repeated back by the line manager to the client.

Insider knowledge

An additional challenge of being an internal coach working in HR or OD is that you may find yourself privy to information about a client or relevant to them that the client does not know. This can happen to internal coaches who are not in HR too – though less frequently – as sometimes line managers tell coaches things about their clients that it would be cleaner for them not to know. Here are some examples.

- "Where a client has shared that they are going for a promotion or intending to leave the organisation, and I have knowledge regarding the situation which would influence their decision".
- "Knowing that an individual I was coaching was going to be made redundant further to an organisational review".
- "I have been told about a coachee's lack of suitability for a senior position, but the coachee has not been told and I am unable to tell them".

These situations can throw up real dilemmas for a coach. Katharine had the experience of coaching someone to help them prepare for a promotion process to a senior position, only to be told privately a month before the assessment board that the client had no chance as the chairman of the panel held the fixed, but unofficial, view that it was essential that the post-holder should be a graduate (and her client was not). Usually, the coach will take the difficult decision not to reveal what they know, meaning that they temporarily cannot be fully authentic in the coaching relationship – an uncomfortable position for any coach.

Rescuing the client

Another aspect of role conflict is the temptation for the coach to 'fix' a problem for the client. As one internal coach working in OD put it:

> "You want to rescue the individual and have to keep checking with yourself: 'Are you sure you're not on your White Charger?' There's a tendency to want to save the individual as there *are* levers that OD could pull".

Coach supervisors confirm that this issue crops up in supervision. The other side of this coin was identified in some research by Wrynne (2011), where the client of an internal coach perceived his coach as "an extension of the organisation that should be supporting him" (p. 33). The client had an expectation that he would not have had of an external coach i.e., that by virtue of her day job, his coach would make something happen for him. Wrynne describes the client as "expecting his coach to use her proximity to organisational power and pull on an organisational 'lever' to actively support him" (p. 58). The internal coach had to disabuse the client of this notion and empower him to shift for himself.

Knowing the same people

It may be hard for you, as an internal coach, to maintain objectivity if the client wants to discuss someone whom you know. This is a common issue. Here are some examples.

- "It's almost impossible not to have your own views on people in the organisation. It's an ongoing challenge not to let that get in the way of the coaching. For example, if your client has a difficult relationship with someone whom you have a problem with too – or who is a friend – you mustn't let it get in the way, but it can be a huge effort".
- "Having knowledge or personal friendships with individuals that the coachee is talking about or having difficulty with, which was unknown when the coaching contract was agreed".

- "Client discussing the negative impact a colleague's behaviour is having on them – the colleague is a personal friend of mine".
- "I knew the manager of one coachee very well through work. Although he is a charming character, I consider him to be a very poor manager. This caused me some problems, in that I had to try to remain neutral during coaching sessions, and to challenge the coachee's equally low opinion of her manager".

Dealing with overlapping work relationships is a fact of life for many internal coaches. How you manage it, though, says something about the way you practise. Will you and your client contract about how you will treat such situations? Or will you wait to see if a problem arises and then discuss it in the moment? Many coaches would say that it would be impossible to maintain the requisite level of impartiality if a client wanted to discuss a difficult relationship with someone they knew really well, or that it would produce unhelpful 'noise', making it hard to give their full attention to the client. Others consider these arguments can be overdone.

An additional wrinkle relates to situations where the coach may have more than one client, and those clients turn out to know each other, and their working relationship may even come up in each other's coaching sessions. As noted in para 2.23 of the Global Code of Ethics:

> "Members will consider the impact of any client relationships on other client relationships and discuss any potential conflict of interest with those who might be affected".

Poaching

A very specific phenomenon that can arise is the temptation for a coach to poach a client or for a client to poach their coach to join their team. This is not as uncommon as it may sound since coaches and clients get to know each other well and may come to admire each other. But it can cause bad feelings if the line manager of the person being poached does not want to lose them, and can give coaching a bad name.

Work life vs personal life

In Chapter 2, we discussed the topic of "what is the internal coach *not* there to do?" including how the boundary between coaching the client on work issues and personal issues is not necessarily a clear one. In Katharine's original research, 91% of the internal coaches answered yes to the question: "Are you content for a coaching conversation to go beyond work issues?"

The sorts of topics outside current work issues that clients had brought to the sessions included family situation/relationship issues, work-life balance, bereavement/illness/fertility treatment and giving up smoking/losing weight. Some of the coaches had shared the following rationales for going beyond purely work issues:

- Because personal issues were directly affecting the client's performance at work ("Home life and other factors often have a bearing on performance, so are legitimate topics if the client wishes to discuss them").
- Because it was important to be holistic ("Life cannot be compartmentalised").
- Because people's pasts shape their present ("People's background, culture and upbringing have significantly shaped their current behaviour. This can come up when discussing values and limiting beliefs and can be helpful to talk through").

As an internal coach you need to be clear what is expected of you. Where are the boundaries in relation to what issues clients in your organisation can or cannot bring to the coaching table? As coaches, we know how a session labelled, say, 'career coaching' can swiftly become a highly emotional exploration of a client's fears about possible redundancy and the impact it could have on their family. Or the client may reveal that they can't see further opportunities to progress in their career, so they need to seek an alternative career path or even leave the organisation.

This whole topic has changed shape since the Covid-19 pandemic because internal coaches now, as a matter of course, find that clients are bringing existential questions into coaching conversations (as mentioned in Chapter 2). Most organisations recognise that and are happy for their coaches to take a holistic approach.

This boundary between work and the personal is reflected at a more strategic level in the debate about "who is the client?". Providing an internal coaching service is not costless to the employer, and Hawkins (2012), Jordan and Henderson (2024) and Peltier (2001), amongst others, have drawn attention to the importance of the coach recognising that they have responsibilities to the organisation as well as to the client.

As Peltier put it:

"To whom does the coach owe loyalty? What happens when a client's interests or intended behaviour are at odds with those of the company? For example, what if a client wants to focus on skills that the company clearly does not need—or skills that the client would like to use in her next job or as an entrepreneur? What happens when the client is angry and contemplating legal action against the company, or is plotting his next move to a new company?" (p. 226)

At what point do your obligations to the organisation kick in for you?

Coaching vs mentoring

What is the difference? While there is considerable overlap in the skills deployed, it is commonly accepted that while coaches are there to use listening and questioning to develop an individual's capability and focus on their personal and professional growth, mentors are:

> "people who impart their own experience, learning and advice to those who have less experience in a particular field".
>
> (Wilson & McMahon, 2006, p. 55)

Mentors often focus on helping the mentee's career advancement, drawing on the mentor's experience, knowledge of the organisation and personal networks.

Why might this boundary be problematic for the coach? Well, many are still trained in the 'pure art' of coaching: that is, to be non-directive, to act as a mirror, to ask 'clean' questions and to provide accurate feedback with the aim of providing an environment in which to help build the client's capacity to think things through for themselves and develop their resourcefulness. But, as mentioned in Chapter 2, clients can try to push their coach into becoming a mentor and offering advice (which can feel comfortable for the coach too and in their happy place) when that is not what their organisation is expecting from them.

One lead coach referred to a manager who pressured the coach into being a mentor and "showing him the ropes", as he had recently been promoted into the grade that the coach held. If that happened to you, would you comply with their wishes? Might your organisation be relaxed about it if you did? Should a coach who has a background in, say, OD and has relevant knowledge and experience of change management be allowed to make this knowledge available to a client who is struggling with managing a change programme? A better approach might be to offer a meeting with that as the agenda rather than as part of a coaching session.

Yedreshteyn (2008) noticed that some participants on a leadership development programme, when assigned their coaches, were:

> "disappointed not to have a more senior leader from their function, someone who could serve the role of mentor and help them grow in the corporation ... [They were] confused as to why they were not assigned a mentor as part of the Leadership Development program and 'checked out' of the relationship after learning they had not been partnered with a mentor". (pp. 86–87)

However, it is for the organisation to take a view on what kind of coaching they want to offer employees and for the coach to deliver that. Julia has noticed that, while some organisations offer their high potentials both a coach and a mentor and regard the roles as different, others are very happy for their internal coaches to move up and down the spectrum between coaching and mentoring as appropriate. The key message is for employers and internal coaches to be on the same page in terms of expectations.

The boundary between a coach and the client's line manager

Yedreshteyn (2008) pointed out that if clients are disappointed that their coach does not play a mentor-type role:

> "this could suggest they just want their manager to be more involved in their development and to help them to grow in their position". (p. 87)

Recent articles, e.g., Southwell (2022) suggest that leaders could be more adept at determining when coaching, mentoring or management techniques can best support their employees' development. This flexibility can address situations where employees seek more involvement from their managers in their professional growth.

Where is the boundary between the responsibilities of the coach and those of the client's line manager? Supervisors report that the topic often comes up in supervision sessions with internal coaches (though rarely with external coaches). As one internal coach said:

> "A lot of people want to be coached on a specific short-term problem, something to do with their current workload, and I think you have to remind them that sometimes this is more appropriate for their line manager, not their coach".

In many internal coaching schemes, the coach, coaching client and line manager will have a three-way contracting meeting at the outset of a coaching programme (for more detail on this, see Chapter 3) to agree goals. Ideally, the coach and line manager will forge an alliance to support the client's progress. The coach can offer them space to be honest about their insecurities and vulnerabilities – which they may prefer not to share with their boss – while the line manager can provide feedback on behavioural or other changes that they notice.

Coaches can, however, sometimes feel that they are simply carrying out the role that a line manager should be doing if they had the time to, interest in, or aptitude for. Robson (2020) highlighted that internal coaches frequently take on responsibilities that overlap with those of line managers, especially in areas like performance management and employee development. This overlap can lead to ambiguity in role boundaries and potential conflicts within the organisation.

Where would you draw the line? What if the client says that their line manager is never there? Or is not prepared to take the time? Or is off sick long term? Is it in the client's and organisation's best interests for you to step in or would it be considered that you are usurping the line manager's role? Situations experienced by internal coaches include:

- "Being asked to coach someone by a line manager who has an ulterior motive of wanting to 'ease' the individual out of the organisation".
- "Being asked to coach an individual to a position where they decide they don't want to become a director: that is, the line manager did not want to have an honest conversation but wanted me to push them to a position where they came to that conclusion for themselves".
- "As an internal coach, I don't want to be linked with the performance management process. Sometimes I have to make it clear to the line manager that that's not my role".
- "I have had an instance where a sponsoring line manager wanted a report on the client's response to coaching. The client had not fully engaged in the coaching relationship, which I suspected was being used as a substitute for performance management".

In such situations, experienced coaches would put the ball back into the line manager's court but power differentials (see later in this chapter) can sometimes make this hard, particularly for new coaches.

Confidentiality

The notion of confidentiality lies at the heart of a coaching relationship. If the client does not believe that what they say will go no further, the much-lauded 'safe environment' disappears. The concept of maintaining confidentiality is an essential ingredient in the relationship. As noted in para 2.13 of the Global Code of Ethics:

"When working with clients, members will maintain the strictest level of confidentiality with all client and sponsor information unless the release of information is required by law".

But what does this mean in practice and how easy will it be for you, as an internal coach, to maintain?

Invitations to break confidentiality by third parties within the organisation tend to be common (St John-Brooks, 2010) and breaches can be a potential issue for clients, e.g., Wasylyshyn's (2003) outcome study about, *inter alia*, the factors influencing clients' choice of coach found that four-fifths said they would not want an internal coach:

"due to coaches' potential conflict of interest, trust and ability to maintain confidentiality". (p. 99)

Jordan and Henderson (2024) highlighted that internal coaches often face complex role boundaries, which can lead to situations where confidentiality is tested. They suggested that internal coaches must navigate their organisational roles and relationships carefully to maintain trust and uphold confidentiality in their coaching engagements.

The point, as noted by Carter (2005), is that confidentiality is particularly salient for internal coaches precisely for the reason that:

"the internal coach has much more interaction (both formally and informally) with other organisational members than the external coach does. In relation to this, internal coaches need to develop a diplomatic way of responding to questions regarding how certain coachees are doing ... This can put the coach in a difficult situation, as they may feel pressurised by senior management into divulging certain sensitive information about one of their coachees". (p. 12)

In most situations, internal coaches find that maintaining confidentiality, when being asked for information, is one of the more straightforward issues to deal with, but managers do sometimes need to be reminded why it must be observed. Comments from internal coaches include:

- "I can be put under pressure to share some of the client's progress with his/her line manager. I never have, and when explained why, the line manager accepts that".
- "I've been asked by the line manager how someone is doing. I said 'great' in response and encouraged him to have the discussion with their direct report (my coachee), reminding him of the contract discussion and expectations laid out re progress updates. He accepted this and was very keen to demonstrate his continued interest and support of the individual".
- "Regularly asked by the sponsor to provide information on how the coaching is going to a level of detail that we cannot provide but we do have clear boundaries around this".
- "Having been an internal coach for nearly eight years, I am now very rarely asked to comment on my clients and there is a trust and respect built up within the organisation whereby the leaders know the sessions are completely confidential".
- "I take the approach that any *perceived* breaches (whether they have happened or not) are a reflection on my professional status. In the past when this has happened, I have challenged and stood my ground as it is about the client's information and my reputation. Once a reputation is lost in terms of confidentiality it is lost forever".

Limits to confidentiality

What limits do you put upon confidentiality? It is essential that at the beginning of the coaching relationship it is made clear exactly what will be kept confidential and what cannot. Para 2.14 of the Global Code of Ethics states that:

"Members will have a clear agreement with clients and sponsors about the conditions under which confidentiality will not be maintained (e.g., illegal activity, danger to self or others) and gain agreement to that limit of confidentiality where possible unless the release of information is required by law".

Coach training programmes normally give significant attention to how to contract with the client and some organisations provide a written contract that includes what the client can expect by way of confidentiality. Others only cover this ground orally. In Katharine's original research (St John-Brooks, 2010), a number of the coaches said that they offered 'complete confidentiality' without specifying any limits – a very risky stance. Others went further than the formulation above saying that they could not guarantee confidentiality if they believed their client was breaching the organisation's own policies.

Examples of violations of organisational policies, cited as reasons for having to breach a client's confidentiality, include bullying (particularly in the form of harassment or inappropriate behaviour), substance abuse and violations of policies related to racial, gender-based, or ableist discrimination. With changes in legislation and growing ethical standards around workplace discrimination and harassment, the line between what constitutes bullying and what is harassment or discrimination based on identity is now more nuanced.

A client sharing information with their coach about a bullying incident or example of open discrimination where they were the victim, or a witness, can place the coach in an uncomfortable position. They are now in possession of information that arguably goes outside the confidentiality agreement, and some organisations place responsibility on every employee for calling such behaviour out. If the client is reluctant to take action – for fear of making the situation worse or finding themselves sucked into an unwelcome formal process – what should the coach do?

Examples from internal coaches:

- "Client told me that she knew a colleague was being bullied, and she had known for two years. Colleague did not want to tell anyone. Client was breaching bullying and harassment policy by not taking any action".
- "A junior client being bullied and feeling intimidated but not wanting to take it any further or talk to HR. I had a concern around what is the duty of care as an internal coach and did the person, by telling me about their situation, feel they had told someone in 'authority'?"
- "A client was referred, and it turned out she had been bullied and was clearly suffering emotionally and confidence-wise. I encouraged her to speak to her boss about it and took it to supervision. I kept asking the question about whether I could get involved in blowing the whistle on the bully but in the end had to accept the person's choice not to take it further. I did encourage her to get some external counselling".
- "During an internal promotion process, my client felt overlooked because of her intersectionality. As a woman of colour with a disability, her contributions often seemed minimised. Even though she had proved herself in her current role, it felt to her that her identity was a barrier to advancement, which was disheartening".

The flipside to promising confidentiality is "whistleblowing". Most coaches would regard this as an absolute last resort but you do need to be clear with the client, when you specify limits to confidentiality, that it means that if they reveal something outside those limits you may feel bound to do something with that information, either with or without their permission.

For the internal coach, whistleblowing is a really difficult area, as you are not only representing the interests of your client, but you have a role in representing the organisation and cannot 'unknow' what the client has shared with you. You need to be cautious, as any action you take can have significant repercussions for the client as well as your reputation and the reputation of the coaching service. By supporting your client in speaking out, you are demonstrating your commitment to ethical conduct, fairness, and advocacy for marginalised voices, which could enhance your reputation in certain quarters. However, it could also have a negative impact: you could be seen as encouraging whistleblowing and interfering with organisational matters. It could damage your professional standing, especially within organisations with a conflict-avoiding culture.

With any whistleblowing matter, you should explore all possible options openly with the client, including potential legal or organisational ramifications. A coach would not normally make decisions for the client but rather help them to explore alternative perspectives and find out what is available in terms of company support. Your role is to help them to explore their options and potential consequences for each avenue explored, ensuring that they feel informed and empowered on the actions they choose to take.

One internal coach, whose day job was in HR, was quite clear that if a client told her about something that breached the organisation's policies, she would offer them three choices:

1   Tell their line manager or HR and provide evidence to her that they had or
2   Go with her to tell their line manager or HR or
3   Understand that she would have to go and tell their line manager or HR

Another interviewee, working as a coach and coach supervisor within the UK's National Health Service (NHS), said:

"Anything around child protection or harm to self or others and it leaves the room instantly".

Strains in maintaining confidentiality

Clients sometimes tell coaches things that are clearly within the boundaries of confidentiality but still result in soul-searching for the coach. You may feel bothered that you are in possession of information that could benefit the client's team or the organisation, but you are unable to share it because it would breach confidentiality. The issue is how to process your feelings about this so that your frustration does not damage your relationship with the client or the effectiveness of the coaching. Two common examples are first, where the client's personal issues are having an impact on their performance, but the client wants to keep them private and second, the coach being unable to use information acquired from the client that could benefit the organisation.

Personal issues

Sometimes clients have problems that have a negative impact on their work performance but they do not want colleagues to know, e.g., the long-term illness of a child or a mental health issue of their own. The coach may feel strongly that the client would be better able to access support if they shared the information, but the client pushes back (and must be allowed to protect their privacy). This is a classic example of something that should be taken to supervision to help the coach work through their frustration.

Information that could benefit the organisation

Coaches can find themselves holding important information, such as knowing that a high performer whom senior managers hold in high regard feels undervalued and is planning to leave. The coach is not in a position to tell anyone of the client's intentions and may despair at finding a way of ensuring that the client, at the least, receives positive feedback from someone senior without breaching their confidence.

Keeping records safe

When it comes to record-keeping, coaches have a professional duty to adhere to GDPR rules on keeping or holding sensitive client information, but there is still a wide variety of practice. Many organisations now use electronic coach management systems to store details of coaches and clients and facilitate matching. Often, there is also a password-protected dedicated space for coaches and clients to keep notes relating to the coaching relationship, e.g., client goals, dates of sessions and summaries of discussions or action points, but only a minority of coaches tend to use this facility.

In Katharine's research (St John-Brooks, 2010), over 90% of her sample of 123 coaches kept records of coaching conversations, but only a fifth of those sometimes shared them with their clients. The others kept the notes for their own purposes (to remember details, help them to prepare for the next session etc.) and a number made a distinction between the notes they took about content and their personal reflections for their own development as coaches. One said:

> "I'm happy to share these notes with my coachees. These would be notes made in the coaching session, but I would choose not to share my learning log with the coachee".

Most of them were unaware of any policy around how long client records should be retained. Typically, coaches retain records for no more than one to three years after the coaching relationship ends. Do you know the policy in your organisation? Clients have the right to request deletion of their data or to ask how long it will be kept, and they should be informed about how their data will be used at the start of the coaching relationship – so do find out what the policy is in your organisation.

Under GDPR, there's no specific time limit for retention. However, it should be based on the purpose for which the data was collected. Once the data is no longer needed for those purposes, it must be securely disposed of.

Using recordings

More and more coaches now record virtual sessions, partly for reflective practice but also because AI now makes it easy to produce summaries of what was discussed. Pedrick (2023) includes an example of a 'request for permission' for the client to sign, which can be downloaded from www.thehumanbehindthecoach.com.

Using email

Another angle that coaches need to be aware of is the potential dangers of using internal email for sensitive exchanges with clients. It does have its risks. Even if you and your client are normally the only ones to see the contents of your in-boxes, be alert if you sometimes need to give access to a colleague – say, if you are out of the office for any significant length of time – to ensure that breaches of confidentiality do not occur.

Managing bias, discrimination and intersectionality

Navigating the complexities of bias, discrimination and intersectionality in the workplace can present significant ethical dilemmas for internal coaches. For example, your client says that their manager is discriminating against them and is making derogatory comments about them to others, but they don't want you to do anything as they think it will only make matters worse. What issues would this raise for you? Here are three areas that you might consider.

- *Confidentiality vs organisational responsibility:* Internal coaches have a responsibility to their client and to the organisation. When a client discloses experiences of discrimination, or systemic barriers, it can cause a dilemma for the coach, as they may struggle with whether to escalate concerns (particularly if there is clear company policy and guidelines for all employees to 'call out' discrimination and report it to HR or Head of Diversity) or respect the client's privacy.

- *Bias vs objectivity:* Coaches need to be vigilant about their own biases and ensure that any unconscious or conscious biases do not influence their coaching. This is particularly challenging when dealing with intersectional issues, as you need to be alert to the multiple layers of discrimination that your clients may face.
- *Objectivity vs advocacy:* All coaches are expected to remain neutral and objective, but when clients face intersectional workplace discrimination, neutrality may feel like complicity with the organisation. You may feel a personal or ethical urge to advocate for change, but this could conflict with your role. For example, a disabled LGBTQ+ employee shares with you that company policies do not adequately accommodate their needs. You, as an employee of the same organisation, see that this is a systemic issue, but you may be unsure if you should push for organisational reform or simply help the client to navigate the existing system.

The following story illustrates just such an issue.

Ngozi Lyn Cole's story

Bias and discrimination in the workplace

Ngozi and her client were working on increasing her client's impact and visibility as a senior executive within their organisation. One day, her client shared a disturbing episode.

'During my appraisal meeting with my CEO, he encouraged me to be more thoughtful about the issues that I raised at Senior Leadership Team meetings. He said that continually raising issues around equity, diversity and inclusion might make me come across as a one-trick pony, less rounded and less professional. He went on to say that the degree of passion that I expressed during these conversations might make me appear as an angry black woman who was always playing the race card. He said that my colleagues were feeling very uncomfortable and asked me to tone it down 'just a notch' for the greater good. This conversation took place on a day when I had gone to my son's school, not for the first time, to complain about the racist abuse that he was continuing to experience in the playground. I was still processing the dismissive attitude of the headteacher and considering what to do next. I was stunned.'

Ngozi was faced with an ethical dilemma. Her client's story was shocking. How should she respond? Could she remain neutral? Would it make her complicit with the CEO's stance?

Ngozi's story helps us to reflect on how we would react to a situation like this. How would we feel and act when hearing about the treatment experienced by both our client and her son? More generally, what is our awareness and understanding of how our organisation treats difference and its approach to ensuring that all employees feel psychologically safe?

The reality is that not all organisations live their values regarding inclusivity. This story goes to the heart of EDI and could happen at any time in our coaching conversations. Can we remain neutral?

In 1986, Archbishop Desmond Tutu emphasised the impossibility of neutrality in matters of justice, stating, "You have to say, 'Am I on the side of justice? Or am I on the side of injustice?' … There is no neutrality". As a coach, is neutrality what we should be aiming for?

We will all have our different views on this and the extent to which we might become advocates. That is, after all, what makes it a dilemma! Some might argue that it is not for us, as coaches, to impose our ideas on others – our role is to ask powerful questions to encourage reflection and raise awareness, to plant seeds that help inclusion to grow. Others might feel, like Desmond Tutu, that 'there is no neutrality'.

Coaches' EDI responsibilities are clearly outlined in the 'Acting Responsibly' section of the Global Code of Ethics (2021), paras 3.1–3.8. The following paragraphs are particularly relevant.

- Para 3.3 Members will abide by their respective bodies' statements and policies on inclusion, diversity, social responsibility and climate change.
- Para 3.4 Members will avoid knowingly discriminating on any grounds and will seek to enhance their own awareness of possible areas for discrimination and bias, including in the use of technology or inaccurate or fake data.
- Para 3.5 Members will be aware of the potential for unconscious bias and systemic injustice and seek to ensure that they take a respectful and inclusive approach, which embraces and explores individual differences.
- Para 3.6 Members will challenge constructively and offer support to any colleagues, employees, service providers and clients who are perceived to be discriminatory or unwilling to take responsibility for their behaviour and actions.
- Para 3.7 Members will monitor their spoken, written, and non-verbal communication for implicit bias or discrimination.
- Para 3.8 Members will engage in professional development activities that contribute to increased self-awareness in relation to inclusion, diversity, technology and the latest developments in changing social and environmental needs.

In navigating bias, discrimination, and intersectionality, internal coaches face ethical challenges that require careful consideration. Balancing confidentiality with organisational responsibility, maintaining objectivity while addressing bias, and deciding between neutrality and advocacy can give rise to dilemmas. The Global Code of Ethics's (2021) guidelines emphasise inclusion, awareness of bias, and the responsibility to challenge discrimination constructively. You will need to uphold these standards while supporting your clients, ensuring that you foster an equitable workplace without compromising your professional integrity.

The impact of power in internal coaching

Power differentials shape our workplaces. Employees with more power have greater control over resources, a bigger influence on outcomes and they shape organisational culture, while those with less power will have limited autonomy and influence. These differences have an impact on how individuals and teams interact, collaborate and experience equality or inequality at work, so it is unsurprising that power-related issues crop up in internal coaching conversations too, especially if the client feels disempowered to act or influence others.

An individual's power within their team, organisation or, indeed, coaching relationship can stem from either 'positional' power or 'personal' power (French & Raven, 1959). Positional power is derived from the person's role – usually their degree of seniority within the organisation. Their position gives them some control over incentives such as pay increases, promotions, recognition and so forth, which they can use to reward desirable behaviour. It also allows them to punish or prevent someone from receiving such rewards. Personal power, by contrast, is the capacity to influence others by virtue of one's personal presence, skills, knowledge and expertise. Charismatic leaders and coaches acquire personal power through earning the admiration of those they interact with and are often skilled at engaging with and motivating others. Both coaches and leaders need to recognise that, in order to be effective, they cannot rely exclusively on positional power. There is a delicate dance between positional and personal power for each to be respected.

For the internal coach, power differentials can throw up all sorts of challenges and dilemmas, both inside and outside the coaching relationship.

Power within the coaching relationship

Whose agenda is it?

It is commonplace for coaches to talk of a coaching relationship as a partnership between the coach and the client. The conventional wisdom is that the client is in charge of the agenda – though the coach may challenge them if they stray from what has been contracted for – and responsible for their own learning. There is an assumption that it will be an adult-adult relationship where the power balance is equal, with coach and client working together to help the client achieve their goals. But is this always the case? Some coaches, particularly when inexperienced, may inadvertently use their power as the questioner to direct the agenda, introduce opinions and offer potential solutions to their clients. And some clients – perhaps intimidated by a perception of the coach as an 'expert' – can find that this affects their willingness to open up, be vulnerable, share feedback and take action. Coaches need to empower their clients, not take power from them, which is why it is so important for them to be aware of how power might be operating within the relationship.

In team coaching, the question of whose agenda it is can be even more complicated. Consider the coach who is requested to deliver team coaching by a powerful stakeholder, such as a senior leader or senior HR professional, who puts pressure on the coach to prioritise the stakeholder's perspective over the team's needs. Difficulties can also occur where some team members wield more power within team coaching sessions – either through seniority or personality – and inadvertently or intentionally dominate the coaching process, influencing the coach's attention and creating a perception of favouritism. The coach's role is to enable all participants to feel safe and engage in open dialogue regardless of the role hierarchies in the room. This can be a tricky process and the team coach needs awareness and agility to think on their feet to make choices and ensure all voices are heard and valued. Planning ahead to contract for and agree ground rules that can encourage and foster psychological safety is imperative.

Tristen's story

The team coach's dilemma: trust, truth and tough choices

As an experienced team coach, I had built a strong reputation in my organisation, both in my coaching role and within OD. This came with challenges. I was tasked with coaching two teams: an IT team and an operations team that relied on them to improve a customer software management system. The operations team struggled to meet targets due to systems issues, but the IT team had been unresponsive. Relations had broken down to the point where communication was limited to email, and the operations team sought to procure external software instead.

The Director rejected this procurement request and demanded that both teams 'sort themselves out'. Neither side was willing to compromise, so the Director, frustrated with the team leaders' rigid stances, urged me to take a directive approach to resolve the issue. I felt the pressure – my reputation as both a coach and employee felt at stake.

Then, a bigger challenge emerged. In a private meeting, the operations team leader admitted that their team had been intentionally delaying some requests to IT. Their goal was to highlight the system's failures and strengthen their case for new software, even if it meant worsening customer delays. They asked me to keep this information confidential.

I faced a dilemma: Should I break confidentiality, exposing the operations team's manipulation at the risk of eroding trust and triggering disciplinary action? Or should I navigate the conflict without revealing this deception, even though it was harming customer service?

As the team coach, I was in a tough spot, balancing confidentiality, ethics regarding the deception tactics and the need to rebuild trust between the teams. Here's the approach I took:

Addressed the ethical breach discreetly: Instead of exposing the operations team's tactic, I facilitated a structured conversation where both teams discussed barriers to collaboration and the impact on customers. By focusing on shared accountability, the operations team acknowledged their role.

Reframed the conflict around a shared goal: Both teams valued customer service, so I guided them to map out how delays affected customers. Seeing the bigger picture helped them shift from blame to alignment.

Offer a structured problem-solving approach: A collaborative session clarified IT's constraints and identified the bare minimum improvements needed. This led to a joint roadmap for system changes within 3–6 months.

Engaged leadership to break the stalemate: The Director's 'sort it out' approach wasn't effective. I used structured mediation to highlight the issue as an organisational challenge, not just a team dispute.

Encourage transparency: Without revealing past tactics, I stressed the importance of honest collaboration to prevent future tensions.

The key was to surface the underlying issues, realign the teams around a shared goal, and create a path forward that didn't rely on deception. By facilitating raised self-awareness and structured conversations, I was able to help both teams rebuild trust, avoided breaking confidentiality and drove real collaboration.

Who is the client?

As discussed in Chapter 2 there is always an issue, for the internal coach, of keeping front of mind the interests of both the client in the room (and, by extension, their manager or a sponsor if there has been a tripartite agreement at the beginning of the assignment) and the organisation. Are there circumstances in which the internal coach might find themselves prioritising the organisation's agenda? Here are three examples that raise questions about the role of power – whether exercised consciously or inadvertently – in directing the agenda and the importance of your being alert to it.

- *A client with autism:* Consider an internal coach who has been asked to coach an autistic client. Autism is often linked with a strong need for autonomy and her client has a tendency to speak his mind and challenge people in a way that does not fit with the organisation's norms. The coach may feel – with the best of intentions – that her role is to help the client to 'fit in' more with the cultural norms. She may be responding to what she unconsciously believes to be in the best interests of the organisation. But is it necessarily in the best interests of the client? You could argue that that approach is a form of control/coercion and that she is unwittingly being a tool to get a neurodivergent client to conform.

- *The coach as change agent:* Amanda Maclean's research (Maclean, 2024) examined the role of the internal coach at a time when an organisation was experiencing significant change and asked the question whether the coach can be a neutral bystander or become an inadvertent change agent. She came to the conclusion that some coaches, without really thinking about it, perceive their role as helping the client to be compliant with the changes – or even to champion the changes. But maybe some of the plans would actually benefit from being challenged/fine-tuned by employees with reservations about them?

- *The coach's role in mergers and acquisitions:* Consider the internal coach taken on by an acquisitive company to ensure that employees from acquired firms fitted in (or conformed?) as quickly as possible. However, the clients were told simply that they are being allocated a coach to support them with their development. The coach knew what the organisation's agenda was. As long as they do help the clients with their development and any other issues, how problematic is the lack of transparency around the agenda?

Power differentials

It is undesirable for either the coach or client to start the coaching relationship already feeling disempowered by virtue of perceived differences, e.g., discrepancies between their positions within the organisational hierarchy; age (potentially resulting in a parent/child or teacher/pupil dynamic being consciously or unconsciously created); class; gender; ethnicity; sexuality; neurodiversity; intersectionality; disability and so forth. Society can be an obstructive force so that a client with, say autism, may already feel at an inherent disadvantage. Here are three examples. All are taken from the academic world.

Powerful client

Marie-Claire, in professional services, was coaching a professor in a science-based department. Her client was male, older than her and senior to her and she struggled with feeling "less than", which was having a negative impact on her ability to coach him well. Her feelings were diverting her attention and energy. There were times when she knew that she should challenge the client (and would have challenged other clients) but felt inhibited from doing so. She took the issue to supervision where, after some quite deep reflection, she concluded that the most challenging aspects for her were a) his being senior to her and b) she thought that, as an academic, he felt superior to her (but without any direct evidence). This gave them something to work with.

Powerful coach

Henry was a senior psychologist working as an internal coach in his university. He became aware that his more junior clients – often MBA students – tried to turn him into a mentor and asked him for advice. They tended to defer to him and were treating him as an 'expert'. As a psychologist he realised that his job title might be conferring prestige and getting in the way. So, he made sure that he worked hard at the beginning of new assignments to frame the coaching relationship as a partnership.

Powerful manager

Helen was a coach and also an OD consultant. She was talking with a head of department about OD matters when he randomly said: "You're coaching Darren in my team, aren't you? He needs to work on delivering to deadlines". This was delivered like an instruction and Helen felt wrong-footed. She said something about confidentiality but was not satisfied with her response. It felt like unfinished business. After discussion with a fellow coach, she went back to him and added that (a) he needed to understand that it wasn't her role to dictate what issues were discussed in her sessions with Darren and (b) if he identified something that Darren needed to improve on, then he should really tell him himself.

Power dynamics within a coaching relationship can affect the trust, rapport, communication and outcomes of the coaching process so, as an executive coach, you need to be aware of how they may influence your coaching and work to equalise the relationship at an early stage through rapport building and being transparent. Intentional coaches might decide to discuss it in the contracting conversation and emphasise how their role is in the service of the client and that the two of them are working as partners so that, if it ever doesn't feel like that, the client will feel able to call it out.

In the majority of coaching relationships, the coach is either senior to the client or a peer. One internal coach related the story of being coached himself, in the noughties, by someone very senior. But far from feeling disempowered, he found the experience a great leveller and reflected on how compelling it had been to hear his coach share stories of her own fallibility. It shifted his understanding of people in positions of authority – that they were human too! As a junior manager he had made all sorts of assumptions that were overturned by the sensitivity with which his coach handled the relationship.

Even where the coach is senior to the client, they may still suffer from a lack of confidence in their role as a coach – particularly when newly trained. It may play on their mind, even if they are highly successful and senior to the client in their day job, that they are a novice in their coaching role. This element of humility could result in their letting go of their sense of being 'leaderly' with positive effects on their behaviour in the day job.

And what about the situation where the client is senior to the coach? Status can be important to leaders and some coach supervisors report quite high levels of anxiety from internal coaches in that situation with worries, mainly, around being judged. The issue is usually in the coach's head rather than in the client's and, generally, recedes once the coaching begins and the coach settles into the role.

Michael's story

Worries about difference in seniority/status

Michael was asked to coach a surgeon, Henry, in his private healthcare hospital. Henry was having problems because theatre staff were avoiding working with him and he had been 'sent' for coaching. Michael was familiar with Henry's reputation for having a big ego.

Henry was unclear what coaching involved and initially assumed that he was going to be told what to do. He was unhappy about this and the first session was difficult for Michael who, amongst other things, was wrestling with imposter syndrome. He felt keenly the difference in status between himself and Henry but he persevered and, over the course of the coaching, Henry – who had a lively intellect – became curious and started experimenting with inviting feedback during operations. He said he asked questions like: "How am I doing?" and "How was that?" and encouraged the theatre team to be honest with him. He was intrigued by their responses and, over time, began to build much better relationships with them. Meanwhile, the positive outcome of the coaching had a major impact on Michael's confidence as a coach and 'slayed the imposter dragon'.

The coach's own power

Internal coaches tend to be aware of their personal power, stemming from their ability to display warmth, build empathetic relationships and help the client to engage fully in the coaching experience. But they can underestimate their power as an 'expert'. An internal coach needs to be aware of their reputation within the organisation, both in their role as a coach and in their day job, and avoid any invitation from the client to wield their personal and positional power.

Wrynne (2011) noted that clients coached by internal coaches sometimes looked on their coaches as being "the embodiment of [the] organisation as if attributed with this power" (p. 59). They cast their coaches in the role of founts of wisdom. Wrynne speculates:

> "it might be suggested that there could be a perceived power imbalance more generally, whereby the internal context might frame the internal coach as distributing organisationally accepted knowledge or truth as an expert consultant rather than a collaborative partner". (p. 59)

This idea of the coach embodying the organisation can also result in the client looking to exert influence over the coach for their own ends. Coaches have cited clients who deliberately sought out a senior coach in order to try to appropriate their influence. Coaches need to be alert to this kind of behaviour. The following are some examples of clients with an agenda.

- "Coachee divulges information about close colleagues inviting me as his coach to collude".
- "One instance where I was asked to coach someone who had received feedback that he had been behaving inappropriately - negative comments about colleagues and excessive criticism about their organisation. He tried to use the coaching relationship to build a case for his defence".
- "Client 'used' coaching to complain about his experience of his line manager".

Impact of power outside the coaching relationship

The power dynamic experienced by internal coaches often extends more widely than the coach-client relationship. One supervisor shared how coaches could feel pressurised by senior managers to break confidentiality and comment on how the client was responding to the coaching. When this was mentioned in a supervision group, several of the coaches chimed in with similar experiences. They decided to put together a document for senior managers about the importance of confidentiality and ethical practice (and how the professional coaching bodies supported this line).

Of course, managers asking questions about the coaching received by their direct reports may often have a benign intent – to support their staff member who is receiving the coaching – but at least one coach suspected that they wanted ammunition to sack the client.

Mackintosh (2003), reflecting on six years' experience as an internal coach, described how uncomfortable it can sometimes be to challenge requests:

> "I remember, on a number of occasions, incurring the wrath of my manager when I refused to answer questions about a particular employee. This was extremely difficult for me to do, as I had always been brought up to respect authority and when your boss said jump … you jumped! It was painful but I stuck to my guns". (p. 1)

Sometimes, the power dynamic can even impinge on your day job as illustrated in Susan's story.

Susan's story

Navigating power and ethics in coaching

Susan was asked to coach Darren, who was perceived to be under-performing. Darren's manager, George, let Susan know that he thought Darren was on his way out of the organisation unless she could 'fix' him and wanted to be kept informed about progress. Susan was quite inexperienced as a coach and conscious of her junior level. She felt intimidated by George but managed to maintain her boundaries and say that her sessions with Darren would be confidential. Meanwhile, she was aware that Darren was sceptical about the value of the coaching as he suspected that decisions had already been taken. Susan felt compromised and very uncomfortable with the situation that she had been put in.

George was senior within the organisation and unimpressed that Susan was not prepared to feed back to him how the sessions were going. He went to her manager and said that she was being uncooperative. He said that if Darren was 'fixable', then why didn't he seem to be improving? Then he asked if Susan could provide him with evidence to demonstrate that Darren wasn't fixable.

Susan knew that it was unethical and inappropriate for her to talk to George, but George continued to put pressure on Susan's manager, who asked Susan to be more flexible and let George know how the sessions were going. She refused. In the end, the client stopped showing up and was eventually let go. The outcome for Susan was difficult. Her relationship with her manager became strained and her self-confidence in her role as a coach took a knock. Fortunately, she received good support from her supervisor and the other coaches in her supervision group, learned from her experience and went on to become an excellent coach.

Here are some other examples of where a power differential threw up a dilemma

- "It became clear fairly early on in a coaching assignment that my client was seriously under-performing, was unlikely ever to perform satisfactorily, and that his line manager was attempting to duck his responsibilities by handing the problem over to me rather than addressing it himself. I knew that I should tackle the line manager about this, but I also knew that this manager, a dominant and somewhat abrasive character, was a rising star who was likely to be increasingly influential in the future and could one day be my boss ..."

- "I was asked by my client, a senior leader in another part of the business, if I would work with his entire team. While it was a massive compliment and would be an exciting assignment, I was already stretched by fitting just one coaching client in on top of my day job, never mind four. I was also concerned about the ethics of it. But I felt hesitant about refusing the client as he was a powerful leader in the organisation who had a reputation for categorising people as 'for him' or 'against him'".

- "I heard stories from three different clients about the same senior person using bullying behaviour. I knew that I should 'speak truth unto power' but also that the person to whom I should take the issue, the HR director, was a close friend of the alleged bully and, frankly, had a bit of a reputation for aggressive behaviour herself".

Working out how to handle issues that throw up ethical dilemmas is the subject of the next chapter.

Ethical dilemmas for team coaches

The ethical codes for one-to-one coaching are now well-established, but they are still evolving for team coaching. Tristen's story above illustrated one issue, i.e., maintaining confidentiality.

Clutterbuck and Graves (2024) list some ethical challenges that came up in workshops.

- How does the coach balance the well-being of an individual team member versus that of the team as a whole?
- The team has been set very challenging goals. They say that they are prepared to work very long hours (despite negative effects on their home lives) for a period because it's a high-profile project and will be good for their careers. The coach suspects that not everyone agrees – they just don't want to let down their colleagues.
- When is it appropriate to advise breaking up a dysfunctional team as against continuing to try to fix it through coaching?
- When is it inappropriate to take on a team coaching assignment?
- The team leader is manipulative and dishonest towards the team. The coach knows his real intentions, but the team does not.
- The coach can see that the team is avoiding a serious issue, e.g., the dysfunctional behaviour of a key member who has special status (such as unique knowledge that the team cannot do without). The team leader has warned the coach against surfacing the issue – but they know that the team cannot make real progress until it is dealt with. (pp. 294–295)

An experienced team coach supervisor shared with Katharine their sense of how "organisations are messy" and how it is normal, in these days of matrix working, for individuals to be members of more than one team. This can add to the complexity of what the team coaches have to make sense of. Where *is* the team? There may not always be a common purpose.

At the diagnostics stage, when you are shaping the assignment with the team, you will need to be mindful of the interests of stakeholders. The team may have different ideas from the team leader about who the stakeholders are and what impact they might have on what the team is trying to achieve. This can cause conflict. Boundaries, too, may be difficult for you. You may have information from stakeholders about the team (or maybe someone in the team) that you cannot share but which can get in your way. Finally, if the team leader does not attend team coaching sessions, it is a red flag and you may have to insist on it. It could be that the leader is trying to avoid their responsibilities and leave it to you to 'fix the team'.

Summary

The purpose of this chapter was to raise your awareness of the practical nature of ethical dilemmas rather than viewing ethics in coaching as an abstract concept. Being able to recognise situations that require you to take a decision or action to avoid compromising your professional integrity as a coach is key. It is important to be aware of who you can go to in confidence when faced with a dilemma, as well as the processes and support mechanisms that should be made available to you to act professionally, responsibly and ethically to minimise the risk of making poor decisions or taking no action when action is needed.

Table 4.1 Questions to reflect on

Ethical dilemmas relating to boundaries

- Where may your functional role have the potential to raise a conflict of interest in relation to the client's, e.g., possible insider knowledge; same professional networks?
- How would you deal with a client's line manager who wishes you to do his/her job as a manager for them?

Ethical dilemmas relating to confidentiality

- Do you have clarity about contracting with clients for one-to-one, three-way and team assignments to ensure that all parties understand the importance of confidentiality?
- What potential threats to maintaining confidentiality do you need to be aware of and what approach will you take if faced with them?
- How will you ensure that your coaching records are safe and secure?
- How will you ensure that your coaching sessions are a safe space for confidential conversations?

(Continued)

Table 4.1 (Continued)

Ethical dilemmas relating to managing bias, discrimination and intersectionality

- What personal conflicts may arise for you if your client shares behaviour or actions towards them relating to bias or discrimination?
- How would you respond to a client who wants you to collude with them to support their discrimination claim when you want to remain objective and non-judgmental?
- You don't know what you don't know so how can you become more ethically aware and sensitive to the range of biases that may arise when clients present unethical practices that they perceive have been visited on them that you have not experienced before?
- How do you see your duty as a coach and as a representative of the organisation to respond to issues around bias and discrimination?

Ethical dilemmas arising from power differentials

- How will you identify clients who have an 'agenda' unrelated to their development needs? If you recognise this is happening, how will you deal with it?
- What can you do to ensure that you do not get caught in the middle of a 'power play'?
- How would you deal with an influential person putting pressure on you?
- How would you respond to clients attributing to you the ability to 'make things happen' because of your position in the organisation?

Chapter 5

Addressing ethical dilemmas

What this chapter is about

This chapter aims to demonstrate the importance of ethics in an internal coach's practice and offer some ideas and a framework for those occasions when you might hit a dilemma that is particularly tricky to resolve. The defining feature of a dilemma is that there is no one 'right' answer – it will come down to context, culture and the personal values and ethical stance of the individual. As Hawkins and Turner (2020) put it, when paraphrasing Solzhenitsyn's (1973) point:

> "If only there were unethical coaches who were abusing their privilege and power for self-interest, and we could divide them from the rest, the ethical coaches. But the line between ethical and unethical practice cuts through every coach and every coaching situation". (p. 166)

We will not all come to the same decision when faced with the same situation, but the important thing is to be aware and thoughtful and to refine our ethical antennae over time (sometimes referred to as 'ethical maturity').

This chapter explores:

- Moral temptation vs ethical dilemmas
- Approaches to thinking about ethical dilemmas
- The three main theoretical stances
- What unethical behaviour can look like and three factors – personal, situational, and organisational – that can make it more likely
- Developing ethical maturity
- A framework for ethical decision making

Some of you may not have had to contend with an ethical dilemma yet or, if you have, you may have been able to resolve it quite quickly. Some dilemmas are more complex than others, but it is likely that an experienced coach who has never detected an ethical dilemma may not be tuning in as well as they might.

DOI: 10.4324/9781003519911-6

Hawkins (2012) referenced this by quoting a key question posed by selectors in an international bank to help them to decide which external coaches they should recruit. The question was: "Please describe an ethical dilemma you have faced in your coaching and how you dealt with it" (p. 53). Any coach who claimed not to have encountered one was discarded. Biquet (2021), in her research with 353 coaches (nearly all EMCC members and the majority external coaches), found that coaches who delivered more than 120 hours of coaching per year declared more dilemmas than coaches with fewer hours.

The thinking underlying Katharine's research (St John-Brooks, 2010) was that internal coaches were likely to be exposed to more dilemmas than external coaches are – and that is why the issue of spotting and resolving ethical dilemmas holds a special place in this book. The acuity with which a coach recognises ethical dilemmas could be considered a mark of their experience, awareness, sensitivity and ethical maturity.

Moral temptations vs ethical dilemmas

Kidder (2009) suggested that, when it comes to making decisions, we are driven by our core values and morals, and that some decisions can fall into one of two categories: moral temptations or ethical dilemmas. His idea was that a moral temptation is a choice between right vs. wrong. He identified three ways of being wrong:

- Violation of the law
- Departure from the truth
- Straying from 'moral rectitude'

The point here is that the coach may have some level of awareness that something is off, or that they are in danger of choosing (whether consciously or unthinkingly) an action that is wrong – or colluding with the client in one – but they do it anyway.

Kidder proposed that ethical dilemmas, on the other hand, arise when two ethical principles collide (so the coach, in effect, needs to choose between right and right). Both potential alternative courses of action have positive and negative elements. Consider the coach who is privy, through her day job, to information about a forthcoming organisational restructure that will affect her client's division. She knows that the client's job is actually safe but can't tell him. At the same time, she is hyper-aware that he is experiencing significant anxiety and having sleepless nights about the implications for his family if he is made redundant. She is torn between her loyalty to the principle of maintaining confidentiality (the details of the restructure are top-secret) and her concern for the psychological well-being of her client to whom she has a duty of care.

Approaches to resolving ethical dilemmas

It can be useful to consider three different approaches to resolving ethical dilemmas: external, internal and relational (Gray, Garvey & Lane, 2016).

External approach

This view sees ethics as an objective set of principles – such as those contained in the Global Code of Ethics (2021) and the International Coaching Federation's Code of Ethics (adopted by the ICF Global Board of Directors in 2019). These codes aim to uphold ethical standards in the coaching profession and provide a level of guidance for coaches. Stating that they abide by the principles in the ethical codes can be helpful to coaches when contracting with their clients around issues such as confidentiality and boundaries – and it is hard to over-emphasise the importance of tight contracting. However, the principles are not articulated in the level of detail that would normally be of practical help to resolve a specific dilemma and are not intended to be a 'rule book'. As Iordanou, Hawley and Iordanou (2017) ask:

> "Can a well-defined list of explicit guidelines cater for the diversity of people and, in consequence, ethical issues that coaches encounter in their daily coaching practice?" (p. 1)

Stokes et al. (2023) refer to research carried out by Fatien Diochon and Nizet (2019) to look at the extent to which coaches used ethical codes to help them resolve ethical issues. They found that their results:

> "confirm that reading and applying the code is rarely enough to solve an ethical dilemma". (p. 278)

Similarly, Biquet (2021) reported in the executive summary of her conclusions:

> "The Global Code of Ethics is a source of information for a number of coaches but still not their first choice when they face an ethical dilemma".

Codes can still be helpful in setting the scene for coaches' ethical practice such as being clear and explicit in contracting and engaging in critical reflection, regular supervision and CPD, and being subject to an independent complaints process, but less so in resolving specific client-related issues.

Internal approach

This is about the coach's internal moral compass and how it guides their approach to resolving client-related coaching dilemmas. What are your values? How have your life experiences moulded them? And what about your biases? Do you have strong views about, say, gender issues, politics or using recreational drugs? Consider the likely difference in approach – to a client's concern about initiating a discussion with a member of their team whom they suspect of regularly drinking at lunchtime – from two coaches, one of whom is a heavy drinker and another who had a close relative die of alcoholism. Understanding your own values and biases and where they come from is an essential part of developing ethical maturity, as explored further in this chapter.

But what if you need help in unpacking the impact of your value system on how you might deal with a specific ethical dilemma? Biquet's (2021) research for EMCC Global asked participants about the nature of the ethical dilemmas they'd encountered. 42% included a "clash between my value system and the value system of my client". She identified this as the most common source of a dilemma. When asked about how they would decide how to handle a dilemma, 72% said that they would take it to supervision, 63% would reflect on the issue themselves and 42% would discuss it with trusted colleagues. Faced with a knotty issue, a coach might deploy all three to decide how to resolve it.

Relational approach

This view puts centre stage the fact that the coach and client are in a co-created relationship characterised by mutual respect and recognition for each other's experiences. As De Vries (2019) pointed out, at the end of the day,

"Ethics is about how we treat and deal with each other". (p. 135)

Ethics in the relational approach are regarded not as precepts (as in the external approach) or where the coach makes a decision for themselves – even if they have used others as sounding boards – based on their own values (as in the internal approach) but as a matter for dialogue and collaboration which privileges the coaching relationship (Gergen & Gergen, 2001).

In this approach, in the event of an ethical dilemma arising, the coach will aim to establish a shared understanding of what the issue is, and what the appropriate ethical response should be. This would combine the perspectives of the coach and the client and the agreed position would be the result of a negotiation. This process will involve understanding the client's values and taking care to avoid appearing to blame or censure them.

In a healthy coaching relationship, coach and client can be honest with one another. From the outset, you will have put energy into building rapport with the client and establishing a close working relationship in the service of making them feel comfortable, in a safe space, and able to broach any issue. Mutual honesty also permits you to hold the client to account and challenge them if they appear not to be following through or deluding themselves about something. It should provide a solid foundation for a discussion of any ethical issue that has arisen.

But what if you're concerned that raising a particular issue might damage that relationship? Or you have a suspicion that the client may be trying to manipulate you or tempt you into a situation where you collude with them? Or if the relationship itself has caused the dilemma, e.g., you or your client have developed feelings that go beyond the professional (or you simply find yourself wanting to agree with your client – because you believe that they have been treated unfairly – which could be seen as collusion on your part)?

Biquet's (2021) research showed that 45% of her coach participants chose to handle dilemmas by discussing them with their clients and, if necessary, re-contracting. But that is not to say that it will necessarily be easy.

A word about contracting

At the beginning of every coaching relationship is a conversation about each party's expectations of the other. It may only be when a difficult situation arises that a new coach appreciates its crucial importance. If you have inadvertently implied that you are offering your client complete confidentiality, with no exclusions, then you will be in a very difficult place if she owns up to something fraudulent and refuses to do anything about it. Or if you have said nothing about boundaries and the client wants to discuss his marriage problems with you in session three - and becomes irate, when you explain that it is beyond your brief, because "you said that the agenda was mine and now you're changing the rules" - you might wish that you had contracted more clearly.

Chapter 3 discusses contracting, including three-way contracting, and Chapter 8 covers in some detail the territory that oral or written contracts might cover. While tight contracting cannot ensure that ethical dilemmas do not arise, you can reduce the scope for dilemmas later by being very clear with the client from the start what the ground rules are. In Katharine's research (St John-Brooks, 2010), she asked the internal coaches what aspects of their role the survey about ethical dilemmas had helped them to reflect on. A number of them said that it had either reminded them of the importance of clear contracting or made them realise that they needed to pay more attention to it.

Ethics – the three main theoretical stances

Many of us would struggle to outline our moral philosophy – though we would probably get further if asked to describe our values. In the context of our work as a coach, we might refer to the code of ethics espoused by our professional body, but how recently would we have read it? Let us look briefly at the dominant theories about ethics. For more about them, particularly how they play out in relation to coaching and counselling, see Carroll and Shaw (2013). For simplicity, we are using Steare (2009)'s descriptors for the three theories.

Principled conscience

Known as "virtue ethics", this school of thought originated with Aristotle (384–322 BC). It proposes that our decisions are driven by the values we live by, such as courage, trust, truth, respect, humility, fairness, loyalty and kindness. We make decisions as much with our hearts as with our heads, and they come from somewhere deep within us. If we successfully live by our values, we can be said to have integrity. However, dilemmas arise if a situation forces us to choose between two (or more) competing values, such as truth and kindness. Say you have interviewed the client's boss, peers, and staff for a 360-degree feedback exercise and are putting together an anonymised report based on the interviews. Usually you quote interviewees' views *verbatim,* but some of the comments are pretty harsh, e.g., "Does this guy ever do any actual work?" and "You ask about his strengths, but I simply can't think of one". Do you include all the remarks, however expressed (truth), or modify them to avoid undermining him too much (kindness)?

Social conscience

Known to philosophers as 'utilitarianism', this theory was pioneered by Jeremy Bentham (1748–1832). His doctrine holds that an action is right if it is useful or for the benefit of the majority, otherwise described as 'maximising happiness and minimising suffering'. If our natural stance is utilitarian, we are likely to take decisions with our heads rather than our hearts, in the sense that it involves a careful weighing up of the pros and cons of any course of action and the likely consequences of what we decide to do. If you take this view, what impact might it have on a decision, say, as to whether to report a colleague who uses bullying behaviour? One problem with the utilitarian approach is: if your action reflects the interests of the majority, how might you protect the interests of the minority?

Rule compliance

This approach, known as 'deontology' (derived from the Greek word for obligation) was first developed by Immanuel Kant (1724–1804). It describes an ethical stance that springs from our perception of our rights and duties. We would aim to take the 'right' decision according to our legal and moral obligations. Within organisations, rights and responsibilities tend to be enshrined in an employee handbook, enforced by HR. Within coaching, the ethical codes play that role.

Steare (2009) notes that rule compliance "tells us what's right" and "helps when we can't always agree on what's right". However, he also points out that:

> "too many rules tend to make us lazy in taking responsibility for our own actions and we can never write enough rules to cover every situation". (p. 31)

If we have a strong sense of the importance of obeying rules, where might it take us in a situation where our client is something of a free spirit and, say, displays what we regard as a rather cavalier approach to what kinds of business expenses can be claimed back?

Here is an example of these three approaches in action. Your boss unnecessarily and, in your view, brutally dresses down a colleague in front of the whole team. The colleague abruptly leaves the room, visibly upset. You are shocked and after careful thought decide to go and see your boss to say that you regard his behaviour as unacceptable. Your grounds for deciding to take this action could be:

- You would rather temporarily damage your relationship with your boss than witness this kind of disrespectful behaviour without speaking up (principled conscience – your boss has violated your values in relation to showing respect and kindness to others).
- Others might suffer from the same behaviour if you do not take action and bring your boss up short (social conscience – your relationship with your boss might be harmed in the short term but a number of your colleagues will benefit if your boss changes his behaviour); or
- There is an anti-bullying policy in your organisation and one of the organisational values that senior managers have all signed up to is "showing respect" (rule compliance – your boss has broken the rules).

On the other hand, you might judge that your boss's response to an intervention from you would result in making your life very difficult while failing to benefit your colleagues. This could still be interpreted as a utilitarian (social conscience) stance, but will result in a different decision from the one cited above. What then? Our purpose in outlining these theories here is that they can act as a catalyst for reflecting on what our own moral drivers might be, and what that reflection might mean for how we usually take ethical decisions and whether we might need to consciously adapt our approach.

Passmore (2009) suggests that most coaches are:

> "ethical pluralists who hold to a few solid principles, but for most of what they do they consider the circumstances of the situation and consider the motives and situations of the characters involved to help them reach a decision about the course of action to follow". (p. 8)

What does unethical behaviour look like?

When thinking about ethical behaviour in the context of coaching, it can be instructive to start with what unethical behaviour looks like. Allan et al. (2011) provide some examples of behaviour that most of us would immediately recognise as unethical.

- Telling your friends and family interesting details about clients.
- Using the names of 'impressive' clients to drum up more business.
- Claiming to have experience you don't have.

- Reading a book about suicide because you have no idea what to say in the next session to a coachee who said she wanted to kill herself.
- Agreeing to coach someone on the basis that "we just need you to deliver three sessions here because we can say we tried, but they are getting the push anyway". (p. 163)

Here are some additional examples of obviously unethical behaviour based on some of the situations raised in the last chapter.

- Encouraging a client to talk about their negative experiences of working with a colleague whom you know well, without revealing that you know them, because of your curiosity about what they might say.
- Omitting to declare that you are coaching one of the candidates in a promotion process where you are one of the selectors.
- Colluding with the client to develop a strategy for undermining a colleague whom the client is having trouble with and whom you don't like either.

It is the huge grey areas, however, that are more of an issue. Take the situation where your client wants to discuss their relationship with a colleague whom you know very well. Have you contracted with the client about what you will do in a situation like this? Do you decide to keep your counsel? Do you tell them that your relationship with the other person precludes your coaching them on this topic? Do you declare your interest but then carry on? Do you refer them to another coach for this particular conversation? Do you discuss with the client the possibility that you may have more than this person in common and whether they should permanently switch to another coach?

Carroll and Shaw (2013) draw attention to factors at three levels that can make unethical behaviour more likely, such as:

- *Personal factors:* A major personal factor is a lack of self-awareness. Others could be self-interest, laziness or a lack of courage. Sometimes we may put our own interests ahead of those of our clients or the greater good or we may take the easier path of doing nothing out of indolence or faint-heartedness.
- *Situational factors:* We all feel the need to be accepted and could find ourselves acting unethically if the alternative is to be out of step with the group. We have to keep working with the other people involved. Many of us also feel some deference to authority and might find it difficult to stand out against the views of a senior colleague (for example, where there's a power differential in a coaching relationship). Both these factors can undermine our good intentions and underline the role of the lead coach in setting a good example and reminding their internal coaches regularly of the importance of behaving in an ethical way.
- *Organisational factors:* Organisations can develop a tolerance for unethical behaviour such as turning a blind eye to minor fiddling of expenses, using

the internet recreationally during working hours or knowingly selling products to customers that do not meet their needs. An organisational culture that tolerates such behaviour can influence an individual coach's reaction to situations that require an ethical response. For example, if HR practices are known to be lax in an organisation, it could be considerably more difficult for a coach to speak up if, say, a client mentioned to their coach that they were having an affair with someone in their team whom they were going to promote.

Demonstrating highly ethical behaviour is particularly important in coaching because of the intimate nature of the relationship. Clients are putting themselves in a vulnerable position by sharing their feelings, anxieties and innermost thoughts, and we must respect the trust that they put in us. Also, the potential for damage, if an internal coach makes an unethical decision or fails to take a decision at all, can be greater than if the same situation arises for an external coach because you could be seen as representing the values of the internal coaching service – or even your organisation.

Developing ethical maturity

Michael Carroll and Elizabeth Shaw write about how we can train ourselves to develop ethical maturity in their book *Ethical Maturity in the Helping Professions: Making Difficult Life and Work Decisions* (2013). They define it as:

"Having the reflective, rational and intuitive capacity to decide actions are right and wrong or good and better, having the resilience and courage to implement those decisions, being accountable for ethical decisions made (publicly or privately), being able to live with the decisions made and integrating the learning into our moral character and future actions". (p. 137)

It is an excellent book for any coach wanting to develop their ethical instincts. The next sections draw heavily on their work.

Carroll and Shaw suggest six component parts to ethical maturity:

1 To foster ethical sensitivity and watchfulness, creating ethical antennae that keep us alert to when ethical issues/dilemmas are present.
2 The ability to make a moral decision aligned to our ethical principles and values.
3 To implement ethical decisions made.
4 The ability to articulate and justify to stakeholders the reasons why ethical decisions were made and implemented.
5 To achieve closure on the event, even when other possible decisions or 'better' decisions could have been made.
6 To learn from what has happened and 'test' the decision through reflection.

Fostering ethical sensitivity

Ethical decision-making in a coaching context is an intensely practical subject, whether it is a dilemma or a moral temptation. We are not conducting an esoteric discussion about how many angels can dance on the head of a pin but rather, recognising and resolving real life issues such as whether we should tell a client that they can stop agonising with a decision about going for promotion because we know, wearing another hat, that the job is already sewn up. Or if we should accept a client because it could be useful to our career in the organisation to build that relationship, even though we suspect another coach may have more relevant skills and experience? Or whether to tell someone that our very stressed client has mentioned, lightly, that sometimes they fantasise about "ending it all"? How good are we at spotting when something *is* an ethical issue?

Depending on your personal ethical stance – irrespective of whether it is articulated – a decision on the examples in the last paragraph might be completely obvious to you or might involve a great deal of thought. Carroll and Shaw's thesis is that we have inherited a particular moral template from our families, peers and communities, and by examining and articulating our values and ethical stance we are in a better position to evaluate them and, if necessary, change them. Do our inherited values reflect what we now, as an adult, believe? This line of thought may also highlight for us that there are some perspectives that do not come naturally to us.

Julia encourages trainee coaches to notice what their guts, heads and hearts are telling them, when facing a potential ethical dilemma. This approach, supported by Kahneman (2011), encourages a balanced evaluation. Here is why it works:

- *Gut (intuition)* represents your instinctive reaction, shaped by past experiences, values, and subconscious processing and can serve as a warning system, alerting you to potential ethical concerns even before you fully articulate them.
- *Head (logic and reasoning)* involves a rational analysis of the situation, considering ethical principles, policies and possible consequences.
- *Heart (compassion and empathy)* reflects the emotional and relational aspects of the decision, considering the well-being of those involved and aligns with care, fairness, and integrity, ensuring that clients' best interests are upheld.

By combining these three perspectives, coaches can make more well-rounded, ethically sound decisions.

Carroll and Shaw float some ideas as to how we might foster our ethical sensitivity. Some of these are:

- Knowing ourselves.
- Raising our levels of awareness.
- Being aware of our values.
- Empathising with others' perspectives.
- Active listening to ourselves and others.
- Reflecting on our actions. (pp. 150–151)

They also quote Mahon (2002) who uses the image of the 'bell ringing' to illustrate what happens when we know or realise something may be ethically wrong. He poses six important questions:

- Review the emerging signals, the bells to which you turn a deaf ear.
- What are your favoured avoidance techniques?
- Hold your own press conference and interview yourself – ask the questions you would hate others to ask you in an open and honest interview.
- Can you get in touch with the 'dark conversations of your heart'?
- Can you unmask the secrets of your own unadmitted attachments?
- Where are your 'evasive concealments' and your 'tranquilised everydayness'? (pp. 149–150)

These activities are familiar territory for coaches. Giving and receiving feedback, developing our self-awareness, reflecting on our core values, beliefs, biases, and actions and empathising with others are central to our training and continuing learning. One could argue that coaches should, in that respect, be ahead of the game. Developing our ethical maturity is partly about consciously taking into that ethical arena our ability to reflect on our practice and to challenge ourselves. Are you confident that your instincts accurately let you know when an issue needs your organised attention?

One way of developing our ethical antennae is to think about how we would respond in certain scenarios, and our intention in providing examples throughout this book is to stimulate thinking. Katharine's research into ethical dilemmas (St John-Brooks, 2010) included a question asking the internal coaches what aspects of their role the questionnaire had helped them to reflect upon. Their responses included:

- "Very helpful in reflecting on my own ethical practice".
- "I realise I need to think more deeply about my ethics and ensure they are clear. I need to write them down".
- "Recognising ethical dilemmas. There are times when I have not fully addressed these and preferred to continue in the hope that they will resolve themselves".
- "My preparedness to deal with difficult ethical issues—I think I would manage, but haven't had much preparation".

The point here is that the simple process of completing a questionnaire had been the catalyst for some helpful thinking. We all need some kind of prompt to ensure that we make the time for conscious reflection. Ring-fencing reflection time immediately after a coaching session and timetabling regular supervision sessions are examples of protecting time for such important thinking.

The next story offers an example of a situation where the coach's antennae accurately picked up that there was an issue that needed addressing and used supervision to work out what to do.

Claire's story

A coach's duty of care

Claire was an internal coach working in the L&D function in a large legal firm. She started coaching Charlotte, a fairly junior client in her 30s working in an administrative role who wanted to develop her professional skills so that she could apply for promotion.

Charlotte had issues around confidence. She found it hard to be assertive and seldom made a contribution in meetings. She became anxious easily and often said that she had a fear of letting people down. Claire encouraged Charlotte to explore where this fear might come from, suspecting that it might have something to do with her childhood. Charlotte said that she was 'very quiet' at home too and then let drop that her husband 'could be a bit controlling'.

Claire had personal experience, within her family, of domestic abuse and had very strong values around kindness and respect for others. She deduced that Charlotte's home situation might well be affecting her self-esteem and how she showed up at work but, at the same time, knew she shouldn't make assumptions. In her head she was in safeguarding mode, and she took the issue to her supervisor where they unpacked her values and also her biases because of her familial experiences.

In the back of Claire's mind was the worry that if Charlotte became more assertive at work, that behaviour might bleed back into her home life with negative results. Her supervisor reminded her that Charlotte was an adult, making adult choices and she had requested the coaching from a desire to become more self-actualising. But she also concurred with Claire's proposal that she check out, with sensitivity, whether Charlotte felt at risk at home.

In the next session, Claire and Charlotte had a frank discussion and Charlotte said that she knew who to contact 'if things got bad'. It was clear that she was fully aware of her situation. She also told Claire that progressing at work would give her more financial security and she was very motivated to change how she came across at work. They did some good work together and a year later, Charlotte achieved her promotion.

Making a moral decision

A decision does not present a dilemma if there is an obvious line to take. Many ethical issues that arise, however, are not clear-cut and each one is unique. Even if the issue is a common one, the culture of the organisation, the context, the client, the interested parties (and what their various interests are), and your own beliefs, values, age, experience, education, and so forth, will differ from those of another coach. You may subscribe to the view that there are objective truths to be discerned, or that you create your own truths based on your own moral values, but either way your challenge will be to find a way forward that will be aligned with those truths.

Fans of the developmental tool MBTI (Myers et al., 1998) will be familiar with the concept of people taking decisions with their heads or with their hearts. It is common for the former to examine the pros and cons of doing something and try to consider the issue objectively, and for the latter to come to a decision intuitively, often driven by their values and their relationships with people who might be affected by the decision. Some would argue that, in fact, the 'thinkers' underestimate the influence of their emotions on their decision (and how their emotions may be skewing the readiness with which various pros or cons come to them) and that 'feelers' will unconsciously bring to bear what they have cognitively learned from past experiences when they get their hunches about what the right decision is.

One of the benefits of a deliberative process, in addition to ensuring that we take a step back and challenge our automatic responses, is that we articulate our rationale, and this allows us to critique it. If we then discuss that rationale with someone we trust, such as another coach or our supervisor, and it stands up, we can begin to have some confidence that it is the right decision or, at least, an ethically defensible one.

The final stage before moving to implement the decision might be to ask yourself the following sorts of questions:

- If the client were to take out a grievance against me, how would I explain my decision?
- What did the person with whom I discussed it think of it?
- How would my professional body (if any) view it?
- If another coach came up against a similar issue, would I suggest they made a similar response?

Then there is the killer question: "If I am reluctant to talk about this or share it with others, then do I need to review my planned decision or action?"

Rushworth Kidder (2009) suggests some useful questions to ask yourself when testing out decisions around moral temptation, i.e., whether a decision is 'right' or 'wrong' but equally applicable to ethical dilemmas.

His three tests are:

1 *The Stench Test:* Simply put, does the potential decision 'smell' wrong? Listening to your gut is a key test of your internal code of morality at a psychological level.

2   *The Front Page Test*: What if the decision that you made in private became very public, e.g., went viral on social media? This tests your social mores and how you feel about your reputation.

3   *The Mom Test*: If your mother knew, what would she think? This is citing a moral exemplar who matters to you. Would you feel ashamed?

Resources, skills and self-awareness

Carroll and Shaw identified the resources that we need in order to make mature ethical decisions.

Resources, skills and self-awareness

Resources

- Knowledge of ethical theories and codes.
- Clear problem-solving model using supervision and others, e.g. peers, to help make clear decision.
- Discussions with others (particularly those with a different viewpoint).

Skills

- Systemic approach (needs of individuals, community, society, and professions).
- Able to integrate emotion, intuition, reason and decision-making.
- Able to reflect deeply.
- Able to be open, stand back from, and keep bigger pictures in view.
- Notice external pressures to make a decision one way or another.

Self-awareness

- Access feelings, hunches and intuition.
- Aware of own ethical stance.
- Alert to assumptions brought to ethical discernment.
- Knowing own vulnerabilities and biases.
- Awareness of usual approach to decision-making (alive to strengths and limitations).

Adapted from Carroll and Shaw (2013, p. 206), published with permission from Michael Carroll and Elizabeth Shaw.

Looking at the components of resources, skills and self-awareness needed to make mature ethical decisions, take a moment to self-assess against each of the requirements using a scale of one to ten, where ten is "fully met"? What would you need to do to get yourself nearer to a ten on all of them?

Implementing ethical decisions

It can be tempting to discuss an ethical issue with your supervisor – or someone else – and decide what to do but then to shy away from it. By the time we next see the client, the situation may have changed or moved on, or the issue no longer seems so significant. We can tell ourselves all sorts of reasons why it is no longer necessary to pursue it, but it may be simply that we lack the courage to follow through. As Aleksandr Solzhenitsyn said:

> "Even the most rational approach to ethics is defenceless if there isn't the will to do what is right".

The subtitle of Steare's (2009) book about ethics is: *How to Decide What's Right and Find the Courage to Do It.* The word courage also appears in Carroll and Shaw's definition of ethical maturity. Sometimes, acting on a decision – particularly if a senior or powerful player within the organisation is involved – can require the coach to dig deep. Clarkson (1997) talks about how we can find ourselves taking the 'bystander stance' and letting things happen. Do you feel that you hold your clients to account? What about a client who makes, say, a slightly racist or sexist remark in a session? Would you let it go (thereby tacitly colluding) or speak up?

We have spoken to many internal coaches who have acted on their ethical instincts. One very experienced coach, with an HR background, said that she had had to take a variety of issues outside the coaching room in her ten years as a coach. They included bullying, sexual harassment, mental health issues, assault and alcohol abuse. She had never had to blow the whistle, as such, but found other ways of resolving the situations.

So why might we fail to implement an ethical decision? Lack of courage could certainly be one, particularly if the client is resisting all attempts to resolve the issue themselves and whistle blowing begins to look like the only option left. But we may also fall prey to simple procrastination. As coaches, many of us will have approaches that we use with clients to help them to conquer procrastination. These are the times when we need to draw on those strategies ourselves. A classic one is to tell someone what we plan to do, to give us that extra little piece of motivation – and accountability – to actually do it.

Carroll and Shaw (2013) suggest some questions to ask yourself if you know you are not implementing a decision as you should.

- What steps do I need to take to implement my ethical decision?
- What people are involved and need to be told?

- What restraints are there on me *not* to implement this ethical decision (internal politics, protection of someone or some organisation, rationalisation, my image, my reputation)?
- What support is needed by me (or others) to implement this decision?
- What risks am I taking in implementing my ethical decision?
- What other ethical issues arise as a result of implementing this decision? (pp. 234–235)

There is also, of course, the classic coaching question to ask yourself honestly, "What's stopping me?"

Articulating your rationale

Carroll and Shaw talk about justifying to stakeholders the reasons why ethical decisions were made and implemented and being accountable for them. Of course, the vast majority of ethical decisions that we make as coaches will not be occasions for major whistleblowing, pose a risk to our jobs or appear in newspapers. They are more likely to be decisions taken and implemented with only ourselves and our clients knowing about them. But Rawls' test: *"Every moral action must meet the test of publicity"* (Rawls, 1971, p. 175), echoing Kidder's 'Front Page Test', is still a helpful one.

If we have thought through our decision from multiple perspectives, discussed it with our supervisor or another experienced coach, articulated a defensible ethical rationale (including, if relevant, what rules, policies, or ethical codes we have consulted) and then implemented it, then we should be in the best possible position to explain why we have done what we have done if the issue were ever to come into the public domain. Carroll and Shaw, in including this element in their steps to ethical maturity, are concerned that we also continue to tell the 'truth' about why we took the action we did and that we should be alert to our natural propensity to present our intentions and actions in the best possible light by massaging the story retrospectively. That is why it is so important to put into words – written down – our reasons for taking the action we have and to check out with a peer or supervisor (or anyone else prepared to give attention to our story and challenge us, if necessary) our real motivations and whether we have enacted the values that we claim to espouse.

At the end of the day, as professional coaches we are responsible for what we do and accountable to others for doing it ethically. Being able to articulate the reasons for our actions is an important element in the process of being held to account.

Living with the decision/achieving closure

Nobody's perfect. We will not always make the best decision when faced with an ethical dilemma, or we might make an excellent decision but then bungle the implementation or fail to implement it fully. Biquet's (2021) research asked participants about the risks of getting a decision wrong, with the following results.

- Losing trust with the coachee or the sponsor (48%)
- Doing harm to the client's development (42%)
- Damage to my credibility as a professional (40%)

But for good or ill, once it's done, it's done. Carroll and Shaw make a bid for our not being too hard on ourselves. We have to live with our limitations as well as the consequences of our decisions. Supervision can be very helpful here. If we fear that we may have stood by when we should have done something, but the time for doing so has passed, then we need to forgive ourselves.

Reflection is good, but there is a difference between healthy, generative reflection that builds our ethical awareness and allowing past mistakes to prey upon our minds. However, if our reflection leads us to realise that there is some ameliorative action or apology that we could make, then that is all to the good and could leave us in a more serene place.

The next story illustrates the value of supervision in help a coach to come to terms with the results of his actions.

Peter's story

Calling out bad behaviour

Peter was a lead coach in a large NHS Trust running a pool of 35 internal coaches. Over a period of four months, three of his coaches came to him to say that their clients had experienced inappropriate behaviours by a very senior manager. She was undermining staff and making hostile remarks and one client had described her as a bully. The staff were feeling intimidated, afraid to speak up and one was thinking of resigning.

Peter knew the manager well – he had worked for her in the past and the relationship had been strained – and was aware that she could be vindictive. He explored a number of strategies for dealing with the situation but none of the coaches nor their clients was willing to make a complaint, from concern that they would be victimised.

For a couple of months, the issue lingered in Peter's 'too difficult' pile but then he heard of an even worse episode involving the same manager, which prompted him to take the issue to supervision. Together they identified that Peter had a clear duty to take the matter further in the interests of the individuals affected and of the organisation as a whole.

The thing holding him back was a fear that he or others might be identified and suffer in consequence. It was a classic case of needing to speak truth to power and, with his supervisor's support, he decided to share his concerns with the HR Director (his boss's boss) since a further complication was that he knew that his line manager socialised with the bullying manager.

The HR Director subsequently discussed the issue with the CEO. Whilst Peter was rightly not informed of the details, the senior manager was moved into a different role, and he heard through the grapevine that she had been given a formal warning. Meanwhile, one of the individuals who had been bullied had left the organisation.

Peter felt ashamed that he had not gripped the issue more quickly. The organisation had lost a valued employee who might otherwise have stayed. But, through supervision, he came to terms with the situation and accepted that, while he could have acted with more speed, he had eventually done the right thing and had learned from the experience.

Learning from the decision

An important aspect of developing ethical maturity is learning from experience. Carroll and Shaw refer to creating new habits of excellence through reflecting on the ethical decisions we have taken and integrating those reflections into our learning. Reflection can be done in many ways, by ourselves or in a dialogue with others. Some people swear by learning journals, others find discussion much more fruitful. Chapter 10 outlines a variety of ways in which coaches might be supported in their reflection (such as one-to-one or group supervision, guided critical reflection, action learning and peer coaching). Supervision provides a particularly fruitful space to reflect on our practice, including how we can use the learning from past decisions to inform our approach for the future. Sometimes we may need some time to elapse after the event to make sense of it and also to establish what the longer-term consequences of our decisions may have been for the people involved.

A framework for ethical decision making

It can be really helpful to have a model to act as a practical tool for working through how we might handle a particular ethical issue that has arisen in our practice. The following eight-step approach draws on Carroll and Shaw's (2013) work on ethical maturity, Duff and Passmore's (2010) ACTION model and Passmore and Turner's (2018) further development of that model into the APPEAR model. When working with any model, the process will often be an iterative one so not, in practice, as linear as it may appear.

Awareness

This involves being aware of:

(a) the fact that a moment of choice has cropped up. Coaches often talk about feeling in their bodies that an ethical dilemma has arisen like a sinking in the stomach or a tightening in the chest. It's all about recognising that there's something now in the room – probably as a result of something that the client has said – that doesn't feel quite right

(b) our own ethical stance, values, and beliefs. Iordanou and Hawley (2020) point out that:

> "as we explore our personal and professional values more closely, we tend to discover new insights, gaining greater awareness of how our values influence our coaching practice". (p. 336)

(c) a relevant code of ethics. In Chapter 8 we discuss the need for organisations to adopt a code of coaching ethics for the guidance of their internal coaches.

Identification

Is the issue an ethical dilemma? What makes it a dilemma? From where does the sense of conflict or competing interests arise? Is there a sensitive power dimension? Who are the interested parties? What would the consequences be if we did nothing? How much would that matter? On a scale of nought to ten how important does it feel that we should do something? What feelings does it raise for us?

Reflection

Taking a multi-perspective viewpoint, rather than playing simply to our own preferences, helps us to avoid missing something important. Carroll and Shaw make the case for consciously using a multi-perspective approach to decision-making. So:

- Reflecting on the issue in a mindful way.
- Being aware of our biases, drivers, and motives.
- Getting in touch with what our feelings are telling us.
- Using our thinking selves to articulate the arguments for different potential ways forward.

The emphasis is on taking care to examine any ethical dilemma from a number of perspectives in a deliberate and conscious way. Fatien Diochon and Nizet (2019) too, say that emotions and rationality need to be interwoven to produce an ethical decision. They use a knitting metaphor, saying that the two are 'fibres' in the ethical decision-making process. Intuition can play a role too, as De Haan (2012) points out:

> "There are convincing indications that many (if not most) decisions are made intuitively before our conscious mind notes, validates and justifies them using reason and language". (p. 108)

The aim of all these reflections will be to identify our options for action.

Consultation

This is the point at which we check out our emerging conclusions with others, whether a supervisor, a fellow coach, or simply someone whose judgment we respect and trust. In some cases, we may need to consider consulting a lawyer. If one of the potential ways forward is "do nothing" then it should be subjected to intense scrutiny, with the aid of the colleague, in case we have been seduced into Clarkson's (1997) bystander stance and are allowing ourselves the excuse that "It's really nothing to do with me" or "I don't have enough information". At the end of the day, if we fail to take appropriate action, our reputation is just as much on the line as if we took inappropriate action.

Evaluation

The options – or 'possibilities' in the APPEAR model – need to be weighed up in the light of your ethical code and any relevant contracting document, such as between you and your client or you and your employer. This is the stage at which the consequences of different courses of action for all the people involved, including yourself, should be evaluated. In particular, how each of those avenues could affect the welfare of each party. Hawkins and Turner (2020) also talk about developing four key capacities:

- Cultural awareness (awareness of our biases and assumptions springing from our own cultural background).
- Listening not only to what is in the room but what is not in the room (hear what the client may not be noticing in their system).
- Wide-angled empathy (compassion for everyone involved in the client's story).
- Holding the future in mind (what the long-term consequences may be). (p. 178)

Decision

Having arrived at a decision as to the best way forward, this is the moment to be making the final check against the sorts of questions outlined earlier in this chapter. Examples are: "Would my professional community support this decision without reservation?" and "If it became public that this was what I had done, would I find it easy to defend?" and so forth. Then we should articulate our rationale as honestly as we can and make a record of how we arrived at our conclusion.

Implementation

As described earlier in this chapter, this may require courage, energy and possibly one or more difficult conversations, so support from a supervisor or colleague can be invaluable in deciding exactly how and what we are going to say and to whom.

Learning

We may not be able to get the full learning until some time later, when we have seen what the consequences of our decision were for all the parties involved. Passmore and Turner (2018) suggest that, after the event, the reflection should be at two levels:

- *Reflection on the process and the various stakeholders:* What have you learned as a coach? You could ask yourself questions like: what resources did I draw on and which were most helpful? What went well and what could have gone better? What was the impact on the client, the organisation and any other stakeholders?
- *Reflection on the issue and themselves:* What have you learned about yourself? You could ask yourself questions like: How has handling the issue affected me at various points in the process? What bearing did my values and beliefs have on my decision-making process? Did I have any misgivings about my decision? How did I deal with them? Have there been emotional consequences for me? Would I do anything differently another time?

A combination of our own reflections and guided reflection with someone else, such as a supervisor, may be the best strategy to get the maximum learning from what happened and to help us to integrate it into our ethical capacity for the future. It is a lifelong journey.

Summary

Acting ethically requires self-awareness and courage. As coaches, it is important that we can define our own values and articulate our personal code of conduct as well as being 'signed up' to our professional body's standards of ethical conduct.

This chapter has sought to help you think about and reflect honestly on how you make and implement ethical decisions. Understanding the personal, situational, and organisational influences that have an impact on how we behave is an important aspect of developing our ethical maturity, as is the learning we take from the experience of handling the ethical dilemmas that we encounter.

Table 5.1 Questions to reflect on

Contracting

- How can you use contracting to reduce the likelihood or incidence of ethical dilemmas?
- How will you contract with your client? What does your contracting process need to include? Do you need a written contract?
- What will you cover in the chemistry meeting or first session to ensure your client has a clear understanding of how confidentiality works and the necessary boundaries of the relationship?

The importance of behaving ethically

- Do you have a sense of which of the three main theoretical stances you share? Principled conscience; social conscience; rule compliance?
- Looking back at a situation when you found yourself with a dilemma, which of the three stances were you drawing on to decide what was 'right'?

What does unethical behaviour look like?

- What type of personal, situational, or organisational factors could make unethical behaviour more likely for you?
- Where may you be in danger of putting your own interests ahead of the client, or take the easier path of doing nothing?
- What situational factors could undermine your good intentions?
- How ethical is your organisation's culture? Will your compliance with an ethical code of conduct require you to stand out against it?
- Where might you find support?

Why do ethics matter?

- What are your personal motivations for behaving ethically?
- When are you most likely to be in danger of justifying what you know to be unethical behaviour?

Where do our personal ethics come from?

- How has your upbringing shaped your behaviour?
- What 'rules' have you inherited from your parents?
- When you think about your values now, do those rules still reflect who you have become?
- How do you hold yourself accountable to your own standards of behaviour?

Ethical maturity

- How will you build your ethical maturity regarding ethical sensitivity, making and implementing ethical decisions, and learning from the decision?
- How clear are you about your own values and your biases or possible blind spots?
- If things do not go well, what support is there for you?
- How do you reflect on your own practice and learn from decisions you have made? Do you need to make this process more robust?

Using a decision-making model

- Could you use the model for making ethical decisions in future?
- What are the benefits to you in using the model and how may it shape your practice when faced with an ethical dilemma?

What Organisations Need to Know

Part II is designed principally for those of you who are – or may become – responsible for internal coaching in your organisation. It aims to distil some of the learning from over 100 organisations' experience of running internal coaching schemes, plus plenty of academic research, with two main purposes in mind:

a To make it easier for you to decide if internal coaching is the way forward for your organisation (if you do not yet have internal coaches).
b To describe many of the approaches that organisations are adopting to setting up and running their internal coaching pools, so as to share the learning (both for organisations that already have internal coaches and those of you who are thinking about it).

Chapter 6

The case for internal coaching

What this chapter is about

There is plenty of research evidencing the value of coaching (De Haan & Nilsson, 2023; Grover & Furnham, 2016; ICF, 2021; Jones, Woods & Guillaume, 2016), showing it to be both popular and effective on both an individual and organisational level. But what are the arguments for training up a pool of internal coaches rather than buying coaching in? It requires a considerable investment of time, effort and resources to make it happen. Why do it?

This chapter highlights some of the advantages and challenges, with the aim of enabling you to decide whether internal coaching would be a good fit for your organisation. For those of you who already have internal coaches, you could also be thinking about whether you are realising the potential benefits and, if not, why not?

This chapter explores:

- The advantages of internal *vs.* external coaches

  - Lower cost
  - Familiarity with the organisation and culture
  - The multiplier effect
  - Networking/breaking down barriers
  - Developing a coaching community
  - Contribution to organisational learning
  - Building a coaching culture

- Potential challenges of using internal coaches:

  - Status/credibility issues for internal coaches
  - The increased scope for ethical dilemmas
  - Being part of the same system

- How reciprocal arrangements with other organisations can work

The advantages of internal vs. external coaches

Any organisation wishing to offer coaching to develop its employees needs to weigh up the pros and cons of bringing in external coaches or developing its own internal

DOI: 10.4324/9781003519911-8

coaching service or, as often happens, deploying a combination of the two. There is no 'right' answer and there are distinct advantages and disadvantages to each. Board members often prefer to use external coaches. The most common reasons given are a perception that external coaches can offer insights from outside the leader's current business environment and that they can provide enhanced privacy, in which the client can be more open and honest about their situation, emotions and feelings, as there are no internal company politics, boundary issues or power differentials at play.

But what about efficacy? The evidence suggests that internal coaches who understand the culture, language and have existing relationships across the organisation can be as effective as external coaches (de Haan & Nilsson, 2023) and a meta-analysis by Jones, Woods and Guillaume (2016) showed that coaching had a positive effect on organisational outcomes overall, with stronger effects for internal coaches.

Schalk and Landeta's (2017) research offers some advantages and disadvantages of using internal coaches vs. external coaches, we have adapted, blended and summarised some of these factors in Table 6.1.

Table 6.1 Internal coaching vs. external coaching

Internal coaching	External coaching
Expectations around confidentiality	
Effective when there is a high level of trust in maintaining confidentiality within the organisation.	Effective when there are concerns about confidentiality, as external coaches are perceived to be in a better position to guarantee it.
Volume of coaching clients and sessions	
Suitable for organisations requiring a large number of coaching sessions, offering cost-effectiveness and scalability.	Suitable for organisations needing fewer, one-off interventions, where the scale does not justify developing an internal coaching resource.
Hierarchical dynamics	
Effective when internal coaches have equal or higher hierarchical status than the executives they coach, facilitating respect and credibility of the coaches.	Beneficial when coaching top executives, as executives may feel more comfortable discussing sensitive topics, such as leadership struggles, career aspirations, or conflicts, without fear of judgement.
Organisational culture	
Suited to internal coaches where a coaching approach is a core part of the leadership style and coaches reinforce this through role-modelling this approach in their client work.	Suitable for organisations where a coaching style is not a common leadership practice and external coaches can bring in fresh perspectives, structured development, and an unbiased approach to leadership growth.
Organisational size	
Suitable for larger organisations with the resources to develop and maintain an internal coaching service.	More practical for small organisations that may lack the capacity to support internal coaching infrastructure.

Now let's explore some of the more significant factors that influence organisations' decisions whether to develop an internal coaching service.

Cost

There are many good reasons for training internal coaches that have nothing to do with budgets, but cost remains an important factor in the enduring popularity of internal coaching. Most businesses are looking to provide coaching at the best possible value. While there is little doubt that cost savings will drive some organisations' decision to develop an internal coaching pool, it should never be seen merely as a cheap alternative. Hawkins (2012) wrote:

> "The journey towards creating, building and maintaining a quality community of internal coaches requires investment, long-term commitment and support, and careful planning. It should not be undertaken lightly". (p. 61)

As Chapters 8 and 10 make clear, setting up a robust coaching framework and supporting your internal coaches with ongoing CPD and supervision are very important to sustainable success but are by no means cost-free so, if cost savings are your main driver, bear that in mind.

Familiarity with the organisation and culture

Surveys of the preferences of clients procuring external coaching services regularly have 'familiarity with the sector' at or near the top. However much external coaches protest that sectoral knowledge is irrelevant to building an effective coaching relationship, it still represents a comfort factor for procurers. By extension, an internal coach can give the client confidence that they understand the organisation and the types of issues with which executives in it may struggle. As Yedreshteyn (2008) put it:

> "This level of familiarity can help create a trusted relationship more quickly and give internal executive coaches more credibility than when working with an external executive coach who is new to an organisation and its idiosyncrasies" (p. 29)

There is something about having a shared knowledge of the environment, history, people and internal politics that can help internal coaches to build a relationship rapidly. And familiarity with prevailing management styles and organisational structures can also be useful.

You cannot assume, however, that your internal coaches will be familiar with your corporate strategy. If that is important, then you'll need to make sure that they have regular briefings (although some may work in positions where this knowledge is part of the day job). Much will depend on the purpose for which the coaching scheme is set up and the seniority of the client. If the purpose is, say, to help a middle manager work out what their personal development plan might include, post 360 feedback, or how to delegate better, then knowledge of organisational strategy may not be necessary. But if the coaches are supporting participants on leadership programmes, then it might well be desirable.

The multiplier effect

The principal aim of most coach-client relationships, irrespective of whether the coach is internal or external, is for the client to be supported to make changes that will be beneficial to them and the organisation. External coaches will then depart, taking their learning about the organisation with them. When you train up internal coaches, however, there will be an additional benefit to the organisation because the coach will be learning too. Internal coaches have reported numerous benefits ranging from learning more about how the organisation worked and how to tackle internal politics to being more effective in their own day jobs.

Mukherjee's (2012) research demonstrated that internal coaches derived many benefits from their coaching relationships. He found that working as internal coaches helped the managers to improve their interpersonal skills, listening capability, work-life balance and self-confidence. The benefits cited by forty internal coaches (all senior managers themselves) were significant and varied. The data came from asking the coaches: "What do you think you have gained personally and how will it benefit you in your professional and personal life?" Responses included:

Improved personal skills: Sixty per cent felt that they had become more effective at dealing with their subordinates, peers and seniors.
Better listener: Thirty-nine per cent reported that they had become better listeners, and calmer. One said he was able to concentrate more and comprehend better.
Increased confidence: Almost twenty-five per cent experienced an increase in confidence even though they were already senior managers. Leedham (2005) mentions that enhanced confidence is a widely recognised "inner personal benefit" of training to be a coach.
Better work-life balance: Thirty-three per cent reported that their work-life balance had improved. When they used the "Wheel of Life" with clients they realised their own low levels of satisfaction on family and personal fronts and started to give more attention to their personal and social lives.
Sense of achievement: Thirteen per cent felt "immense joy in contributing to bringing various changes in the personal and professional areas of the coachees".
Broader vision: Fifteen per cent reported that their overall vision had broadened and they could understand better their role as a manager in building organisational capabilities.

Mukherjee noted:

"From these findings it can be argued that when an organisation develops high-quality internal coaches from successful leaders or managers within the organisation, besides addressing cost containment pressure, the organisation develops their leadership competences and confidence". (p. 85)

Julia would very much corroborate these findings. Over her 13 years of training internal coaches, she has noticed, in the testimonials of managers completing their professional coach training, how becoming an internal coach has benefited them in their day jobs. Here are a few of many examples.

- 'I have come to understand just how much of my daily work interactions can be improved through the judicious application of coaching approaches - it can effect a subtle but positive change in terms of empowering people to achieve their potential'. (2025)
- 'I have seen how coach training has changed people's working lives and the way they behave towards others. It is a skill that I have certainly taken into my work and non-work life and find myself using in everyday interactions'. (2024)
- 'I have learnt a lot about common workplace issues including the value of assertive communication, the value of feedback, drivers of workplace motivation and issues around conflict'. (2024)
- 'Within my role (as Head of HR) people have commented that I have changed my approach and seem far more inquisitive (asking questions) and reflective than I was before the coach training. I have become a better listener and more adept at giving feedback and seeking it from a wide range of sources to continue my self-development journey'. (2025)

The multiplier effect from investing in internal coaches can extend even beyond the coach and their client since additional beneficiaries of the coach's enhanced skills can be their team, the client's team, the wider organisation and sometimes even customers/clients.

Networking/breaking down barriers

Training to be an internal coach provides employees with the opportunity to deepen connections across the organisation and strengthen internal networks. In Chapter 2, we refer to this as one of the personal benefits that internal coaches say they get from coaching people in other parts of the business (and being part of a coaching community from all parts of the business) but there are clearly also organisational benefits.

Most large organisations have a concern about internal communications. People refer to "silos" or "baronies" that can be created in different functions that have to compete for resources. Employees often do not fully understand how the different parts of their own organisation fit together, resulting in poor consultation and a lack of joint working simply because of that failure to comprehend who else might usefully be involved. Organisations try to address this problem in many ways, whether by full matrix working or a series of one-off project groups involving diagonal slices of employees from across the business. Having internal coaches with a day job in one part of the business working with clients in other parts of the business can play a very positive role in helping to break down these structural barriers.

Developing a coaching community

The benefits of having coaches working across departmental boundaries can be greatly amplified if you build a coaching community involving all your coaches. The additional benefits of this are the support that the coaches can offer each other, the additional development that they get from training together, being supervised together and undertaking CPD together, and the contribution they can jointly make to growing a coaching culture (more on this below). The coaches learn from each other what is going on in other parts of the organisational forest and those sessions bringing them together to update them on, say, organisational strategy, discuss a new coaching book or do some skills development, can be time very well spent. Some organisations go further by involving their external coaches too and arranging annual or biennial events such as a one-day conference or workshop where the coaches share their experiences. While some external coaches might seek to charge for their time attending such an event, many would view it as a development and relationship-building opportunity and make no charge.

Building a coaching community is important. Not only can internal coaches feel quite isolated otherwise, but you might be surprised at the number of organisations that do not actually know how many active coaches they have or who they are. The coaches operate independently and informally and are never brought together. Such a missed trick for developing coach connections and shared learning.

Two case studies follow telling the stories of newly appointed lead coaches and how they approached building coaching communities.

Tony's story

Building a coaching community in a university

It is not uncommon for a new head of internal coaching to discover that there is no community, common purpose, or sharing of know-how among the members of the coaching pool. This was Tony's experience when he was recruited to a Northern university. Two faculties had introduced internal coaches, eight years previously, to help students cope and stop them dropping out. The initiative was successful so other faculties had followed suit, but there was no central co-ordination.

Tony talked to each coach individually, asking about their motivations, experiences, what they wanted and potential barriers to achieving a unified approach. He identified many challenges. First was tribalism. The coaches were loyal to their faculty, not to the university, so there was no sharing of experience of what worked. The faculty heads did not recognise the value of a university-wide strategy either. And there were real tensions around the possibility of being 'measured', specifically the comparative student retention rates for the different faculties.

He asked about practices and found that there was no consistency in terms of support for the coaches, expectations around numbers of student clients per coach or methods for recruiting them. Even the role descriptions were different, and the quality of the coaches was variable.

Tony arranged an event for all the coaches, aiming to engender a common sense of purpose. He included some CPD, two hours of group supervision and discussion of how to introduce consistency across faculties. Feedback was very mixed. The coaches appreciated the CPD and supervision but Tony received considerable push-back to the idea of introducing consistency of practice: there was no appetite for standardisation or even a common definition of what constituted success. The tribalism was even stronger than he had expected.

Tony regrouped. He badged the coaching resource 'The Coaching Academy', helping to give the coaches status. The Academy had its own portal on the university's intranet onto which he put learning resources. He offered all the coaches quarterly supervision – initially as a pilot – and regular CPD opportunities. He established a monthly newsletter giving the dates of CPD and supervision sessions, and profiling individual coaches. He featured testimonials from satisfied clients and provided links to interesting webinars. Finally, in an effort to break down the silo mentality, he introduced a mentoring programme with more experienced coaches mentoring less experienced ones across different faculties.

Progress has been made. Bringing the coaches together regularly has resulted in more sharing of experience. Trust is being built between coaches in different faculties and barriers are gradually being broken down.

Learning

- It is a real challenge to build a coaching community where there is a silo mentality and pre-existing multiplicity of practices.
- Coaches, like anyone else, can dislike change. Building a real sense of community takes time.
- Tony wonders if his starting point of providing CPD and so forth was a 'safe' way to begin rather than a 'good' way. He was appealing to the coaches' sense of professionalism rather than addressing their lack of organisational citizenship. He wonders if he was colluding and avoiding the real issue.

Case study

Building a coaching community in Network Rail

Network Rail used to rely on external coaches to provide coaching to senior leaders when required. In 2015, they decided to build an internal coaching resource for two key reasons:

- *Financial*: As a publicly funded organisation, they wished to adopt a more cost-conscious approach, allowing them to offer coaching to more employees.
- *Cultural*: With a large front-line employee base, Network Rail's strategy was to empower line managers, relying less on direction from above.

In 2020, a new lead coach was appointed to build a coaching commu- nity from a pool of 50 'job-plus' coaches with a variety of qualifications, inconsistent practices and no contracts. She began by gathering information about the coaches' qualifications, which ranged from Foundation level to a Masters. She set a minimum standard of a six-month accredited course and introduced good practices, starting with a soft touch:

- Adhering to the Global Code of Ethics.
- Attending a CPD session every two months (coaches were also given mem- bership of the Association of Coaching for additional CPD opportunities).
- Attending quarterly supervision for restorative and developmental purposes.

Then she developed an Internal Coaching Agreement, which included:

- Attending CPD and supervision.
- Coaching one to two clients at any one time.
- Offering clients a 6–12 month program of six 60–90 minute sessions, equating to around 36 hours of coaching over 12 months.
- Organising co-coaching groups every two months.

It soon became evident that some coaches weren't adhering to the agree- ment. Two new cohorts of coaches were locked into the new arrangements, but around twenty of the original coaches left, leaving around eighty en- gaged coaches.

By 2022, the lead coach was in regular contact with the coaches, encourag- ing them to attend supervision and CPD events and establishing good prac- tices. She focused on building the reputation of the coaching pool internally, starting with the leadership development team. Initial caution about allocat- ing internal coaches to leadership development programmes disappeared and they began supporting Network Rail's Emerging Leaders programme before progressing to more senior leadership programmes. Participants in senior programmes highlighted the value of coaching to the Executive Leadership Team, who themselves became advocates for coaching.

Challenges along the way

- Arriving at a suitable supervision model: internal supervision offers the best value for money, but external supervision is 'cleaner'. The outcome was quarterly external group supervision plus *ad hoc* internal 1:1s.
- Embedding the coaching contract with 'job-plus' coaches who had to balance coaching commitments with busy roles.
- Encouraging coaches to keep up-to-date with CPD and supervision.
- Encouraging coaches to log their hours/sessions on the automated system.
- Balancing supply and demand.

Learning

Keeping the coaching pool engaged was key. The lead coach employed the following strategies:

- Annual one-to-one meetings with coaches to check their support needs.
- Monthly newsletter to coaches which included positive feedback from senior leaders and reminders to log hours/sessions.
- Offering internal CPD which allowed for networking within the coaching community.
- Funding all CPD and (external) supervision, offering *ad hoc* (internal) supervision, paying for Association for Coaching membership and offering accreditation to those with significant coaching hours.

The service is fully used and valued within the organisation and coaches are highly motivated but this does require constant attention to keep them engaged and functioning as a community.

Contribution to organisational learning

One significant benefit of having an internal coaching resource is the opportunity offered for harvesting generic themes emerging from coaching sessions to contribute to organisational learning. Hawkins (2012) writes about how he asks CEOs and HR directors of companies that employ many coaches this question:

"How does your organisation learn from these thousands of coaching conversations?" (p. 3)

This learning does not happen by itself. Failure to set up a mechanism for extracting this systemic information is a missed opportunity.

Katharine's research (St John-Brooks, 2010) suggested that 50% or fewer of organisations had any kind of mechanism for collecting organisational learning. The simplest way of doing it was via group supervision sessions or facilitated action learning sets but not all organisations offered these. There was a variety of destinations for the information, once gathered. These included the OD team, the L&D team, the HR Director, the organisational sponsor for the coaching and the CEO. In Chapter 7, we do a deeper dive into how organisational learning can be harvested and used.

Building a coaching culture

Much attention has been given over the past twenty years to the idea of building a 'coaching culture' in organisations and the benefits of developing leaders' and managers' coaching skills in terms of improved performance, motivation, commitment and engagement (Athanasopoulou & Dopson, 2018; Gormley & van Nieuwerburgh, 2014).

Clutterbuck and Megginson (2006) proposed that an organisation had achieved a coaching culture when coaching has become the predominant style of management but Passmore and Crabbe (2023) argued that culture is more than just behaviour: it flows through to artefacts, such as organisational policies and practice, and to mindsets which underpin the behaviours. They offered the following definition:

> "A coaching culture is one where an organisation's people have a coaching mindset and use a coaching approach, both with each other throughout all levels of the organisation and beyond into relationships with external stakeholders, to protect each others' wellbeing, maximise each and every individual's potential and create organisational value". (p. 4)

In the ILM's report titled "Creating a Coaching Culture' (2019), they emphasise the importance of embedding coaching practices across all organisational levels to foster a high-performance culture, highlighting that while 80% of companies utilise coaching for staff development, it is predominantly directed at senior management, with only 52% extending coaching to non-management staff. They advocate a more inclusive approach, suggesting that coaching should be accessible to all employees to maximise organisational benefits.

But how to get to that position? Some would claim that internal coaches alone can have quite an impact on the system:

> "Teaching managers to coach is not only cost-effective for sustainable long term organisational benefits, but there are deep benefits in terms of their personal and professional gains. Focusing managers on their coaching skills and making them deliver formal coaching ... has a broad systemic impact across the board".
>
> (Mukherjee, 2012, p. 85)

But it is important to be aware of any perceived or actual barriers to introducing a coaching culture. Brook (2015) identified some potential barriers to coaching in the workplace, adapted and summarised in Table 6.2.

Table 6.2 Possible barriers to coaching and strategies to overcome them

Possible barriers	Strategies to overcome the barriers
Lack of leadership from the top to support and articulate the value of coaching	Senior leaders and managers tell their stories and lead by example by having quality coaching conversations with individuals and teams.
Lack of understanding of the value of coaching in the workplace and the impact and benefits it can offer	Position coaching as part of leadership development activities, to ensure top talent is attracted, developed and retained by the organisation as well as supporting existing employees in their career aspirations and professional growth.
Lack of time to learn, practise and coach others	Organise action learning sets and peer coaching groups for managers who have attended leadership coaching training for them to share, discuss and explore solutions for coaching challenges, successes and learning.
Fear of over-complicated techniques	Train employees to be skilled and confident in applying basic coaching techniques and models, providing a common language for developmental techniques to address a range of work situations.
Insufficient reward and recognition	Introduce coaching behaviours and outcomes into the performance management system and make it an essential requirement in job descriptions for leadership roles.

A blended approach

A common approach to building a coaching culture is a judicious mix of external coaching, internal coaching and opportunities for all managers to learn coaching skills. Passmore and Crabbe (2023) have built on this approach in their LEAD (Leaders, Everyone, Approach, Distributed) framework. They propose four zones.

Zone 1 (Leaders): Leaders should have 'managed access' to executive coaching. While they do not specify that external coaches are used, that will be the case in most organisations. They make the point that the leaders should not source their own coaches, rather they should be centrally recruited and evaluated by the organisation (and, crucially, receive supervision). They also recommend three-way contracting (coach, client, HR representative or line manager) and that arrangements should be made for harvesting organisational learning.

Zone 2 (Everyone): This zone envisages coaching being made available to all managers. (sometimes referred to as the 'democratisation' of coaching) with internal coaches being a key method of delivery. Passmore & Crabbe suggest that personal choice in the selection of the coach is important since it results in a stronger commitment to the coaching process and the coach-client relationship (Graßmann et al., 2020). Attention is given to the value of ensuring diversity in the coaching pool in terms of gender, age, race, ethnicity, disability, seniority, time zone and language.

Something not mentioned by Passmore & Crabbe is the possibility of providing AI-powered coaching chatbots – already available though still evolving – for staff who are not allocated an internal coach. This could get them into the mindset of setting goals and thinking through their options for achieving them.

Zone 3 (Approach): This zone is all about ensuring that coaching becomes the default style of management. In practice, this is about ensuring that coaching skills feature in leadership and management programmes, but internal coaches have a role here too in modelling a coaching approach for their teams and clients. They suggest that organisations offer group supervision for leaders using a coaching style to "support a transition towards a culture of learning and reflection" (p. 12). We are not aware of organisations where this is already happening but it is a great idea.

Zone 4 (Distributed): This final zone relates to the idea of an organisation 'coaching across boundaries', e.g., with customers or commercial partners.

The next case study illustrates a company supporting culture change through coaching.

Rand Merchant Bank

Putting internal coaching at the heart of company strategy

Introduction

In 2009, the banking community was still reeling from the global financial crisis. Rand Merchant Bank (RMB), based in South Africa, recognised the need to rebuild trust and strengthen relationships. Executive Committee (Exco) members, familiar with executive coaching's benefits, decided to support culture change through coaching. Leaders were expected to be "leaders of stature, leaders who spoke up, leaders of character".

The newly promoted Head of Human Capital – an enthusiastic leader – established a Coaching & Mentoring Centre to encompass executive coaching, internal coaching, mentoring, and leadership programmes. Internal coaching was considered to provide better value for money than external coaching and the internal coaches were aligned with the company's culture and understood career paths from personal experience. A Head of Coaching and Mentoring was appointed full-time within the Human Capital Division.

Getting up and running

After the first cohort of 24 internal 'job-plus' coaches, including pioneers and leaders, was launched internal coaching quickly became a sought-after service and further cohorts were trained. A high-profile leadership programme allocated internal coaches to participants and when some Exco members expressed doubts about using them, the CEO strongly backed the internal coaches. Leaders soon derived immense value from the coaching and external coaches became a fallback.

The strategy evolved to include coaching skills for leaders and managers, group coaching, coaching circles, personal mastery programmes and systemic team coaching. Coaching expanded into areas such as parental transition coaching, resilience and wellness coaching and diversity work. Managers used their coaching skills with teams and customers, promoting a culture of self-leadership and "building leaders of character".

Coaching maturity

Fifteen years later, coaching is embedded in RMB's culture. In 2019, internal coaching was extended to the First Rand Group, including the largest franchise in the Group: First National Bank (FNB), with 44,000 employees across Africa. By 2024, RMB had 80 coaches and a waiting list for coach training, bringing new challenges. Greater diligence was required to target resources effectively.

Challenges/learning along the way

- Introducing policy and governance around the coaching practice to ensure that all stakeholders are aware of their role in sustaining the coaching practice.
- Ensuring people are allocated a coach for the right reasons. Do they truly need a coach, or should they be mentored or be performance managed?
- Embedding a three-way contracting process.
- Ensuring internal coaches participate in CPD, coaching supervision and the community of practice.
- Getting the coaches to log all their hours.
- Scaling the coaching effort to meet demand.
- Exploring technology solutions and coaching platforms.

Outcome

The internal coaching resource is fully used and valued within RMB but keeping coaches engaged and functioning as a community requires constant attention.

Potential challenges of using internal coaches

Chapter 3 outlined some of the challenges of being an internal coach from the perspective of the coach. But what are the downsides of using internal coaches, as opposed to external coaches, from an organisational perspective?

Status/credibility

Frisch (2005), Jarvis, Lane and Fillery-Travis (2006) and others have suggested that one of the key challenges for internal coaches can be their potential lack of credibility with senior managers. Yedreshteyn (2008) expressed it like this:

> "External executive coaches come into organisations with advanced degrees, training and broad coaching experience, which is likely to afford them immediate credibility, something that internal coaches may not receive". (p. 29)

Wrynne (2011) raised a related idea that coaches can be perceived by some as a status symbol and that an internal coach confers less status than an external coach. The issue from the coaches' point of view is a suspicion that some potential clients think external coaches are 'better'. Internal coaches can feel undervalued and it is the responsibility of the lead coach to address this.

In practice, internal coaches working within mature schemes may be very experienced. Ten per cent of the internal coaches that took part in Katharine's research (St John-Brooks, 2010) coached executives in the top team, and there is probably a similar distribution of experienced and inexperienced coaches in both internal and external coaching populations. Interestingly, in CoachSource's 2018 report, credibility – compared with their external coach counterparts – while still an issue for internal coaches, declined in importance between their 2013 and 2017 surveys (from 50% down to 32%), which may reflect the increasing maturity of some internal coaching services.

To address this potential challenge, take care to position internal coaching as a high-quality service, provide your coaches with excellent training, CPD and supervision, and ensure that there are champions within the business who can market the internal coaching service with enthusiasm and authority. There is more about positioning and marketing the service in Chapter 8.

Increased scope for ethical dilemmas

Chapters 4 and 5 described the numerous varieties of ethical dilemma that can arise for internal coaches. Some managers can have concerns around a possible lack of confidentiality if they have an internal coach, worrying that they and their coach may have colleagues in common. It is important that your coaches check out, during the chemistry session, whether their networks may unhelpfully overlap with the client's, and provide the reassurance the client may seek about confidentiality. Evidence suggests that while some very senior leaders may prefer to discuss their personal and professional issues with an external coach rather than an internal one, confidentiality is not, in practice, something that internal coaches' clients tend to have concerns about.

Despite the potential challenges relating to ethical dilemmas that can crop up for internal coaches, as Hawkins (2012) put it, they "can be addressed by an organisation that is willing to invest in the appropriate training, development and supervision of internal coaches" (p. 62).

One approach that alleviates potential problems relating to confidentiality and overlapping networks is to develop reciprocal arrangements with other organisations. These can work really well. At the end of this chapter, we give some examples of successful collaborations.

Being part of the same system

Working in the same organisation as their coaching clients can be a two-edged sword for internal coaches. As Hunt and Weintraub (2006) put it:

> "... the internal coach does swim in the same political and cultural waters as the coachee, at least to a degree. While this can be informative, it can also represent a trap for the unprepared". (pp. 2–3)

Or as an internal coach expressed it:

> "In some ways we can be less objective, as the issues that affect all staff also affect us. It can be more difficult to step back and take a third-party view about an issue that also causes concern for you as an employee".

Organisational restructuring is one example of something that can really test internal coaches' ability to put their own concerns to one side and give their full attention to the client. Below is an extract from *The Listener*, a coaching journal (no longer published) developed by Ken Smith, who used to be an internal coach in a government department before setting up his own coaching practice. It illustrates the real difficulties that internal coaches can find themselves in, by virtue of being part of the same system as their clients. Smith is a very experienced coach with a sophisticated understanding of the dynamics. Less experienced practitioners might be less aware (or unaware) of how their own feelings about their organisation being in turmoil may be playing out unhelpfully within the coaching relationship – particularly if they do not have access to supervision.

Ken's story

Navigating uncertainty: the internal coach's challenge

Internal coaches are of course caught themselves in the change net. It may easily be that our own futures are very uncertain, and we must deliver a professional coaching job while at the same time knowing that we are at risk of redundancy. So how good are we at recognising our own emotions and managing them productively within the coaching session, drawing on them only in a way that enhances rapport and avoids a parallel process of distress? We need to learn from the emotions we ourselves experience in uncertainty that can deepen our self-knowledge and so help build our practice. The challenge of this can be compounded when the psychological contract we have as employees within our organisation is broken. When this happens, how then can we, as internal coaches, congruently represent our organisation to our clients, no matter how directly or indirectly we are asked to do so? We need to ask ourselves honestly: "Where is my own energy right now and where do I want to put my energy?" and from the answer conclude whether we can take the coaching assignment.

Reciprocal arrangements

Given the downsides in terms of potentially overlapping networks, confidentiality issues and the coach being part of the same system as the client, a popular approach – particularly in the public sector – is to set up reciprocal arrangements with other organisations.

These arrangements work as networks of organisations that can pool resources, share training, supervision and CPD arrangements and release their coaches to coach in each other's organisations. This approach has been wholeheartedly picked up by the NHS, which has developed a national platform with portals for each of its regions. The past twenty years has seen networks come and go, both in the private and public sectors. The following are two examples of thriving coaching networks – one very mature network and one set up more recently.

Reciprocal arrangements (1)

Public Sector Coaching & Mentoring Pool

The Public Sector Coaching & Mentoring Pool (formerly West Midlands Coaching & Mentoring Pool) was established in 2007, becoming one of the longest-standing networks offering cross-organisational coaching in the UK. It aimed to share coaching and mentoring services across member organisations and evolved into a significant vehicle for learning and development. By 2025, it had expanded from 13 to over 45 organisational members, with 130 coaches coaching across the network, alongside 200+ internal coaches working in their own organisations. In 2023/24, 429 individuals registered for coaching, and 961 hours of coaching and mentoring were delivered.

Sam Darby (Consultant, Coaching and Mentoring at West Midlands Employers), attributes the pool's success to continuity, introducing a subscription model in 2010, and the dedication of the coaches and coaching leads.

What are the benefits and challenges in supporting such a large and mature network?

Benefits

- *Breadth and depth:* Employees in member organisations have access to a wide variety of coaches with diverse skills, experience and backgrounds. Many original coaches continued to coach *pro bono* even after retirement or setting up their own coaching practices.
- *Diverse backgrounds:* Initially, all coaching leads were coaches themselves. By 2025, a mix of perspectives reduced the risk of groupthink and blind spots.
- *Training and support:* Coaches receive extensive training and support, with investment in supervision and CPD.
- *Regular evaluation:* Client evaluations are taken seriously, with high satisfaction ratings. In 2023/24 the answers to: "How would you rate your experience of the coaching relationship?" averaged almost 10/10.
- *Annual conference:* The annual conference showcases thought leaders. 170 coaches attended in 2023.

Challenges

- *Churn of coaches:* There is a constant need to train new coaches, although some move to new employers within the public sector and remain in the pool.
- *Churn of coaching leads:* The L&D leads also move on, requiring continual relationship-building by Sam Darby and her team.
- *Marketing:* Limited resources can affect promotion of the pool by member organisations, leading to under-utilisation of the coaches. Marketing materials are provided to them to help.
- *Profiles:* The quality of coach profiles varies, affecting client matches. Comprehensive guidance has now been made available.
- *Quality assurance:* There is a baseline minimum qualification (Level 5 certificate) plus a commitment to a minimum of 10 hours of CPD and supervision annually. Attendance is monitored and followed up.
- *CPD:* The network offers CPD but there is discussion whether external opportunities – meeting a certain quality threshold – should qualify.

- *CMS:* Maintaining accurate and timely records in the coach management system (CMS) is challenging. Non-compliance is followed up (telephone calls are most effective) but this is time-consuming.

The pool has evolved over time to reflect changing contexts and demands.

- *The offer:* The service has broadened to include business coaching and mentoring, mostly delivered online.
- *Communication:* Initially, meetings with lead coaches from member organisations were bi-monthly. By 2025, they had reduced to twice a year with CPD included (to encourage engagement).
- *CMS development:* The pool has used three CMS providers and gradually developed the functionality. Potential clients can now request a shortlist of suitable coaches based on their requirements. Many functions are now mechanised, e.g., evaluation forms automatically sent to clients.
- *Coach profiles:* In response to demand, coaches now include personal characteristics, such as neurodiversity, gender, sexuality, religion or belief, ethnicity, disability and family responsibilities in their profiles as well as their experience.
- *Coaching approach:* Flexibility has been introduced to provide mentoring, if requested.
- *Supervision:* Initially external, supervision can now be provided by trained internal supervision facilitators.

Reciprocal arrangements (2)

NHS North West Leadership Academy

NHS North West Leadership Academy (NWLA) is a member-led NHS organisation providing leadership development and consultancy for NHS North West's regional workforce. The aim is to develop compassionate and future-focused leaders to secure better health, care and wellbeing outcomes. Coaching and mentoring (C&M) is offered to leaders at all levels.

The NWLA provides access to a coaching and mentoring hub – an online platform that matches mentees with trained mentors and coachees with experienced, qualified coaches. Leaders can use the NWLA portal to create a profile, manage relationships and gain access to CPD opportunities. This platform is accessible to all NW members including NHS providers and Integrated Care Boards (plus six other NHS regions, each with their own portal). In 2025 the NWLA had over 200 active coaches and 400 active mentors, with over 100 active relationships.

Terms and conditions for users are underpinned by the Global Code of Ethics and all registered coaches must sign up to:

1 Completing accreditation toward a Level 5 qualification (incorporating minimum levels of coaching and supervision hours)
2 Maintaining the log of coaching hours and evaluation of completed coaching relationships
3 Attending CPD (logged six monthly)
4 Accessing coaching supervision (minimum annually)

The seven regional/national leads for the C&M hub meet regularly to share good practice and develop shared strategies through the Coaching & Leadership Community of Practice (COP).

Challenges

- It is important to keep the coaches and mentors engaged and ensure that the portal is meeting everyone's needs.
- The hub permits clients to select coaches from other regions. When coaches are coaching in other regions it presents challenges for local data gathering of coaching activity and demonstrating impact.
- The Hub is technology driven, but the data is only as good as the information entered by the coaches. The evaluation questionnaire gets sent to clients when the coach 'closes down' the relationship on the Hub, but this often does not happen.
- Only around half the coaches take up the offer of supervision. More work needs to be done to encourage take-up.

Learning

- In 2024, the Coaching and Mentoring COP conducted a review of what worked well and less well in the coach management system. Suggestions for improvements included:

  - Improved reporting – pre and post C&M; difference made; impact achieved
  - User-friendly interconnected regional system access
  - Questionnaire reviews – to gain further engagement on evaluation process
  - Enhance automated processes in all aspects of relationship to gain better understanding of active relationships status

- Once a year, the NWLA ask coaches to cleanse their records to gain a better reflection of coaching activity happening.
- The NWLA stay connected to provider coaching training offers, to ensure they support their CPD and provide them with access to coaching

relationships on the hub to complete their training, which then also increases hub coaching capacity.
- There are plans to upskill coaches to become supervisors in the future to promote further engagement and support for this community.

Summary

There are distinct advantages to organisations in using internal coaches. They provide good value and, in addition to providing a coaching service, internal coaches become better managers and leaders themselves and can make a significant contribution to the development of a coaching culture. As long as care is taken to address challenges such as confidentiality, overlapping networks and role conflicts, an internal coaching service can provide many benefits. Becoming a member of a coaching network can provide organisations with more flexibility of resource as well as reducing some of the downsides associated with the coach and the client being part of the same system.

Table 6.3 Questions to reflect on

Advantages of internal vs. external coaches

- Are you making a compelling case for having internal coaches in your organisation?
- Is there a financial benefit to using internal vs. external coaches when training, on-going support, time away from the day job, etc. are taken into account?
- What value do you place on your coaches having a shared knowledge with their clients of the environment, people, culture, internal politics, etc.?
- Would an internal coaching resource add value to other business initiatives that are going on in your organisation?
- What needs to happen to ensure the benefits are optimised?

Potential challenges of using internal coaches

- What do you need to do to ensure that your coaches are as seen as professional and credible as external coaches?
- What do you need to take into account when matching coaches to clients to set your coaches up for success?
- How do you see the disadvantages of your coaches being part of the same organisational culture as their clients? Are there any aspects of this issue that need to be addressed in the training and support you give your coaches?
- There is an increased scope for ethical dilemmas. What support can you provide for your internal coaches if this occurs?

Reciprocal arrangements

- Would your organisation benefit from a reciprocal arrangement? If so, how could you find potential partners?
- Is there already a local network that you could join?
- What needs to be put in place to ensure that the costs to your organisation are outweighed by the benefits gained?

Chapter 7

Developing a coaching strategy

What this chapter is about

As Diane Newell put it: "Building a coaching and mentoring strategy with policies and resources that deliver against the organisation's purpose and priorities is one of the most powerful contributions to organisational agility and adaptability that HR can make. It's akin to increasing the talent bandwidth; change and adaptation flow faster and allow much more to be done by more people simultaneously, which ultimately drives organisational success" (Newell, 2024).

This chapter explores:

- The reasons for developing a strategy
- Governance
- Securing commitment from senior leaders
- Identifying the strategic purpose
- Targeting your coaching resource
- Deciding who will receive coaching
- Scope and approach of the coaching scheme
- Budgets
- Harvesting organisational learning
- Sustainability

Developing a strategy is the first step in setting up a sustainable internal coaching resource so before we begin, consider the flowchart on the next page which presents all the key components. They will all be addressed in the chapters that follow.

Why have a strategy?

It is not at all uncommon for an internal coaching pool to be set up by a coaching enthusiast in HR, L&D or OD who successfully argues for a slice of budget, trains up some employees and sets off, on a wing and a prayer. The rationale would often be that coaching is a great addition to the L&D offer but that might be as far as it goes.

DOI: 10.4324/9781003519911-9

Step 7: Monitor, evaluate coaching impact and ROI
Create mechanisms for feedback and review of coaching service impact
Define return on investment to promote more continuous learning
Foster coaching culture, embed it into organisation's DNA

Step 6: Launch and deliver coaching services
Develop coach and coachee profiles and communicate process for matching
Set up coaching assignments and monitor how many clients and number of sessions
Ensure coaches are supported through supervision and create a coach community

Step 5: Training and selection of potential coaches
Appoint training provider and build training programme
Create and market selection process and provide accredited training
Determine what supervision and CPD is required for ongoing development

Step 4: Identify target coaches and agree training professional route
Decide on relevant qualification or accreditation route to train coaches
Market coach application and selection process
Identify coaches already working in organisation; how do they comply with standards

Step 3: Design the coaching process and methodology
Create standardised documentation to support the coaching process
Define coaching offered, approaches and coaching journey
Build coaching management system (software or manual)

Step 2: Who are the sponsors and stakeholders; communicate their roles
Agree budget and resources needed
Define roles, responsibilities, accountabilities for steering group, stakeholders, coaches, coachees
Create internal marketing campaign to launch the coaching initiative and engage sponsors and stakeholders

Step 1: Develop coaching strategy and its integration into organisation activities
Why is coaching needed; how does it support organisation purpose and values
Define tangible metrics and success criteria, what measurable outcomes are expected
How will coaching align and integrate with other development strategies, plus performance reviews, succession plans & talent management

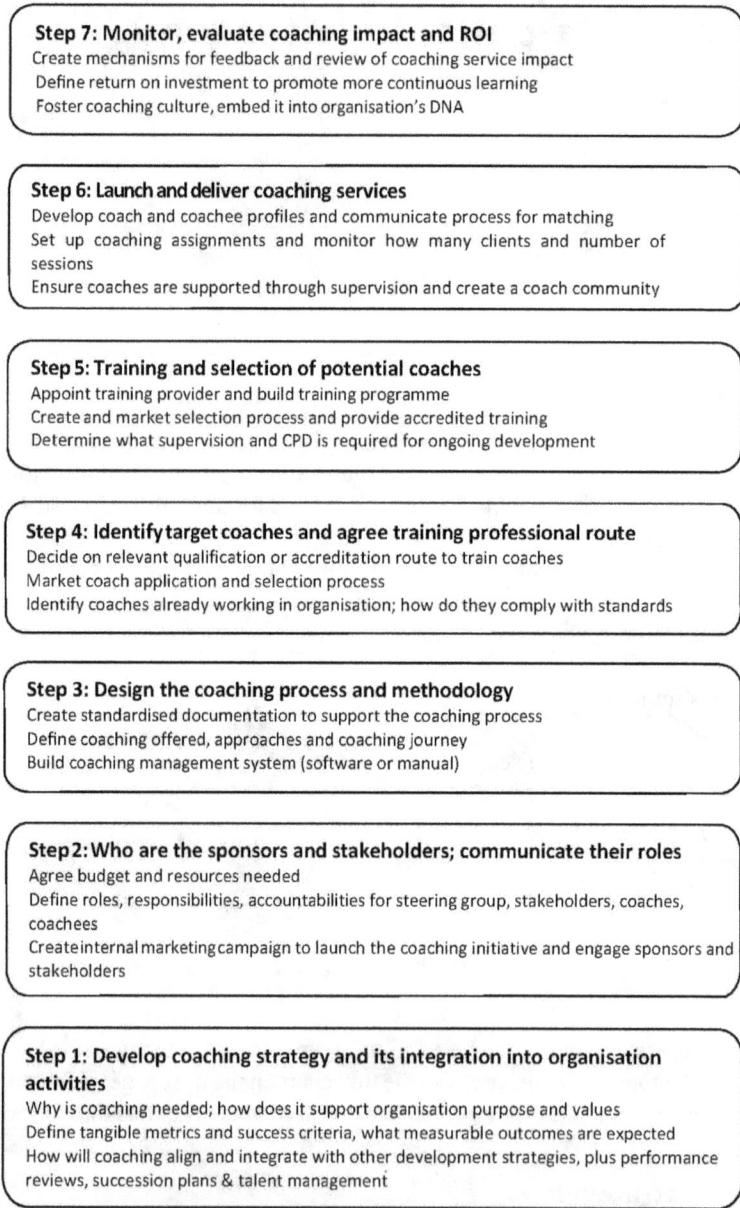

Figure 7.1 Coaching framework flowchart

How much better, surely, to have a proper coaching strategy? Formalising your ideas and putting them into words has many benefits (St John-Brooks & Isaacson, 2024) such as helping you to really think through what you want to do, when and how; ensuring that you're aligning what you're doing with your organisation's priorities; identifying the key elements of your business case; and offering a vehicle to get everyone necessary on board so that, finally, you have a basis for evaluating the effectiveness of whatever you're planning to deliver. Remember the old saying: "If you don't know where you're going, how will you know if you've got there?" The aim of this chapter is to help you to do the necessary thinking to put a strategy together.

Internal coaching schemes come in all shapes and sizes. Consider two scenarios:

1 Your internal coaching resource consists of five people who were already qualified coaches when they joined your organisation and who co-supervise each other. They subscribe to a coaching professional body, adhere to its code of ethics and access its CPD events. They find their own clients, coach on top of their day jobs and cost your organisation virtually nothing.
2 You are the lead coach for a multinational company with 80 internal coaches. You have a steering board chaired by the People Director, a state-of-the-art coach management system for matching coaches with clients and monitoring activity, provide regular supervision for your coaches from an external provider, arrange bi-monthly CPD sessions, and put on an annual conference to which you invite both your internal and external coaches in order to capture organisational learning. Your budget is substantial.

Clearly, strategies can look very different in their scope, scale, sophistication and cost. When you reflect on the various elements of a strategy described in this chapter, your response to them will be proportionate to the scale of what you are running (or proposing to run).

Some organisations simply provide interested managers with a few days of coach training, match them up with anybody expressing an interest in being coached, and say "Go to it!" with no clear strategic framework for what they are doing or any further support for the coaches. You might argue that any coaching in an organisation is better than no coaching, but such a hands-off approach:

- Fails to maximise impact because there is no strategic purpose for the coaching.
- Misses a trick by not getting the coaches together to develop a supportive community or harvest organisational learning.
- Risks grievances or employee tribunals if a coaching relationship goes wrong with no process for dealing with it.
- Neglects the continuing growth and development of the coaches.
- Provides no data about what coaching is taking place, whether it is effective (or even ethical) or if it demonstrates a return on investment.

In many organisations you will need to make a business case for an internal coaching service in order to get approval for a budget. Having a clear strategy will help you to write it.

Governance

At the outset, consider the need for a formal or informal steering group to develop and govern your strategy. There are numerous arguments for and against. Lead coaches in the 'for' camp see a steering group as a crucial aspect of governance, i.e., getting clarity around who is accountable to whom and for what. If the group includes influential managers from across the organisation then it can provide heavyweight input to and critiquing of the coaching strategy, champions for the scheme around the business, a process for ensuring that the coaching is linked to business need, support if the scheme comes under threat when budgets are tight, necessary challenge around effectiveness and value for money and an incentive for the lead coach to keep on top of monitoring and evaluation. One coach lead said that if she were to start again, then she would "pay much more attention second time around to governance".

An alternative point of view is that as long as the scheme is run by a pro-active, energetic lead coach with the freedom to make decisions, access to funding, buy-in from a strong champion who can provide support if required, and good lines into stakeholders around the business, then all a steering group would add is a layer of bureaucracy. It would likely want monitoring reports and to meet regularly, arguably taking the lead coach away from 'the real work'.

Perhaps the key to this issue is scale. If you intend to develop a substantial number of coaches in the future then, even if the scheme has small beginnings, it might be worth setting up a steering group from the outset. The value of having individuals from around the business invested in the success of the scheme should not be underestimated.

The Co-op Group

Why have a steering group?

In 2018, the Co-op Group trained a cohort of 12 employees as internal coaches to ILM5 level, which became the core of a formal network, then invested in training more coaches and a coach management system but kept a 'light touch'.

Ownership of the coaching pool moved, in 2021, to Learning & Development (Leadership Design). The new manager found plenty of good things – the coaches were well trained and there was a lot of experience within the pool – but only about 20 of the 80/90 coaches used the coach management platform properly so much of the coaching went unrecorded and many of the coaches were inactive. There was no CPD or supervision. An early action was to whittle numbers down to an active 51 coaches.

Collaboration and co-operation are key values for the Co-op Group, so it was a natural step to set up a steering group of coaches. The manager cast the net widely, reaching coaches across the business, and chaired it himself. His approach was pragmatic – What's working? What isn't? – and he was keen that members should really add value.

The steering group started work in 2022, initially with 12 members that eventually settled at eight. An early task – after writing some simple terms of reference – was to develop a coaching strategy. The coaching effort had been stand-alone and was not integrated into the general L&D offer: that needed to change. The manager was keen to articulate a strategy that recognised the varying needs of the different business units and that 'one size doesn't fit all'. He also wanted answers to key questions like: How many coaches do we actually need? How is our coaching different from mentoring? Within the first three months the group discussed important principles including accessibility – rooted in a company value about being fair to employees – and decided to make coaching available to all junior and middle managers. They also introduced CPD and supervision, adopted a Code of Ethics and arranged indemnity insurance cover.

The steering group was advisory. It didn't itself have authority to make financial decisions but there was a 'check-in' process with the finance business partner or Procurement for some decisions with budgetary implications. While the steering group was not part of the formal governance framework, it was recognised as providing a vital layer of scrutiny when the annual budget was agreed.

The steering group met virtually, every four weeks. It operated informally – there wasn't always a formal agenda – and Copilot (an Office 365 AI-enabled tool) produced a summary of agreed actions. A Teams channel was set up for the group to share any outputs and progress against actions, such as drafts for comment, etc.

Key benefits of having a steering group were the diversity of views and opinions which allowed for rich discussion and collaboration; sharing of the workload – all members were involved 'side of desk' and no-one had to take on an unreasonable amount of additional work - and harnessing internal expertise and networks. The steering group capitalised on the skills and contacts of group members, some of whom sourced or delivered CPD. The main challenges were commitment and finding the right size for the group. Too many members slowed down the pace of discussion. Scheduling meetings that the majority could attend was also difficult, although technology – like Teams and Copilot – has helped.

Securing commitment from senior leaders

Having an influential, enthusiastic champion can make a significant contribution to the success of an internal coaching service. As Dr. Martin Read said, in his foreword to the CMI/Penna report on the business benefits of management and leadership development (McBain et al., 2012):

> "We cannot leave management development solely to HR teams and training specialists. They have an important role to play but throughout my career I have seen the difference that the chief executive's commitment to development can make. So I urge CEOs and MDs – of companies large and small, of public services, and of charities – to look closely at how they personally promote better management and leadership throughout their organisations". (p. 3)

Support could take the form of the CEO, or another board member, agreeing to chair your steering group, or saying publicly that they have benefited from coaching, or promoting the service at an all-staff event. One professional services firm has short video clips on their internal network of board members talking about the positive impact that coaching has had on them.

Another route to securing visible commitment from senior figures is to train them as internal coaches. When the NHS introduced internal coaching, the first cadre of trainees included a number of CEOs of hospital trusts who became energetic advocates.

You need to nurture that commitment from the top through regular meetings and reports – written or oral – so that the added value being provided by the coaching service is always kept front of mind. The lead coach at one large consultancy used to provide a quarterly report to lead partners across the business including:

- A summary of coaching activity (how many being coached; at what grades; from what parts of the business).
- What proportion of the budget had been spent.
- Evaluation results.
- A 'forward look' covering ground like plans for expanding the pool, running a conference for the coaching community or extending the offer into a new area (e.g., onboarding).
- Insights about systemic issues gained from feedback.

At the other end of the spectrum, many lead coaches simply go and see a key champion at regular intervals to keep them in touch with developments.

Identifying the strategic purpose

If you do nothing else, at an early stage give some real thought to why you're setting up your internal coaching resource. What problem are you seeking to resolve or organisational benefits are you hoping to deliver? How does it fit with your organisation's mission, business strategy, learning and development strategies and plans, and talent management processes? Who or what is it *for*? Perhaps your internal coaching strategy is part of a broader strategy, together with deploying external coaches and training managers in coaching skills, to build a coaching culture within your organisation? The answers to these questions form your strategic purpose.

Jarosz (2023) highlighted how many organisations introduce coaching without a clear strategic rationale, leading to inconsistent application and diminished impact. She argued that organisations must explicitly articulate their coaching objectives, aligning them with business goals. In a similar vein, some evaluation research carried out on behalf of the Learning & Skills Improvement Service (LSIS) that listed the "top ten essentials" that internal coaches working in further education said they needed, showed that seventy-seven per cent of the coaches needed a "clear organisational purpose" (Turner, 2012, p. 8). So, what will yours be?

Here are three examples from 2025, with kind permission from the coaching leads:

"At Accent, we believe in creating a workplace where everyone can thrive. Our coaching network is a key part of this, supporting colleagues to develop their potential, build confidence, and navigate challenges in a way that aligns with our values - caring, inclusive, smart, and driven. Coaching is not just about growth; it's about enabling colleagues to take ownership of their careers, enhance their wellbeing, and contribute to a culture of continuous learning. As we embed coaching into our strategic talent approach, we ensure it is accessible to all while also supporting leaders, high-potential colleagues, and those facing career barriers, reinforcing Accent as a place where everyone belongs and succeeds".

Gwen Jefferson, Accent Housing

"The staff coaching network was set up with the underlying principle of equity, is available to anyone across the organisation and aims to: support staff potential, engagement and wellbeing by providing a tailored approach to varying staff needs and equip a range of staff with skills and behaviours to promote performance, self-care, motivation and responsibility. Over time this has expanded so that coaching is becoming an integrated part of our strategic talent management approach and as well as being available to all staff, is also targeted to staff in key leadership roles, to high potential employees and to staff facing additional barriers to career progression".

Kate Elliot, Bath University

"At Nottingham College, two of our strategic priorities are investing in our people and fostering a positive, inclusive, supportive, and productive culture. Setting up a colleague coaching network is a purposeful step towards achieving these goals, and forms a core part of our People Strategy. Regardless of role, department or level in the organisation, our mission for every member of the workforce is to 'unlock potential through learning'. As a college we have recognised the contribution that coaching and mentoring provides for our colleagues to do just that, whether that's for newly promoted managers, more experienced senior leaders or supporting colleagues in their solution focussed thinking".

Debra French, Nottingham College

Targeting your coaching resource to achieve your strategic purpose

Every internal coaching pool has to start somewhere. When your first cohort of coaches emerges from the qualification process, there are clear benefits to having some well-defined objectives for the internal coaching scheme sitting under the broad purpose. So, for example, under a purpose articulated as "growing your own leaders" (for a company with a history of hiring senior managers externally), you might have some more specific objectives around providing coaches for members of your talent pool, for under-represented groups, for participants on leadership courses and so forth. Such objectives give focus to the coaches, simplify the task of explaining the rationale for the scheme, make decisions around selection and training easier and help the targeting of resources (and then appropriate evaluation measures and metrics). Hunt and Weintraub (2006), amongst others, are sceptical of the unfocused approach. They say:

"Organisations would do well to make sure that they don't have internal coaches without portfolio, wandering around, looking for work. Coaching in an organisational context needs to be tied to organisational goals and needs, otherwise it will ultimately be viewed as a fad and lose its credibility". (p. 4)

The following case study tells the story of a company that tied its coaching effort into key organisational priorities.

Eide Bailly LLP case study

Aligning coaching strategy with business needs

Eide Bailly LLP is an American accountancy and business advisory firm with 49 offices in 15 states plus an office in Mumbai, India, and 3,500 employees including around 400 partners. In the early 2000s the firm took on a full-time internal coach and by 2025 there were four.

When Jason Miller joined the firm as an internal coach in 2023, the new CEO was seeking to understand the ROI of the coaching effort and the Chief HR Officer asked the coaching team to formulate a strategy.

Until then, the partners were the principal client group, but the team recognised that the next level down merited more attention. Moreover, there were concerns over the rate that senior managers were leaving the company. Partners were asked to nominate for coaching those whom they regarded as being on track for partnership. In the first year there were 15, six of whom became partners in the next promotion round. One of them specifically cited the coaching as why she hadn't left the firm. The 'high potentials' list became a key focus for coaching support.

Seeking to support Eide Bailly's mission: "One Connected Firm", the coaching team started offering newly promoted partners six months of group coaching followed by one-to-one coaching for a year. The goal was to build a supportive cohort of new partners that would last beyond the coaching engagement.

The firm had developed eight competencies for partners, and the coaching for partners and senior managers often revolved around those themes, thus tying it to the firm's needs and values. Also, the four coaches attended town hall meetings and all-staff calls by the CEO, so they could refer to issues that came up and check with their clients if they should be on the agenda.

Over time, the strategy extended its scope.

- The firm was growing through acquisitions, bringing new partners who didn't always transition in their 'hearts and minds'. Coaching groups were set up for them using the Bridges Transition Model.
- Partners who had been promoted into business-critical roles needed more support, so coaching groups were created for new Department Heads. Some also accessed one-to-one coaching.
- Retiring partners sometimes found it hard to let go and transfer knowledge to the next generation. One-to-one coaching was offered to help them do so in a timely way, cement their legacy and prepare them for the next phase.
- In common with many other firms, the senior roles were dominated by men, so a coaching group was established for high-potential women to help the firm grow its own female leaders.

The business drivers for the coaching strategy could be summarised as growing their own leaders, retaining talent, improving transitions, promoting the firm's mission of "One connected firm" and navigating change in the Firm and accounting industry.

There were many benefits to overtly aligning the coaching strategy with business needs. It made it easier to demonstrate the value-add of the coaching pool and justify the spend, showed the partners the value of coaching (inspiring them to consider it for their own personal and professional growth) and gave the coaches a sense of what they were achieving for the firm.

This case study exemplifies how strategies can grow and develop while still being closely tied to organisational priorities. There's nothing stopping you from pivoting your resource or adding additional objectives as circumstances change. The Covid-19 pandemic introduced strains and stresses into many organisations, not least – in the UK – in the NHS where a major programme of coaching for wellbeing and developing resilience was introduced in 2020 in response to the significant pressures on employees (for an evaluation of the effectiveness of this programme, see the case study in Chapter 11).

The following section offers examples of targeted support, drawn from many, many internal coaching schemes, and grouped under five headings:

- Support for business change
- Support for transitions
- Support for HR initiatives
- Support for L&D programmes
- Support for employee wellbeing

Support for business change

Strategic support: One London-based consultancy offered its internal coaches for what they called 'thinking partnerships', supporting partners to reflect regularly on their business and people strategies. The lead coach specifically positioned her internal coaches as change agents.

Supporting business-critical projects: Some organisations focus their internal coaches' efforts on supporting managers heading up major new client projects or change programmes.

Supporting new teams: Examples have included coaching managers responsible for leading a new product development team, leading a project to improve the way that customer relationship managers interacted with customers, and establishing a new team to deliver a flagship government policy. Team coaching can help here too.

Support for transitions

Transition to senior leadership roles: Targeting coaching on people who have gained promotion – sometimes beginning before they make the move so that they can hit the ground running – and then for the first 100 days is a popular approach.

Onboarding: New recruits at a senior level can find it especially helpful to be supported by an internal coach, as the coach's familiarity with the system and the culture helps the client up the learning curve fast.

Career break transitions: Losing high-flying managers mid-career can be costly for organisations and maternity coaching has become popular, particularly in high-pressure legal, financial and consultancy environments where it can be difficult for new parents to balance their family commitments with client-facing roles. The period between six months and eighteen months after returning can be a crunch time when the employee decides whether the juggling is sustainable or not.

Support for HR initiatives

Improved retention: Sometimes organisations hit a period of losing staff at a rate beyond 'normal' wastage. Managers may have lost sight of what their options are within the organisation. Internal coaches can help to re-engage them.

Career development: Internal coaches can be used very productively in career coaching as they understand the organisation and where the opportunities might be. Research by Levenson et al. (2004) in 55 large organisations found that using external coaches actually increased the risk of losing staff that had 'derailment risks'. Internal coaches are often in a better position to help a client think through their options within the organisation and develop a career plan.

Supporting diversity: The EDI agenda has rightly moved much higher up organisations' priorities over the past 10–15 years and internal coaches can play a powerful role in supporting members of under-represented groups to develop self-confidence in their personal identity and break through the glass ceiling.

Embedding new HR systems: Organisations have found internal coaches to be a valuable resource when managers are struggling to implement new HR systems. Problems can range from managers not having engaged with a new system at all, to their not appreciating the opportunity that it might offer to manage their staff more effectively or even save them time.

Improving implementation of existing systems: Most organisations expect managers to conduct regular development interviews with their direct reports, but they can fail to grasp this opportunity. Some ask their staff to write their own development objectives or interpret the word development simply as 'training courses'. Internal coaches can help managers to reflect on how they might approach the task more positively and effectively.

Support for L&D programmes

Leadership and management development programmes: Participants on leadership programmes can find themselves completely overwhelmed by what they are exposed to. A coach can help them to process and embed what they have experienced and think through how they can translate what they have learned back into the workplace. Having support while trying out new approaches or behaviours can make a significant difference.

Talent management schemes: These can take many different forms. They can involve a mix of access to training, work shadowing with senior people, development opportunities like short-term secondments and regular meetings with a mentor. Support from an internal coach alongside these experiences can be the 'glue' that maintains the development focus.

Specific initiatives: From time to time, L&D departments recognise a systemic need. One organisation trained half a dozen internal coaches specifically to deliver 360-degree feedback based on leadership competencies to dozens of managers and then to help them write a development plan. The process was test-driven with the board and then rolled out through the organisation.

Support for employee wellbeing

Mental health and stress management: Coaches can help employees with strategies to manage workplace stress, prevent burnout and build resilience. This may include mindfulness techniques, emotional regulation and coping mechanisms for high-pressure environments.

Work-life balance and boundaries: Some employees need support to maintain a healthy balance between professional and personal life – particularly challenging in the post-pandemic world. Coaches can help them to develop time management, prioritisation and boundary-setting strategies.

Career development and purpose: Coaching can support employees to find meaning in their work, set career goals and navigate transitions. It can also build motivation, job satisfaction and long-term engagement.

Interpersonal relationships and workplace communication: Coaching can help employees to build stronger relationships with colleagues, improve their communication skills and manage workplace conflicts more effectively, ultimately contributing to better employee wellbeing.

These are all examples of targeted coaching support. It can be useful, when identifying specific programmes or targeting groups as part of your overall coaching strategy, to frame some tangible outcomes that are measurable. Chapter 11, which focuses on evaluation, explores this issue further.

Deciding who will receive coaching

Identifying who will be eligible to access your internal coaching service will flow from your strategic purpose. Sometimes, it will be obvious. If you are aiming to support managers who have recently transitioned into new roles on promotion, then they are the employees who are eligible. If, however, you have settled on a broader purpose, such as developing the leadership potential of your middle managers, then you will need to find a way of identifying who, within that group, can access a coach. Do you want to publicise the availability of coaching, then leave it in the hands of interested individuals to apply? Or ask leaders to identify people in their team who might benefit? Or hand-pick people running business-critical projects?

Most lead coaches position the coaching as being an investment in the organisation's talent to help them to reach their potential. One lead coach commented that they do not have the resources to make coaching available to anyone who might like it so have identified certain groups such as:

- All executives above a certain level.
- Managers on specific development programmes.
- Those making transitions to director level.

Another approach is to see an internal coaching pool as the ideal opportunity to accelerate the development of more junior managers, not merely the élite.

Scope and approach of the coaching

Your strategy needs to make clear what you are expecting your internal coaches to deliver. For example, how results-driven do you want them to be? Will they mentor as well as coach? Will they need to involve the client's line manager? Will they offer team coaching?

Business objectives vs. personal objectives

How results-driven are you expecting your coaches and their clients to be in their coaching relationships? Are you happy for coaching sessions to offer a rare opportunity for the client to draw breath, reflect on their work, and go wherever their thoughts take them? Or are you keen for specific, work-oriented goals to be agreed, possibly in a three-way meeting with the line manager, and not to be deviated from? Are you intending that employees get professional development, personal development or both? Where, as an organisation, do you want your coaches to put the boundary between the needs of the organisation and the needs of the individual client, in the sense of work vs. personal issues? Chapter 4 briefly explored the issue of "Who is the client?" (i.e., the client in the room or the organisation) from the perspective of the coach. It is something that you too, as lead coach, need to think about, and it might deserve a place in your coaching strategy. Would it be okay if a client devoted a coaching session to, say, losing weight, because they felt that their size was having an impact on their self-confidence at work?

To some lead coaches this is a non-issue. They would say that they train their internal coaches to be professional and to use their judgement on how to use their time effectively. However, coaches can experience uncertainty around this issue as illustrated by this remark from an internal coach supervisor:

> "The purpose is often pretty woolly - or it may have started off by being clear but then that purpose disappeared, and the coaches just turned their hands to whatever came up. Coaches often had to make it up as they went along when deciding whether a personal issue could be on or off the agenda. As a supervisor I would often ask my coaches 'How clear is your mandate and how could you find out?'"

Coaches often tell clients that the agenda is theirs, without overtly putting much of a boundary around that. This can translate into clients' believing that any topic is permitted. Snape's (2012) research mentioned: "... everyone was clear that the coachee should be able to discuss anything they wanted to" (p. 50) and Wrynne (2011) wrote: "All the coachees either display a tension between their personal goals and organisational goals or express difficulty in separating the two" (p. 42). As lead coach you may or may not want your internal coaches to put rather tighter boundaries around what coaching time can best be used for.

Wrynne points out that the CIPD's definition of coaching talks about aiding an "individual's private life" but, as he says:

> "[This] indirectly asks the question as to whether the organisation is responsible for an individual's broader development and if this should be facilitated on organisational budgets. This problematic notion, whereby individuals might engage in learning or development outside the parameters set by the organisation, channels into the broader debate on the tensions between individual and organisational learning". (p. 2)

An interesting piece of research was undertaken by Carter (2009). She analysed 88 client action plans as part of a wider evaluation study of internal coaching in an organisation. The plans had been completed during the first or second coaching session. Some 225 objectives were listed, an average of 2.5 each. She categorised the objectives by primary outcome expected into 'individual' or 'organisation' objectives. The 'individual' category included self-awareness, personal effectiveness, and career and skills development outcomes. The 'organisation' category included customer service, reputation, and culture change and business strategy outcomes. Only 37 objectives (17%) were fully aligned to business outcomes.

When Katharine interviewed Carter about this research, she said that she recognised that there was a chain of impact, i.e., working on a personal goal such as raising the client's overall confidence is likely to have an impact on the client's work performance. But she felt that a key issue that can be overlooked by organisations when setting up coaching schemes was the line of sight with business strategy:

> "If your company is looking to accelerate the personal development of its people, that's fine, but be clear that's what your coaching programme is about. If on the other hand your organisation expects specific business impact, then I suggest thinking about giving guidance to your coaches and line managers to encourage their clients/staff to include relevant business-oriented goals".

(Carter, 2013)

Mentoring vs. coaching

How do you feel about your coaches doing some mentoring along the way? What kind of coaching do you want from them – 'pure' coaching or something more flexible? Coaches sometimes experience their clients putting pressure on them to play the mentor role, and Chapter 4 discusses the ethical dilemma that this can present for the coach.

Snape (2012) quotes one client saying, about whether a coach should give guidance or advice: "I know they're not meant to, it being a coaching session, but I would still like it" (p. 50). Yedreshteyn (2008), too, notes this topic being discussed by clients who were being supported by internal coaches on a leadership programme:

> "There was a lot of conversation about preferring to work with coaches or mentors. Some clients wanted an independent and objective coach from another

business while others were disappointed not to have a more senior leader from their function, someone who could also serve in the role of mentor and help them grow in the corporation".

Some would argue that internal coaches are uniquely well placed to pepper their coaching with a little mentoring, and Julia has noticed that many organisations are increasingly flexible about coaches operating along the whole spectrum between coaching and mentoring.

Macann (2012) also felt that coaching clients often looked for coaches with experience of their business area and, rather than 'pure' coaching, were after elements of mentoring in the coaching conversations.

So, should an internal coach who has skills in, say, OD and who may easily be able to offer a consultancy perspective, be allowed to play that role if a client is struggling with managing a change programme? That may not be what you want – indeed you may have a mentoring scheme specifically to meet this need or would prefer the client to arrange a separate meeting with someone in OD to discuss this – and you expect your coaches to maintain strong boundaries and keep mentoring firmly off limits. But it is worth sharing with your coaches how flexible (or not) you expect them to be. For clarity, many organisations now provide written guidance about what clients can expect from their coaches (see Chapter 8 for more on this).

Involvement of line managers

What role do you, as lead coach, expect line managers to play in the coaching? Invariably, employees wanting to train to be an internal coach need permission from their line manager to carve out time for coach training, coaching sessions with clients, supervision and continuing professional development.

Many businesses look for the active involvement of the client's line manager in the coaching process, beginning with authorising participation in the scheme followed by involvement in a three-way contracting meeting at the beginning of the coaching assignment. There can subsequently be a check-in partway through the process and finally feedback at the end on any changes or progress observed. For line managers to be able to play their part, it is important that they are given guidance about the process and what is expected of them (see Chapter 8).

The picture just painted, however, is of a fairly "hands on" variety of coaching scheme. In some organisations, the line manager may have little or no part in the process at all (or even know that their direct report is being coached). You will want to think about what makes most sense in your organisation. How much line manager involvement do you want?

Team and group coaching

More and more organisations are training their coaches to be able to offer team coaching as part of their coaching strategy to enhance collaboration, improve communication and boost overall team performance. As teams increasingly work on complex tasks and projects, coaching can help team members to manage conflict and strengthen interpersonal relationships which are critical in today's fast-paced work environments. Team coaching can be particularly effective when a dysfunctional team needs (and wants) to change or when it is important that a newly formed team hits the ground running. However, team coaches need specialised training to understand group dynamics, manage diverse personalities and tailor strategies to meet team needs.

Group coaching is something different. Team coaching enhances a unified team's collaboration and performance, focusing on shared goals. By contrast, group coaching supports individuals from different parts of the organisation who are looking for personal and professional development. Here the coach encourages peer learning and self-reflection rather than a team approach and collective outcomes. There are a number of examples of group coaching in the Eide Bailly case study, earlier in this chapter.

Table 7.1 highlights the distinct characteristics and approaches to team coaching versus group coaching, helping to clarify how each method is applied in organisational settings.

Table 7.1 Characteristics and approaches to team coaching versus group coaching

Aspect	Team coaching	Group coaching
Focus	Enhancing team dynamics, collaboration and performance.	Helping individuals with similar personal or professional goals.
Objective	Aligning collective goals and improving team effectiveness.	Supporting individual goal achievement within group setting.
Participants	Members of a single team working toward shared outcomes.	Individuals with diverse backgrounds or goals but similar themes or objectives.
Approach	Facilitates collaboration and cohesion to function as one entity.	Each individual works on their own goals within the context of the group.
Coaching Style	Focuses on team dynamics, conflict resolution, and collective decision-making.	Emphasises personal growth, peer support, mutual accountability.
Duration	Ongoing, often tied to team development goals and project timelines.	Typically shorter, goal-specific sessions.
Coach's Role	Coaches use specific methods such as team-building exercises, to facilitate teamwork and ensure that they are working towards the same goals.	Coaches support individual progress while maintaining group engagement.
Outcomes	Improved team synergy, productivity, conflict management.	Achievement of individual goals and learning through group interactions.

Offering group coaching can be a very cost-effective way of reaching more people and can operate a little like an action learning set (for more on action learning sets, see Chapter 10).

Budget allocation for the coaching scheme

No strategy would be complete without some indication of the financials and you'll need a precise idea of costs if you have to put together a business case. The size of budget that you'll need to set the internal coaching scheme up and then run it will depend on the answers to questions like these.

- How large will the initial cohort of coaches be?
- Will your coaching service be made up of part-time or full-time coaches (or both)?
- How high profile will the initiative be?
- Will you be offering team coaching as well as one-to-one?
- Will the coaches be trained from scratch, or can you draw on qualified coaches already working within your organisation? Will the training (or validation of existing employees with coaching skills) be delivered in-house or outsourced?
- What level of qualification do you require? And will you seek to have your coaches accredited?
- Is the matching to be done individually (resource-intensive for the lead coach or coaching team) or via an electronic coach management system (involving a set-up cost if custom-built or an ongoing cost if leased from a provider)?
- Will a major and ongoing communications/marketing plan need to be resourced or is the coaching to be lower-key or 'by invitation only'?
- Will the supervision offered to your coaches be one-to-one or group and will it be delivered in-house or outsourced?
- Will time and energy will be invested in building a coaching community?
- How much CPD will you offer to your coaches? How will it be sourced?
- Will you join a coaching professional body as an organisation and/or will you offer individual membership to your coaches?
- How much monitoring/quality assurance/evaluation will you do?
- How much resource will be required to service your steering group, if any?

Many of these issues are explored in more depth in Chapters 9–11.

Piloting your scheme

One useful approach, if you want to prove the concept before devoting significant funds to an internal coaching scheme, is to pilot your coaching scheme in one part of the organisation, conduct an evaluation into its effectiveness, and only then roll it out across the organisation, as in the next case study.

Case study

Piloting your coaching scheme

A large public sector organisation decided to pilot an internal coaching scheme within one business area. The trigger was a staff engagement survey that showed that staff in that part of the business (numbering some 2000 people) were noticeably less engaged than in others. The head of Learning & Development for that business partner suggested that an internal coaching scheme could contribute to the solution and a business case was made for training eight 'job-plus' staff as internal coaches. Before the pilot, only senior staff had had an opportunity to receive one-to-one coaching, and always from an external supplier. The purpose of the coaching pilot was "to empower middle managers and make them feel more supported and valued".

ICF accredited training (at Associate Credentialled Coach level) was chosen, contracts were drafted and agreed between the organisation and the coaches, and between the coaches and the coachees, expectations by all parties were clarified and boundary issues discussed. After the pilot programme had been running for eighteen months, it was decided to train a further thirty-six coaches. At this point the importance of ongoing support for the coaches was recognised and the programme added in coaching circles and two days per annum of CPD (including group supervision and triad work).

After three years, an evaluation questionnaire was launched for clients to complete. Most of the questions involved a seven-point Lickert scale (from strongly agree to strongly disagree) and covered a lot of ground (feedback for the coach; the coaching process; personal learning development; impact on the job; organisational impact; and support received). Those running the scheme were conscious of the need to demonstrate its value and were therefore very pleased when consistently ninety per cent of the clients answered "Strongly agree" to the following two statements:

- Coaching, compared to other learning activities, is a worthwhile investment in my development.
- Coaching, compared to other learning activities, is a worthwhile investment for the organisation's development.

Responses to the statement: "The provision of coaching demonstrates to me that the organisation is committed to developing its people" were also very positive, demonstrating that clients were feeling more valued. They also reported feeling more motivated, engaged in their job, empowered, and able to take actions forward. Some line managers who were interviewed similarly reported that their wider teams had benefited from a staff member's coaching because of the client's positive behavioural shifts and the impact these had on ways of working.

In the two years following the evaluation, more internal coaches were trained. Six years on, there were over 100 internal coaches coaching throughout the organisation.

Harvesting organisational learning

Having an internal coaching resource offers a terrific opportunity for gathering systemic learning and feeding it back into the business. Fletcher and Macann (2011), Passmore and Crabbe (2023) and others have written about the benefits. As Alison Maxwell said in a particularly colourful metaphor: "Coaches can reach into the bowels of the organisation in a way that other interventions cannot" (Maxwell, 2013). However, you need to decide on what collection mechanism works best for your organisation and where the information can be fed back for maximum impact. The most popular method for harvesting organisational learning is via supervision groups.

Here are some examples.

- In the NHS, when strategic health authorities still existed, the coaching leads would meet quarterly as the 'SHA Coach Network'. As part of the meeting, anonymised themes from coaching supervision groups would be circulated for discussion. These would be used to inform what CPD sessions to provide for the internal coaches.
- In a pharmaceutical company, the lead coach met with the People Director twice a year to talk non-attributably about themes emerging from the coaching sessions provided to participants on leadership development programmes.
- A lead coach in a legal firm regularly picked three themes to feed back to the managing partner. This was done in an *ad hoc* way. "Sometimes he listened, sometimes he didn't. I would know if he'd listened because I'd hear about some conversation that he'd had or some action that he'd taken".
- At one media organisation, the supervisor asked the supervision groups to come up with the "top three organisational issues" every six months and then shared these with OD.

There seem to be two main categories of helpful data: information shedding light on possible improvements to the coaching service and information suggesting ways in which the organisation could work more effectively.

Examples of harvested themes for improving the coaching service

- Supervisors reported back that some of the coaches were struggling to get enough clients and were becoming deskilled. The lead coach increased publicity for the scheme and streamlined the "matching" system.
- A supervisor spotted that issues around boundaries kept cropping up and suggested a refresher CPD session around that.
- Coaches fed back to their lead coach that their line managers were becoming disgruntled at the amount of time that the coaching was taking up. The lead coach spent the next few months systematically contacting the line managers of all the coaches to remind them of the benefits and also to express personal gratitude for the contribution their direct reports were making to the organisation.

Examples of harvested themes for improving the organisation

- Coaches in an engineering company noted a significant number of senior clients needing support in taking decisions. Managers appeared to be afraid to put their heads above the parapet in case they got it wrong. The issue was fed into a board awayday.
- Coaches in a consultancy company became aware of conversations at all levels around the poor gender mix in recent promotions to partner. It was demotivating high-flying women and sending a negative message throughout the organisation about attitudes towards diversity generally. The partners took it on board for the next promotion round.
- Senior managers coaching clients in a local authority reported feeling that top-level decisions were not being properly communicated to them, which left them feeling disengaged. It resulted in more attention being given to internal communications.
- In a professional services company, coaches coaching returners from maternity leave were able to feed back some very specific problems. When women reached the 'unpaid' element of their maternity leave, their security passes and email access were automatically disabled as though they had left the company. In addition, on their return to work they had to be escorted into the building as though they were a visitor. They found this very unwelcoming. The company acted on the feedback.

Sometimes coaches pick up issues that people are disgruntled about, which can shed light on a dip in retention rates or poor employee engagement scores.

However, the fact that data is collected does not ensure that it is actioned, so it is important to check that the information is reaching the people who can act on it and that they are actually doing something with it. Some years ago, Katharine came across an example of a lead coach who was dutifully providing data quarterly for OD's regular management meetings only to discover, three years in, that it was not actually being included on their agenda.

Edward's story

Systematically gathering organisational learning

Edward took over responsibility, within the People Department, for running the internal coaching service (which was distributed around a number of business units), procuring external coaches and providing coaching skills training for managers.

Edward's steering group was moribund so he decided to re-engage and re-energise the members by reviewing and renewing the coaching strategy. While all the internal coaches used the same coach management system and adhered to the same policies, he noticed that there was no process for harvesting organisational learning from their activities and proposed to the steering group that he put that right.

So he developed a variety of approaches. First, he asked the lead coaches in each business unit to meet regularly with their internal coaches and invite them to share knowledge including any emerging organisational themes. Then, he talked to the two external supervisors who ran supervision groups four times a year and asked them, at the end of each session, to identify three or four organisational themes emerging from the group discussions and let him have them. Edward also ran coaching skills for managers training sessions and he noticed that data about systemic issues surfaced in them too, from time to time.

Once a quarter, Edward synthesised the learning from all three sources and fed it back to the steering group, who were surprised at the depth and breadth of the messages that were being brought to the surface by the coaching. Over time, Edward acquired funding for an annual all-day coaching conference and invited both internal and external coaches. The question "What are we seeing in the organisation?" was always asked as a way of sense-checking the high-level organisational themes that had been identified during the year.

Sustainability

Over the past 15 years, listening to stories about successful and less successful internal coaching schemes, asking lead coaches about what has gone well and what less well, Katharine has frequently noticed a 'wave' effect. Schemes tend to wax and wane. Schemes can go 'underground' for a few years until someone new arrives and regenerates the internal coaching effort. This section is all about sustainability. How can you set up an internal coaching service that survives into the long term?

Where schemes have faltered, the dominant narratives tend to be:

a Pools set up by a passionate advocate for coaching (almost always a coach themselves) who moves on and is replaced by someone who lacks the seniority, energy, influence, or personal experience of coaching to keep the profile high and the coaches engaged.
b Pools that start with a burst of enthusiasm but then hit a wall because – say – a restructure results in the coaches having less time available for their coaching, lose motivation and impetus and become inactive.
c Pools that have a senior champion, so the lead coach does not feel the necessity to collect evaluation data. But then that champion leaves the organisation and is replaced by someone who does not understand the value of coaching and closes the coaching service down because the lead coach cannot provide evidence that the coaching was providing benefits.

The following case study tells the sad story of a thriving coaching service that gradually disintegrated.

Case study

How internal coaching pools can fail

In 2010/11, a multinational information and communications company with over 120,000 employees had an internal coaching service boasting sixty active internal coaches, six internal supervisors, a charter, a code of ethics and a coach/client matching platform. By 2024, there were only half a dozen active coaches left in the company. They were operating as a self-managed group, with no central direction or monitoring of their activity and no access to CPD or supervision. What happened and what can we learn from it?

Sponsorship/governance

In the early days, the internal coaching service was sponsored by an enthusiastic HR Director. She had been coached herself and was supportive of offering internal coaching to employees, but she did not commission a strategy or provide any real governance. When the lead coach left the company, the HR Director allowed responsibility for the coaching service to pass to someone who was not a coach and had other pressing responsibilities. When the HR Director herself left a few years later, there was no one to fight for the budget so it disappeared, leaving no money for CPD or for training any new coaches.

Balancing supply and demand

While considerable thought was given to the supply side from the outset – ensuring that the coaches were well-trained and supervised – virtually no attention was given to generating clients. Little consideration was given to how the coaching effort might best be targeted and the result was a lack of demand. Gradually, the coaches had fewer clients so they lost confidence and, when requests did come in, were reluctant to take them on.

Marketing

Recognising that publicity of the service was called for, a new lead coach put together an impressive marketing pack with slides, an explanation of what coaching was all about, business cards to give to managers, testimonials from internal coaching clients, etc. But rather than marketing the coaching service via a central initiative, the coaches were expected to use the marketing pack to find their own clients or, as one coach put it, to 'prostitute themselves'. They didn't see it as their job to market the coaching service. Those that did, assembled a random collection of clients, but there was no strategy.

Coach management system

Eventually, the company invested in a user-friendly portal on a commercial coach management system containing coach profiles and resources like videos, books and CPD opportunities. CPD and supervision sessions went advertised on there too but, when coaches failed to attend them, they stopped. Gradually, the internal supervisors drifted away as many of the coaches were inactive and few actually used the new portal. Some of them continued to find their own coaching clients but didn't engage with the centre. When an effort was made to encourage the coaches to use the portal, there was pushback. Eventually, there was nothing left.

Lessons

- Where there is no strategy or governance, there's little to glue the system together.
- Internal coaches need to be nurtured and integrated into a community or they may disengage.
- The funding for coaching pools can be vulnerable if there is one champion and that person departs and there is no evidence of organisational value.
- Attention needs to be given to demand as well as supply.

The following represents a few thoughts on strategies to deploy to ensure the sustainability of your internal coaching resource.

Leadership

Having a senior champion is very important, but a key benefit of having a steering group is that the energy behind a coaching scheme does not rest simply with two key people: the champion and the lead coach. The steering group should be a nexus of people committed to ensuring that the scheme flourishes. Members of the group can help to make sure that the purpose is kept fresh and relevant to the needs of the organisation and to support the lead coach if they show signs of flagging. It can also help to have not one lead coach, but a small team, either distributed through the organisation or in a cluster at the centre. They can support each other and take it in turns to take the strain when activity in their day jobs is particularly demanding. It also means that if one of them moves on for whatever reason, the infrastructure will not collapse.

Balancing supply and demand

Organisations often concentrate on the supply side: selecting, training and supporting the coaches to the detriment of the demand side: recruiting clients. There are many organisations with under-employed internal coaches, which is a criminal waste of talent and has a very negative impact on return on investment. Quotations from Katharine's 2010 research – and, sadly, little has changed – include:

- "My organisation's invested a lot of money in training me but has then failed to give me anyone to coach. I feel as though I'm deskilling and already need a top-up. I'm losing confidence".
- "We were trained up and only then did my firm start looking for coachees so there was a hiatus. It should be a seamless process - not leaving us twiddling our thumbs".
- "I feel a lack of connectedness with the people running the scheme. They don't seem to be marketing internal coaching - perhaps to protect us from being overwhelmed by requests - but it's bad news from where I'm sitting. I'm losing motivation, enthusiasm, connectedness".

Many lead coaches are nervous of being swamped by demand and therefore under-market the scheme, so the initial take-up can be very slow. The result of that can be that the coaches become deskilled or lose interest and anyone who asks for coaching gets it, even if they are not in an influential position or wanting to work on business-critical issues (but just because the coaches want the practice).

Chapter 8 suggests many ways to promote an internal coaching service. One approach is to market enthusiastically and simply run a waiting list if demand outstrips supply. This is likely to result in a more sustainable service.

Building a coaching community

There are many benefits to building a coaching community. Sometimes, the team spirit becomes so strong that the internal coaching effort continues even if the L&D

function that ran it is completely dismantled. In the public sector, there have been a number of examples of this over the past ten years. Where internal coaches have been encouraged to become a real community, they have a much better chance of making a go of being self-managed and continuing to deliver coaching within their organisations. This could include making referrals to each other, getting together regularly for co-coaching or coaching practice sessions, or even taking it in turns to organise a lunchtime CPD session with an external speaker happy to donate their services. But if they have been isolated from each other that is most unlikely to happen.

The bottom line is that coaches really appreciate being part of a coaching community. See Chapter 6 for examples of how organisations have gone about building them.

Valuing your coaches

Retention of coaches can be another sustainability issue. They may leave the organisation because a restructure or staff cutbacks lead to redundancies or because they want to work as a freelance external coach or join a coaching consultancy. Or their job may simply change shape, so they have less time available for coaching. Training new coaches takes time and resources so you need to keep those who remain in your organisation – with their coaching experience plus knowledge of the organisation and the people in it – for as long as you possibly can. Sometimes a coach may become inactive for a year or two but then return to the fold. One lead coach uses a system of providing the coach with a one-to-one supervision session before, during and after their first assignment back in the role. If all goes well, the coach returns to the active pool.

Given that you do not have the lever of offering them promotion or a pay rise, the best way of keeping your coaches is to make them feel valued and supported. As Long (2012) puts it:

"In many organisations, the internal coach has to fit coaching around their day job. Their contribution as an internal coach may not even be recognised at appraisal. While coaching can be a rewarding "escape" from other parts of their role, unless there is encouragement and support from somewhere within the organisation then it is easy to see how the commitment to coach can wane, and for internal coaches to go off the radar". (p. 3)

So, what ways do organisations find to demonstrate that they value their internal coaches? The following are some examples.

- The lead coach takes every opportunity to say thank you to the coaches (such as at CPD days or regular get-togethers), affirming what they do, and acknowledging the commitment they show by coaching on top of their normal jobs.
- Some lead coaches collect the feedback from evaluation forms and hold annual one-to-ones with their internal coaches to pass on the feedback, thank them for their dedication and ask if there is anything more they could be doing to support them.
- A senior champion, ideally at board level, sends an annual thank you email to all the internal coaches for their contribution to improving organisational

effectiveness. One HR director sends a handwritten Christmas card annually to every internal coach saying thank you.

- In some organisations, the coach's development objectives as a coach will form part of their individual development plan, so their coaching work is acknowledged as part of their annual performance review.
- Investing in supervision, holding regular CPD sessions, and arranging get-togethers for the internal coaching community are all seen by coaches as demonstrating that the organisation values what they do.

Demonstrating effectiveness via evaluations

One tried and tested way of ensuring that a coaching scheme continues to be funded is by demonstrating its effectiveness. Katharine worried about the lead coach, one year into his role, who told her that he did not plan to do any evaluation, rather trusting his coaches to do a professional job and his very influential champion to argue successfully for the funding each year. But what would he do if his champion moved on and the finance director asked for evidence that the money was being spent well before committing any more funds?

There are many other good reasons for evaluating the effectiveness of your internal coaching scheme, but ensuring that it is sustainable is one of them. Evaluation is explored in depth in Chapter 11.

Summary

This chapter has examined the need for a coaching strategy and the areas you might cover in it. A good strategy becomes your blueprint for implementing your internal coaching scheme and ensuring its success. We have discussed a number of different issues ranging from how you will ensure commitment from the business, which is essential for sustainability, through to the scope of the scheme, including targeting your coaching resources plus the need to evaluate it. If you have clarity on all these issues your communication to the business will be clear and consistent, and that is paramount to the success of your internal coaching programme.

Table 7.2 Questions to reflect on

Do we need a coaching strategy?

- If your scheme is small, what are the consequences of not writing a strategy for the future?
- Who is your audience for the strategy? What do you need to consider so that it is best positioned to gain their support?
- What is going on in the organisation at present that has implications for your coaching strategy? Are there other development initiatives/talent management initiatives/change programmes to take into account?

(Continued)

Table 7.2 (Continued)

Governance

- If a steering group is appropriate for your organisation, who would be best to chair it and to whom should it be accountable?
- How can you ensure that the members have credibility and influence within the business?
- How does the makeup of the group reflect your coaching strategy?
- How will you frame the members' role and what will their practical commitment need to be?

Commitment from the business leaders

- Who in senior management is supportive of coaching and how will you gain commitment and support from them?
- How can you engage line managers in supporting members of their team who are internal coaches?

Strategic purpose

- Do you have clarity on the business drivers for your internal coaching resource?
- What are the benefits that coaching will deliver to the organisation and potential clients?
- What are the problems or issues that coaching could help to address?
- How could coaching contribute to business priorities?

Organisational learning

- How might you go about harvesting organisational learning?
- Who could make best use of it?

Positioning

- Have you included a communications plan as part of your coaching strategy and what channels of communication are most effective in your organisation to tailor messages to engage different groups?
- Do you need to target clients in particular parts of the business to ensure equality and fairness and ensure there is alignment with your strategic purpose?

Scope and approach of the coaching

- Do you want to link clients' coaching objectives with their personal development plan?
- Are you expecting your coaches to do any mentoring?
- Would three-way meetings between client/coach/line manager be beneficial? If so what support and guidance needs to be in place to make the process easy for all?

Targeting your coaching resource

- How can you make best use of your internal coaches to meet business needs?
- On which areas of the business or ongoing programmes do you need to target your coaching resource?

Budget allocation for the coaching scheme

- Will you fund the internal coaching training centrally or expect individual business units to contribute?

Sustainability

- How are you engaging with the business to ensure internal coaching will continue even if there is a change in top management?
- What are the 'drivers' that will help create a proactive coaching community? And what do you need to put in place to sustain the energy and enthusiasm of your internal coaches?
- What do you need to do in terms of 'succession planning' to ensure you have continued support for internal coaching if your business champions leave or you leave?

Chapter 8

Creating a coaching framework

What this chapter is about

Organisations often overlook the importance of establishing a solid coaching framework, including policies, procedures and communication strategies, in favour of immediate benefits. Yet it is an essential ingredient in sustaining the coaching effort. As the CIPD (one of the leading HR and development bodies in the UK) put it:

> "A coaching framework provides clarity and structure, ensuring that coaching is aligned with the organisation's goals and values. It ensures consistency in approach, which leads to better outcomes for individuals and the organisation as a whole".
>
> (CIPD, 2023)

This chapter offers guidance on establishing your coaching framework, including sample templates, agreements and guidelines accessible via the QR code on page 3.

This chapter covers:

- What is meant by a coaching framework
- Integrating your coaching framework into organisational strategies
- Roles, responsibilities and accountabilities
- Guidance on contracting
- Record-keeping and GDPR
- Remote coaching and use of technology
- Standards, ethics and quality of service
- Internal marketing and business engagement

What is meant by a coaching framework

Coaching frameworks are structured approaches designed to guide, inform and standardise the environment within which your coaches work (Connor & Pokora, 2012). The target audiences for the guidance you provide are primarily the coach, client and sponsor (who will usually be the line manager), and this chapter aims

DOI: 10.4324/9781003519911-10

to explore who needs what guidance and the documentation required to support it. Figure 8.1 highlights examples of the range of organisational policies and strategies that may sit within a coaching framework.

Strategies and documents supporting...	
...the organisational framework	**... the coaching framework**
	• Coaching strategy: purpose, positioning, people
	• Roles and responsibilities guides
• People and OD strategies including future skills analysis.	• Differences between coaching and mentoring
• Organisational competencies	• Coachee self-assessment /selection form
• Professional coaching standards and accreditation	• Matching process documentation
• Equality, Diversity and Inclusion Policy	• Coaching feedback and evaluation forms
• HR policies including disciplinary, bullying, harassment.	• Contractual engagement
	• Team coaching process
• Well-being policies including occupational services	• Global Code of Ethics
	• Ethical charter
• Sustainability strategy & risk assessment	• Data Privacy and security guidelines
	• Professional indemnity insurance policy

Figure 8.1 Strategies and documents supporting the organisational framework and the coaching framework.

Integrating your coaching framework into organisational strategies

A number of studies highlight the growing role of coaching in organisational development, leadership development, talent management and retention, performance enhancement, cultural transformation and effective succession planning plus how a coaching framework can be integrated into organisational strategy (CIPD, 2008, 2023; ILM, 2024).

Four ways to achieve this integration

Alignment with strategic goals: Making sure that your coaching strategy is directly aligned with the company's strategic goals helps to identify where coaching can have the most significant impact. Integrating it into the 'leadership pipeline' is one, very visible, way of showing how coaching can help managers to develop the competencies they need. Charan et al. (2011) describe how leaders can best be supported when transitioning between different levels, and the competencies required at each stage. Coaching support is a key tool within this strategy.

Employee learning and development programmes: Where coaching is positioned as an ongoing learning opportunity rather than a one-time intervention, it can support leadership, team and career development. Structuring coaching to complement training programmes, i.e., giving each participant a coach to work with, can encourage employees to apply their learning in real-time while receiving support on overcoming obstacles or improving performance.

Succession planning and talent management: One tangible way of integrating coaching is to support high-potential employees to accelerate their growth and readiness for more senior roles. Coaching often focuses on developing their people skills, emotional intelligence and strategic thinking to get them ready for higher-level responsibilities.

Create a coaching culture: One of the most popular ways to integrate coaching principles and practices is to encourage managers both to access coaching themselves and to receive training in a coaching approach so that they can coach their own teams, creating a shift in leadership style to being less directive.

Roles, responsibilities and accountabilities

It is desirable to articulate the roles, obligations and expectations of everyone involved in the coaching process from the outset. These will include:

- Steering group, if any
- Lead coach/scheme administrator
- Line manager/sponsor
- Coaches
- Coaching clients

Role of the steering group

The primary role of a steering group responsible for internal coaching services is to provide governance, strategic oversight and guidance to ensure that they deliver what the organisation needs. A case study, illustrating the benefits of having a steering group, appears in Chapter 7. Key responsibilities typically include the following.

Purpose and objectives: Being the voice of clarity on what the coaching seeks to achieve and ensuring that it helps to deliver the organisation's strategic goals.

Governance: Approving policies, guidelines and standards of coaching practice to ensure that the service is professional and ethical.

Resource allocation: Gaining approval for investment in the coaching service.

Stakeholder engagement: Acting as a bridge between the coaching service and senior leadership as well as promoting awareness of the coaching service throughout the organisation.

Performance monitoring: Reviewing metrics on results and impact – in the form of coach, client and stakeholder feedback – and identifying generic anonymised themes that can contribute to organisational improvements.

Ethics and confidentiality: Upholding ethical standards. The steering group may take a role in addressing any issues that arise, e.g., as part of a complaints process.

Championing a coaching culture: Being the advocate for fostering a culture that values all coaching (external coaches, internal coaches and leaders using coaching skills) across the organisation.

Role of the lead coach/scheme administrator

The lead coach is the key contact for all operational matters and supports the coaching process and the coaches. Often, they will also hold a strategic role. Their key responsibilities typically include the following.

Development of the coaching strategy: The lead coach will frequently have responsibility for writing the coaching strategy. Sometimes external coaching is also within their remit. They are the conduit between the coaching service and the steering group (if any) and, where anonymised feedback is harvested from coaching conversations, will convey these messages back into the business.

Developing the coaching framework: The lead coach would normally set up the administrative infrastructure and develop policies to underpin the coaching service, advising on processes, procedures and communication activities necessary to launch and support the coaching offer.

Selection, training and development: They will lead the selection of employees to be trained as coaches, then source the training, supervision and CPD.

Allocating coaches: If an electronic Coach Management System (CMS) is used – putting the client in the driving seat for finding their coach via an index of coach profiles – the lead coach will source it. On occasion, they may decide that a client needs a specific internal coach, for example if a neurodivergent client requests someone with a relevant background.

Evaluating the coaching service: It is generally down to the lead coach to decide (or propose to the steering group) how best to evaluate impact.

Role of the line manager

Line managers have two distinct roles in an internal coaching scheme:

1 Agreeing to release – and then support – a direct report to be trained as a coach.
2 Supporting a direct report who might benefit from being coached.

Supporting a trainee coach

The line manager needs to understand what they are being asked to authorise in terms of the time commitment expected from the trainee coach. Explaining the benefits to them is key – as not only will the coach become a valuable asset to the organisation, but the development of their coaching skills directly correlates with performing more effectively in their day job.

In Julia's experience, the most common reason for trainee coaches failing to complete their training is not down to their motivation but due to the lack of line management support as they struggle to balance study time with work demands. The role of line managers in protecting the trainees' time is crucial. Clear communication about training commitments, including workshops, study hours, client coaching sessions and supervision is essential to ensure that trainees succeed and the organisation benefits from having qualified internal coaches.

Once the coach has completed the training, it is equally important that their line manager continues to support them in making time to deliver coaching to their internal clients.

Supporting a direct report receiving coaching

One cannot assume that line managers will automatically understand the benefits of a direct report receiving coaching, so part of the internal communication is to explain their role as sponsor – and key stakeholder – in the coaching process. Some organisations require little involvement from line managers to support clients (indeed some systems are entirely client-led with no involvement from the line manager at all), while others may ask them to:

- Authorise the coaching.
- Get involved in the client's goal setting and defining success criteria.
- Participate in initial three-way contracting with the coach and client.
- Take responsibility for giving the client support and feedback between coaching sessions.
- Take an active role in closing down the coaching assignment and supporting any continuing development.

To access "The line manager's role in the coaching process: A Guide", use the QR Code on page 3.

The role of the coach

Your coaches' role will reflect the purpose that you have defined in your coaching strategy, the training that they receive, the clients they coach and the coaching process and model you adopt. One thing to be clear about from the outset is whether you expect your coaches to deliver 'pure' coaching or to operate along the coaching-mentoring continuum. You may have a separate mentoring scheme so need to have clear boundaries between the two. There is guidance via the QR Code that outlines the differences between coaching and mentoring.

To access "Key differences Between Coaching and Mentoring: A Guide", use the QR Code on page 3.

Coach responsibilities would normally include the following.

Contracting with the client(s): This may be one-to-one or with a team and, as expanded on below, where there is a single client, the contracting meeting may include the sponsor/line manager.

Coaching sessions: Conducting one-to-one, group or team coaching sessions, taking ownership of the process of coaching while using the skills of active listening, questioning and feedback techniques to support client or team growth.

Goal setting and action planning: Helping the client to define clear, achievable goals, develop actionable plans and review progress.

Support and building trust: Encouraging the client to be honest – in a confidential safe space – and develop self-awareness, self-reflection and responsibility for their own development.

Alignment with organisational goals: If the coaching offered is part of an organisation's talent development approach, leadership programme or change initiative, ensuring that the coaching outcomes align.

Skills development: Supporting clients to improve specific skills (e.g., leadership, communication, resilience, priority management or problem-solving) including referring clients to, or providing resources and tools for, self-directed learning.

Feedback and evaluation: Offering constructive feedback to the client based on observations during the sessions with regular evaluation of the effectiveness of the coaching and adjustment to the approach, as needed.

Most organisations specify how many sessions they expect their coaches to deliver. This is often up to six sessions and it is important that the coaches do not become a permanent crutch for their clients. Some coach management systems allow for a maximum of 12 sessions but that doesn't stop the coach and client arranging additional sessions without logging them. In one company, to guard against this, the lead coach has an annual session with every coach to discuss contracting, dependency and setting expectations.

The coach's role in multi-stakeholder contracting

The primary role of the coach in a multi-stakeholder contracting meeting (generally three-way: coach, client, sponsor) is to facilitate the process by which each person understands their role in the coaching relationship plus what coaching can and cannot deliver.

Chapter 3 has more on three-way contracting from the perspective of the coach. Three key benefits of three-way contracting are setting clear and specific goals with clear outcomes, ensuring that these goals are aligned with organisational needs and obtaining a commitment from the sponsor to help the client to apply their development back in the day job. It is for you, as lead coach, to decide if you want three-way contracting to be the default process and to ensure that your coaches receive the training they need in order to facilitate the process confidently.

Role of the coaching client

It is often said that the most important ingredient in effective coaching is how committed the client is to changing. It is common for lead coaches to focus mainly on the coaches, and less so on the clients and their suitability for coaching, but research (Haden, 2013; Norman, 2024; Stokes, 2007) suggests that the success of coaching assignments relies to a significant degree on the 'coachability' of the client. This is something to think about when establishing the organisational framework. How might you assess the clients' readiness to be coached, their willingness to engage fully in the coaching process and their commitment to achieving outcomes? Is your valuable coaching resource being used to best effect, targeting the people who will benefit from it most?

There are two schools of thought. One is that no one is uncoachable, the issue is rather whether a particular coach is the right one for the client. Might a sociopathic manager, viewing the coach as one more person to manipulate, be more responsive to a coach of higher status than themselves? The other view is that some clients are simply unable to engage substantially with coaching process – a key factor being an inability to be honest with themselves so that any change can only be external (whereas successful coaching relies upon internal change).

Steinberg (2020) suggests seven core characteristics that differentiate leaders most likely to profit from coaching from those who are less likely to. The characteristics are tolerance for discomfort while embracing new ways of being and behaving; openness to experimentation and taking risks while trying out new ideas; the ability to look beyond the rational and connect with their feelings; a willingness to take responsibility rather than blaming others; the capacity for forgiveness (making peace with the past and moving on); applying self-discipline by sticking with new behaviours, e.g., learning to say no and, finally, preparedness to ask for support including accepting and acting on feedback.

Stokes (2007) developed the concept of the 'skilled coachee' (Stokes, 2007). He identified the skills and attributes that enable clients to engage effectively with the coaching process. You could use these attributes to construct a questionnaire for potential coaching clients to complete.

To access "Desirable Attributes in the 'Skilled Coachee': A Guide", use the QR Code on page 3.

Guidance on contracting

Clear contracting at the outset is the bedrock of a successful coaching relationship. It involves agreeing on well-defined expectations between the coach and the client and, if three-way contracting with the sponsor is involved, the coach needs to facilitate that process to ensure that there is agreement on issues such as how confidentiality and boundaries will be handled and what involvement the sponsor will have in the process before the coaching assignment commences.

It is the coach's role to define the purpose, process and expectations of the first three-way meeting so that there is clarity. For example, there may be both open and private goals, some goals being agreed with the line manager and others just between the coach and client. It is common, for example, for the client to want to do some work on their relationship with their line manager, but they may not want to be explicit about that. We looked at the importance of contracting in setting up the relationship in Chapter 3 and paid attention to the three-way approach.

Not all organisations provide their coaches with a written contract to share with their client. Rather they rely on the coaches to cover the ground orally in the first session. Having an agreed, written agreement before the coaching sessions get underway, however, is a professional and ethical way to establish the ground rules for the coaching relationship. It is desirable that, as lead coach, you provide your coaches with an approved written agreement to discuss with their clients.

There are potential downsides if you don't provide a written agreement.

Unclear expectations: No common understanding of the responsibilities, process or scope of the coaching can lead to confusion between the coach and the client. Sometimes there can be 'scope creep'.

Compromised confidentiality: A contract outlines confidentiality terms. Without one, clients might feel hesitant to share sensitive information, limiting the effectiveness of the coaching process.

No accountability: A written contract helps to establish accountability for both the coach and the client. Without this, there might be no clear boundaries around commitments, session frequency, or follow-through on agreed actions.

Disputes and legal risk: If something goes wrong, e.g., miscommunication, dissatisfaction with the coaching process or ethical issues, there is no clear legal framework without a contract to protect the interests of both parties or resolve disputes.

Boundary issues: There may be unclear boundaries around the coach's role – what they are and are not there to do.

Conflict of interest: A contract can help clarify any potential conflicts and establish ethical guidelines.

The coaching agreement provided via the QR code is one example of a coaching agreement/contract.

To access "Coaching Agreement: An Example", use the QR Code on page 3.

Record keeping and GDPR

The two things for coaches to be ultra-careful about are confidentiality and data protection (Rogers, 2011), and you need to ensure that your coaches understand their responsibilities. The Global Code of Ethics (June 2021) helpfully describes the professional standards of ethical practice regarding record keeping.

What records might you ask your coaches to keep?

It is good standard practice for coaches to maintain accurate records to track their clients' progress, while being mindful of GDPR implications. For full guidance on ensuring that both your coaches and your organisation comply with GDPR, please refer to the UK Government website for full details of the Data Protection Act (2018). The following focuses on the coaching records that your coaches may keep.

Client information: Your coaches will need to seek client agreement for them to store their contact information, enabling them to get in touch by phone or email.

Initial assessment: To gain a full picture of their client's development needs and goals, your coaches may need to gather information about the client's current situation, challenges, and desired outcomes, including their strengths and areas for growth. This may include assessment tools, e.g., completing a personal SWOT analysis or asking them to undertake or share recent performance appraisals or 360-degree feedback.

Goal setting and tracking: Your coaches may wish to document the short-term and long-term goals that the client wishes to achieve, exploring what success would look like. After each session they may make a record of what progress is being made and, if adjustments are necessary, making a note of key milestones and achievements reached by the client along the way.

Confidentiality and ethical documentation: This includes the signed contract (promising to ensure the privacy of the client's information) as well as a record by your coaches of any ethical issues that the client raises regarding role conflicts, confidentiality or boundary issues during the coaching assignment.

Coaching session records: It is up to your coaches how detailed their session records are – it comes down to how good a memory they have and personal preferences – but they need to have a good recollection of each coaching session including key points discussed, challenges faced, and insights shared. It can be helpful to keep a record of any specific actions, reflections or learning that their clients have committed to doing and also any important questions they have posed and responses by the client that need to be revisited in future sessions.

Feedback and reflections: The coach may choose to make a record of any oral or written feedback or observations that the client provides about the coaching process, the relationship or their experiences. The coach can also record their own reflections.

Ending the coaching programme: To capture the whole experience of coaching the client, your coaches might find it helpful to write a short summary at the end of the assignment to describe the coaching journey, including key achievements, lessons learned and recommendations for the client's continued growth. Generally, the client is also sent a feedback form about their experience of the coaching. It can include how they would describe their coach and whether they would be willing to offer a testimonial. With permission from the client you, as lead coach, would generally keep any testimonials as they can be used to support and market the coaching service.

Paying attention – from a relational perspective – to the coaching relationship is reflected upon in Chapter 3. There is also an ethical record-keeping aspect to it, referenced in the Global Code of Ethics.

Ideally, your coaches should give their clients the Global Code of Ethics (2021) to read, so that they understand the professional and ethical practices that their coach abides by, paying particular attention to the following elements in the Code regarding contracting and confidentiality.

"Para 2.13: When working with clients, members will maintain the strictest level of confidentiality with all client and sponsor information unless the release of information is required by law. Coaches will:

Para 2.14: Have a clear agreement with clients and sponsors about the conditions under which confidentiality will not be maintained (e.g., illegal activity, danger to self or others) and gain agreement to that limit of confidentiality where possible unless the release of information is required by law.
Para 2.15: Keep, store and dispose of all data and records of their client work including digital files and communications, in a manner that ensures confidentiality, security, and privacy, and complies with all relevant laws and agreements that exist in their client's country regarding data protection and privacy".

In Katharine's original research (St John-Brooks, 2010), the period that coaches kept their records for varied widely, from destroying the notes after the final session to three years or more after the end of the coaching. And a key insight was that most of them had been given no guidance on this by their employer. While the safest approach might be to destroy them as soon as the relationship has reached a conclusion, coaches were often reluctant to do this in case the client returned for coaching at a later date. It's worth bearing in mind that electronic records that are 'deleted' may still be accessible somewhere on the server.

Para 2.25: Members will respect the client's right to end the engagement at any point in the process, subject to the provisions of the coaching service agreement.
Para 2.27: Members will prepare clients for the ending of the service including having a service continuity plan if the member is unexpectedly unable to complete.
Para 2.29: Members understand that their professional responsibilities continue beyond the end of the professional relationship. These include:

Maintenance of confidentiality of all information in relation to clients and sponsors with careful and ethical management of confidential, personal, or other data.

The Global Code of Ethics (2021) also shines a light on the ethical practice of record keeping by stating that coaches should:

"Para 3.2: Demonstrate respect for the variety of practices used by coaches and all the different ethically informed approaches to coaching, mentoring, and supervision, including the use of data technologies and AI".

(Global Code of Ethics, 2021)

GDPR implications

When providing internal coaching services, it is important to pay attention to key record-keeping practices, being mindful of GDPR (Data Protection Act 2018). See the guide for compliance with GDPR and the implications for coaching services.

To access "Compliance with GDPR: A Guide", use the QR Code on page 3.

This is a short summary of some aspects to consider:

Consent: During the contracting phase, your coaches should ask the client for consent to keep records to support the coaching process, explaining what information will be recorded, how it will be used and how long it will be retained. Explaining this up-front supports professional practice and provides reassurance to the client about the privacy of the data.

Record maintenance: Consider both hard copies and password-protected notes if stored on a company laptop or PC.

Storage and access control: Implementing a secure filing system for easy retrieval and monitoring of coaching records is key. Coaching records should only be accessible to those who have a legitimate need and permission from the client to view them, e.g., your coaches, HR/L&D personnel. Use password protection, encryption or other security measures to safeguard digital records. For physical records, ensure they are stored in locked cabinets. Anonymising or coding clients' names is an added protection for the privacy of client information.

Considerations relevant to GDPR compliance

By ensuring your record-keeping practices are aligned with GDPR principles, the organisation and the client can feel assured that your coaches are abiding by and complying with data protection legislation. Here are some relevant additional considerations.

Training: Ensure that your coaches receive training on GDPR compliance and data protection to supplement their initial training, possibly with input from HR.

Data Protection Impact Assessments (DPIAs): Some organisations may be required to conduct DPIAs when processing personal data that may pose high risks to clients' rights, identifying and mitigating potential risks (especially in organisations like the NHS and social care services).

Professional Indemnity Insurance: Coaching carries some risk, however small, so professional indemnity insurance is advisable. It provides legal protection if a coach's actions lead to harm or financial loss. Given the sensitive nature of coaching, misunderstandings or dissatisfaction can arise, leading to potential claims. This insurance covers legal fees, compensation and damages, safeguarding both the coach and the organisation. Even well-intended coaching may have unintended consequences, impacting a coach's reputation and practice. Insurance ensures a structured response to disputes, preserving professional credibility. It is desirable to discuss with HR whether it makes sense to put such cover in place.

Use of coaches' notes in court cases: There is no legal coach-client privilege like lawyer-client or doctor-patient privilege (Williams & Anderson, 2006). Coaches may promise confidentiality but, in practice, could be compelled to disclose notes as part of legal processes, such as in employment tribunals.

Remote coaching and use of technology

In recent years, researchers and coaching professional bodies have been doing a lot of thinking about the impact of technology on coaching – variously called TEC (Technology Enhanced Coaching), Coach tech or Digital coaching (Bajpai, 2024; Diller & Passmore, 2023; Isaacson, 2021).

There are five key ways in which technology will have – or is already having – an impact.

The first four categories can benefit the way you and your coaches run the coaching service. The fifth affects what happens inside the virtual coaching room. Where particular products are mentioned, we are not endorsing them, simply offering examples to clarify what we are talking about.

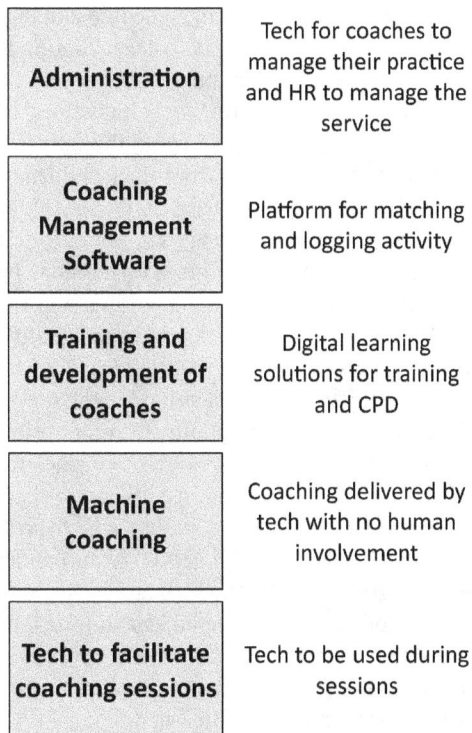

Administration	Tech for coaches to manage their practice and HR to manage the service
Coaching Management Software	Platform for matching and logging activity
Training and development of coaches	Digital learning solutions for training and CPD
Machine coaching	Coaching delivered by tech with no human involvement
Tech to facilitate coaching sessions	Tech to be used during sessions

Figure 8.2 Technology in coaching.

Administration

Task and project management systems can help you to manage the coaching programmes, and your coaches to manage their practice, e.g., diarising sessions or recording dates of sessions. Other tools include:

- *Assessment and feedback tools:* SurveyMonkey and Clarity Wave, for example, can help gather feedback to measure progress or conduct evaluations.
- *Communication tools:* Slack, WhatsApp and Telegram are all communication platforms that can provide a space for coaches and clients, or you and your coaches, to communicate efficiently, collaborate, share resources and track progress.

Coaching management software (CMS)

Many organisations use coaching management software, either by building their own platform or leasing access to a portal on a commercial platform. Functionality varies but the more sophisticated versions allow clients to request what they want from their coaching and then to receive a shortlist of matches from the index of coaches on the platform; schedule and log meetings; store notes; automatically send out evaluation forms to the client and stakeholders and analyse data, e.g., levels of activity. When purchasing access to a portal, ask the provider to demonstrate how they deal with bias – 'matching' algorithms can be discriminatory, e.g., sexist or racist. Also give some thought to whether the portal software is compatible with your own. More than one lead coach told Katharine that they were not going to renew the lease on the portal they were using because it couldn't be integrated with the company's systems, e.g., Teams. While functionality existed to use the platform to enter notes on sessions hardly anyone did. They were looking for other solutions.

More of an issue, though, can be the quality of the data that your coaches provide (or, more commonly, don't provide). Katharine has found it hard to identify any organisation that does not struggle with getting their coaches to log the data on the CMS that is needed centrally for monitoring purposes. It is particularly difficult to introduce a CMS to a cadre of coaches that was formerly free-wheeling. They often push back. The best results are in those organisations that have introduced a 'licence to practice' or similar which lays down that the internal coaches can only practise if they fulfil certain requirements like attending supervision and fully engaging with the CMS (so that all their coaching relationships are on there, the number of sessions delivered and so forth). Even then, many organisations have to chase the coaches to update their records every quarter so that the activity records are accurate. There is often a requirement for coaches to formally log the 'end' of their coaching relationships to trigger the CMS to send the client an evaluation feedback form to complete. If they fail to do that – which often happens – the feedback form does not get sent and the opportunity for feedback is lost.

Training and development of coaches

Online learning platforms have transformed corporate training, e.g., digital learning solutions, including AI-driven and adaptive learning platforms for self-directed learning. In the coaching space, technology provides webinars, videos of TED talks, virtual CPD sessions arranged by coaching professional bodies, YouTube videos of coaching demonstrations plus the opportunity for your coaches to view or listen to recordings of their own sessions by themselves or with a supervisor to learn from their own practice.

Machine coaching

There are a number of products on the market – both paid for and free – offering coaching with no human in the room. Virtual coaches, using chatbots or AI assistants, can offer personalised coaching by analysing data and using algorithms (Plotkina & Sri Ramalu, 2024). Key benefits include scalability, accessibility and constant feedback, and there are a number of large companies currently experimenting with making such coaching available to all their employees. This is sometimes referred to as the 'democratisation of coaching'. Some coaches have privacy and ethical concerns as AI coaching systems rely on personal data which, if mishandled, could be misused or exposed.

There is no readily available research yet on how effective AI coaching is. Some clients may like the anonymity it provides but anecdotal evidence suggests that, while AI coaching certainly provides a useful structure of questions to help clients work through issues and can provide helpful data-driven insights, it cannot (yet) replicate emotional intelligence or the nuances that human coaches perceive.

Technology to facilitate coaching sessions

Zoom, Microsoft Teams and other messaging and communication platforms are already widely used for virtual coaching sessions, with features like screen sharing, session recording and virtual whiteboards easily available. For those ready to experiment, there are also plenty of tools popular with coaches looking for ways to engage their client(s) in creative ways: AI-generated artwork, emergent soundscapes and 3D representations of metaphors can all be used and even virtual rooms – or landscapes – where your coaches and their clients can play. The extent to which your coaches will be able to use advanced technologies, such as wearable tech, will depend on whether you think it will enhance the client experience; the adaptability of your coaches, and if your organisation is willing to invest in it.

The impact of technology on your coaches

At an individual level, many coaches feel simultaneously fearful of becoming irrelevant from the speed of technological change and excited about the opportunities that digitalisation offers. Clients may feel similarly, with some uncomfortable about using technology. This can create a barrier, particularly for less tech-savvy individuals or those with limited access to high-speed internet or sophisticated devices. Studies on digital literacy, e.g., Selwyn (2007) have suggested that clients who are not comfortable with technology – this is less correlated with age than with openness to new experiences – may disengage or struggle to use it effectively. So your coaches will need to take care with how they use it.

Virtual coaching is now the norm. 78% of the coaching undertaken by the 137 coaches in our 2024 survey was virtual. It was driven by the move to remote working during the Covid-19 pandemic, which introduced even the most technophobic of employees to virtual technologies, and advances in technology have made the whole process cheaper and easier.

Studies comparing digital, face-to-face and blended coaching have shown similar effects in terms of success, as perceived by clients and coaches (Doyle & Bradley, 2023; Michalik & Schermuly, 2023). However, Diller and Passmore (2023) and others have identified a variety of pros and cons of virtual coaching and other digital tools, including:

Pros

- Eliminates travel expenses and travel time, reducing costs for both the coach and client, supporting sustainable practices and lowering carbon footprints.
- Enables access to coaching anywhere in the world.
- Offers flexibility, convenience, privacy.
- Opens up opportunities for people from diverse backgrounds and work patterns, e.g., clients with disabilities, single parents or caregivers, clients living in remote areas and clients from under-represented racial, ethnic or gender groups may feel more comfortable working in their own safe space.
- Provides easy access to sharing resources like videos, podcasts, and articles, to enhance the learning experience.
- Makes scheduling of sessions easier by providing a calendar for clients to choose a time convenient to them.

Cons

- There's a risk that coaches could over-rely on digital tools, potentially reducing the coach's focus on using human intuition and emotional understanding.
- A reduction in the visibility of non-verbal cues can have an impact on developing trust and adversely affect the coaching relationship.
- Intensive use can lead to 'Zoom Fatigue' (Shockley et al., 2021).
- Interruptions in the physical space (e.g., cats) or in the digital room, (e.g., technical faults or time lags), can disrupt sessions.

Patrick's story

Potential impact of coaching virtually

Contributed by Dr Brajesh Bajpai

Patrick, an experienced executive coach who specialised in board-level engagements, shared a story illustrating how coaching virtually can reduce understanding, potentially impeding the coach's ability to discern situational nuances and hinder the development of a robust working alliance.

"I had a female Indian coachee whom I coached for 9–12 months. We got into some very profound issues – helping her to understand why she was stuck and why she was grieving about a previous role. She had this deep script about being a woman. Coaching virtually didn't mean that we couldn't get to a level of depth and emotionality ... that did happen. But then I met her in real life, and it was extraordinary! When I met her in person with her full physical presence and being able to see her in three dimensions, she was a very lively, vivacious, and energetic person which had not come across online at all. If we had been coaching face-to-face, how might that have made the coaching different?"

Patrick expresses uncertainty about whether gaining a more comprehensive or, as he described it, a more accurate perception of the client's persona might have influenced the coaching process. The fact that he was able to explore deep-seated issues with the client suggests that, in this instance, the virtual setting might not have hindered the development of a meaningful connection or a strong coaching alliance. But the insights he gained into the client's personality during their face-to-face interaction surprised him. It is clear that the mental representation Patrick had constructed of the client in the virtual space differed significantly from the reality he encountered in person.

Bajpai (2024)'s research identified both direct and indirect impacts on coaches of developing technologies. The direct impacts stemmed from the range of technologies now available to them and the indirect impacts related to the issues that leaders were bringing to their coaching sessions resulting from the challenges of the digital age, namely managing distributed teams, virtual interactions and informal, digital methods of communication and collaboration. Another issue was the extent to which modern leaders were having to deal with the changes driven by digitalisation, namely hyper-connectedness, instant interactions and constant contact from teams. So there is a lot for coaches to contend with.

Finally, coaching with technology can raise new ethical considerations. EMCC Global has undertaken considerable work in this area.

To access "EMCC Global Code of Ethics Guidance for Providers of Coaching using Technology and AI (July 2023)", use the QR Code on page 3.

Standards, ethics and quality of service

Standards and ethics

There are three significant reasons for highlighting, in your coaching service's principles and practices, the importance of professional standards and ethics and making sure that your coaches do too.

1 *Duty of care:* Your internal coaches need to take very seriously their duty of care towards their clients. The coaching relationship is an intimate, self-revealing, trusting space and your coaches may be given privileged information by the client who may be emotionally or psychologically fragile or in an unresourceful state. Your coaches may also have position power and may be perceived by the client to have a hotline to centres of influence in your organisation. With the increasing emphasis on wellness, coaches need to have their ethical responsibility for the client's welfare at the forefront of their minds. The ICF's Insights and Considerations for Ethics document (International Coaching Federation, 2023) highlighted how unethical boundary violations or role confusion can undermine the coaching process, leading to negative outcomes such as burnout, disengagement or mistrust.

2 *Dealing with ethical dilemmas:* Chapters 4 and 5 focused on the probability that internal coaches encounter more ethical dilemmas than their external colleagues because of the increased likelihood of role conflicts, overlapping networks and being part of the same system. Familiarity with ethical principles enhanced by training and CPD around ethics will provide a strong foundation for your coaches to deal with any dilemmas that arise and giving them access to supervision is also highly desirable.

3 *Signalling your professionalism:* The coaching industry is not currently regulated, but all serious, practising, professional coaches sign up to a Code of Ethics and, by doing so, you are showing that your internal coaching service is professionally run and trustworthy.

For all these reasons, it is important that your organisation prioritises the needs and wellbeing of your coaches and their clients by subscribing to an ethical code. Ensure that your coaches are aware of it and abide by it, as it provides an essential foundation for promoting a safe coaching environment. The ideal would be for your organisation to become a corporate member of one of the coaching professional bodies and adopt the Global Code of Ethics or the ICF's Code of Ethics. All stakeholders and sponsors of the coaching services in your organisation should also be made aware of your ethical code, know how to access it and, ideally, have read it! The basic point is that they understand that the coaches in your internal coaching service are professionals, guided by the principles outlined in the code.

Complaints processes

Complaints about coaches are very rare, but as a lead coach it is in your interests to ensure that you have a clear procedure for dealing with any complaints rather than being caught out if one arises. The ethical codes of all the professional coaching bodies have complaints processes, so that's a good place to start. But if you decide not to become a corporate member of one of them, you will need to develop one of your own. In Katharine's original research (St John-Brooks, 2010), 20% of respondents said that their organisation had a separate, specific procedure for dealing with complaints about coaches, sitting outside the normal grievance or disciplinary procedures; 55% said it did not; and 25% did not know. Examples of comments at either end of the spectrum were:

"There is nothing established, and I don't think the organisation has considered this possibility. I suppose it would be via the usual grievance policy".

"If this was to arise, the contracting document with the coachee specifies whom they should contact – so the procedure is set out".

Once you have a complaints procedure in place, do communicate it clearly to all parties, while ensuring that you also have professional indemnity insurance to protect the coach and the organisation (just in case).

Ensuring a high quality of service

Having thought through your policies and procedures and established your framework for delivering an effective internal coaching service, it is worth building in processes to ensure that the quality of what your coaches are delivering is high and, ideally, improving over time. The following are some things to be thinking about.

Maintaining alignment: Defining the specific purpose of your coaching service and aligning it with what your organisation needs is a given, but organisations' needs change over time so you should check in regularly to ensure that the coaching service is still relevant. Having a steering group with membership from around the business is one way to keep your finger on the pulse. Another is to have an annual check-in with interested parties around the business.

Qualified, skilled coaches: Do your best to ensure that your coaches have the appropriate qualifications, certifications, accreditations, experience, ongoing supervision and CPD to enhance their skills and keep up with new coaching methodologies and trends.

Regular monitoring and evaluation: Collecting feedback from clients at the end of their coaching programme will help you to assess their satisfaction and the effectiveness of the coaching, though it is worth bearing in mind that clients will have built a close relationship with their coaches and may be wearing rose-tinted spectacles immediately after an assignment finishes. Feedback methods can include the use of surveys, interviews, or follow-up assessments with the coach, the client and the line manager or sponsor. Chapter 11 explores many options for how to evaluate the effectiveness of the coaching.

Extending your coaching offer: It is worth considering how you might expand your range of services through introducing different formats such as group or team coaching. During the pandemic, some organisations introduced on-demand, one-off sessions lasting an hour that were publicised through word of mouth. Variously called express coaching, spot coaching or coaching 'surgeries', this format has become quite popular.

Accessibility: Who is your target market for coaching? Does it align with your policies on EDI thus ensuring that coaching services are accessible to employees at all levels, in different departments or locations? It is worth remembering that some people – who could be your future leaders – may lack the confidence right now to seek coaching, so some kind of communications exercise to get the message out there to encourage 'access to coaching for all' might be a positive step.

Staying updated with trends: Try to keep abreast of new developments in coaching approaches and organisational best practices, adjusting your procedures, practices and training and then communicating these to all your stakeholders.

Internal marketing and business engagement

In Chapter 2, we mentioned that it was all too common for individual coaches to be under-utilised and that having too few (or no) clients can have a major impact on internal coaches' confidence and skills: use it or lose it. Then in Chapter 7, we highlighted how an imbalance of supply and demand (too much supply, not enough demand) contributed to some coaching services gradually withering on the vine. This usually comes down to poor marketing of the coaching service. Publicising the offer requires strategic communications that send clear messages about the benefits of coaching. There are a number of approaches and communication tactics that you can deploy to help employees understand what you are offering and to drive up engagement – as illustrated in Figure 8.3 on the next page.

The extent of the internal marketing that you need to do will, of course, depend on the scope and scale of your coaching service. If you are training half a dozen internal coaches and plan to target them purely on supporting participants on leadership programmes, you may not need to do very much marketing at all. But if the scope is much bigger and broader than that, and you want to make a splash, it can be helpful to enlist professional help from your own marketing

Figure 8.3 Key internal marketing activities

department to help you refine the wording for your communications and design your branding. For example, some organisations brand their coaching pool 'The Coaching Academy' or something similar. Be aware that any campaign to launch your coaching service may need to comply with company branding guidelines. Your steering group may commission this work, and the messages will need to be updated and supplemented as the coaching service develops and gains more traction in the organisation. Here are some pointers to consider when planning your campaign.

Communicate the benefits: Explain the value of coaching, such as increasing employee engagement, raising performance, supporting disadvantaged groups or developing talent. Highlight how coaching can support personal and professional development and have an impact on business results.

Clear messaging around where coaching will have the most impact will get people's attention.

Showcase success stories: Share real examples of employees or teams who have benefited from coaching. This is always a winning formula. The use of case studies, testimonials, podcasts and getting employees to speak about the benefits they have noticed is a great way to connect with people. If you send feedback forms to clients at the end of assignments, it is worth including a question asking if they would be willing to offer a testimonial for use in internal marketing of the service.

Leadership endorsement: Ask senior leaders and executives to promote the coaching service actively to encourage wider participation. Might one of them record a short video describing their experience of coaching?

Targeted communications campaigns: Use brochures, posters and newsletters – distributed through email, intranet, or internal social platforms – to explain how the coaching service works and its benefits. Regular communications covering coaching offerings, success stories, upcoming sessions and how to request coaching keep the service alive and engaging. Creating a dedicated coaching page with resources, FAQs, coaching packages and registration details on your organisation's internal network makes it easy for employees to learn more and consider applying.

Integration with employee development activities: Annual or interim performance reviews can be a great way of promoting coaching as a key element of employee development, linking it to career growth plans, skill gaps, or leadership development programmes. It can be a productive strategy to remind managers of your coaching service when performance review time rolls around.

Interactive experiences: There are lots of ways that you can help potential clients experience what being coached is like. You can offer introductory workshops or webinars – live or recorded – where employees can learn more about it and what to expect. Offering short coaching 'taster' sessions is a quick and easy way to experience the process firsthand. Julia and her colleague, Jonathan Whitham, organised speed coaching at a Learning and Development conference for the Training and Development Agency in Manchester (now part of the Department for Education) which was hugely successful in building employee understanding of what coaching is and how valuable it can be – and in only a 15-minute conversation!

Tips on how effective communications can support business engagement

- Keep communication regular and consistent, so employees are always aware of the coaching offer and how to access it.
- Simplify your messages to avoid confusion, using language that resonates with the employee audience.

- Promote two-way communication by encouraging employees to ask questions and provide feedback, making them feel heard and valued.
- Use a variety of communication methods, such as emails, intranet posts, team meetings and organisation-wide events, to ensure the message reaches as many employees as possible.

Case study

Approaches to internal marketing/publicity

One public sector organisation deploys a variety of approaches to ensuring that employees know what the internal coaching service has to offer.

- Bi-monthly coaching drop-in education sessions (what coaching is; what it can do for you) with the dates for the whole year publicised in advance. Each session can accommodate ten people – usually with two coaches there to answer questions. The coaches take it in turns to lead sessions. Some coaches have led a 'silent coaching' session so that people can get a feel for it. There is a 60–70% conversion rate.
- The coaches themselves put effort into publicising the scheme. They help to build the brand and are seen as champions of coaching. They look for opportunities to remind people of the coaching offer, and there are coaches in the senior leadership team, in the women's inclusion network, in the neurodiversity network and in the BAME network who keep the kettle boiling.
- At certain times, opportunities are spotted for coaches to promote the service, e.g., around staff appraisal time the coaches might say to their networks "Don't forget that you can get help from a coach around having difficult conversations" or "Remember that if you identify a weak area that your direct report needs to develop then recruiting a coach for them might be a way forward".
- Every month the coaching champion leads by example by making a pledge to the other coaches about how they are planning to promote the coaching pool that month, e.g., "This month I'm going to talk to recent graduate recruits about their next step and how they could have support from a coach to plan it".
- The coaching champion has an L&D channel and sometimes satisfied clients are asked to provide soundbite written testimonials.
- They have held a 'Let's Talk Coaching' live discussion within one of the organisation's leadership networks, where the topic was leadership and confidence. Two of the coaches led this with two willing coachees who shared the impact that coaching had had on their overall effectiveness and performance.

Summary

By creating a coaching framework, you will be building the foundation of the principles and practices of your coaching service. The policies and processes you develop will translate your strategy into deliverables, building the infrastructure that will drive a valuable and sustainable programme of internal coaching. The aim is to ensure that great coaching is delivered in a safe, supportive, professional and ethical environment, where all parties involved in the internal coaching process understand their roles and their responsibilities and that there are mechanisms, processes and standards in place to provide ongoing quality assurance to deliver an excellent and valuable service that the organisation can be proud of.

Table 8.1 Questions to reflect on

What a coaching framework is and how it is integrated into organisational strategies

- Are you clear about how the coaching service aligns with your organisation's business strategies?
- How will you identify and agree on what organisational policies and procedures will support your coaching framework?
- Have you informed your coaches of the policies and procedures that can support them and their clients if boundary issues arise in the coaching conversations?

Roles, responsibilities and accountabilities

- **Steering group**: Have you considered its role, members and accountabilities, e.g., communicating progress, value and ROI, commissioning budget, resources, internal marketing, etc.?
- **Lead coach**: In what ways are you connecting with the trainee coaches and those already providing the service to ensure you are getting their feedback on what they need from you to operate effectively?
- **Line manager**: Is there clear guidance on their role that is clearly understood?
- **Coach:** Do you have a broad representation of coaches with a wide range of expertise and attributes to meet the needs of a broad spectrum of clients?
- **Client:** What guidance do you offer to support their full understanding of what to expect and their engagement in the coaching process?

Contracting

- How will you reinforce the critical importance of contracting to all parties?
- Will you promote the use of three-way contracting?
- How can you make all coaches aware of the action and the process to escalate a matter where they believe that they must breach confidentiality?

Record-keeping and GDPR legal implications

- How can you provide clear guidelines for coaches on the importance of record keeping that adheres to GDPR?
- How will you ensure that all coaches keep their coaching records secure and safe and for how long will you ask them to hold them?
- Do you have company professional indemnity insurance set up to protect your coaches?

(Continued)

Table 8.1 (Continued)

Remote coaching and use of technology

- What is your approach to remote coaching and what guidance will you provide on what platforms to use?
- What is your stance and guidance on the use of AI and other technologies to support the coaching process? For example, use of AI in the matching process or using AI in identifying resources to support clients?
- What coaching apps and learning platforms can you recommend to your coaches to share a range of tools and techniques to support them and their clients' development?

Standards, ethics and quality of service

- How will you ensure that your coaches, stakeholders and sponsors involved in coaching activities are aware of and abide by the Global Code of Ethics?
- In what ways can you ensure an ongoing quality of service from your coaches in the methodologies, processes and the tools they use to support their coaching practice?

Internal marketing and business engagement

- What is your unique selling proposition for having an internal coaching service?
- What actions will ensure that you have professional branding, regular communication campaigns and information to promote the value of coaching to the business?
- How can you engage coaches and stakeholders to showcase and promote the coaching service?

Chapter 9

Selection and training

What this chapter is about

Your coaches *are* your coaching service. They need to be credible, professional and ethical, and provide a high standard of coaching to build, enhance and uphold the reputation of your coaching offer. This depends to a significant degree on selecting good people and training them well.

This chapter covers:

- Developing the application and selection process
- Identifying the right people to be potential coaches
- Qualifications, accreditations and apprenticeships
- Training content and skills development
- Team coach training
- Matching coaches to clients

"Those organisations that scrimp on the careful selection, training and supporting of internal coaches run serious risks. Ultimately, their greatest risk may be that they undermine the perception of coaching as a learning tool because of the lack of credibility of their internal coaches" (Hunt & Weintraub, 2006, p. 4).

Developing the application and selection process

So, your coaching strategy has been approved and you have the budget and resources in place. Now it's time to find your coaches by identifying individuals with not only the right skills, qualities and aptitudes to make great coaches, but also the potential to contribute positively to building a coaching culture.

Getting started with your recruitment campaign

People will need to know exactly what they'll be signing up for, so construct a clear statement about what coaching is; why you want to develop a pool of internal

DOI: 10.4324/9781003519911-11

coaches; what the focus of the coaching will be (e.g., will it be accessible by all employees or more targeted to support, say, leadership development or improve employee engagement?); what sort of skills you are looking for and whether their coaching role will be recognised as part of their formal job description. It is only in a minority of organisations that this last happens, but it can be an important way to recognise their contribution to the organisation, so it is worth thinking about from the outset.

You will also need to make clear what your expectations are, in terms of how many clients they will be expected to coach at any one time and for how many sessions, and what development activities they will need to make time for, such as supervision and CPD. Your new recruits will need to ask for approval from their line manager to apply, so they too will need to be clear about what the time commitment is likely to be – both during the training and afterwards.

Creating an application form

You will probably want to attract applicants from all areas of the business and with diverse capabilities so that your pool of coaches supports your equality and diversity values. To do that, it is important that you create a transparent and accessible application process. Are you looking for specific things like leadership experience, emotional intelligence or a track record of organisational influence, or can you broaden your criteria to ensure that a wider cross-section of your employees feels able to apply? The questions that you ask on the coach application form will need both to identify people with the sorts of aptitudes that you are looking for and establish whether the applicants have a genuine interest in developing people. Are they willing to invest in personal learning and growing their coaching skills and, post-training, to dedicate the time and energy required for continuing development? Here are some examples of what you might ask.

Table 9.1 Examples of types of questions to ask on your application form

1 What motivates you to pursue training as an internal coach, and what do you hope to achieve from the coach training programme?
2 What specific skills or strengths do you possess that you believe will make you an effective coach and how do you demonstrate these qualities in your professional life?
3 Can you describe a time when you successfully helped someone overcome a challenge at work? What approach did you use?
4 How do you approach giving and receiving feedback?
5 How do you typically manage conflicts or differing opinions in a team or work setting, and what strategies would you apply as a coach?
6 How do you typically approach personal or professional growth and self-improvement?
7 What do you believe is the role of a coach in our organisation?

There is a variety of routes open to you, with pros and cons to each. In all cases you should request that the application is endorsed and authorised by the applicant's line manager.

Send an open invitation to all staff: This offers everyone in the business an equal opportunity to apply. The upside is that you should get a broad response; the downside is that you will need a bigger resource to process the applications.

Ask business leads: You could send a carefully worded invitation to business leads/ heads of divisions with an indication of the qualities you are looking for, the time commitment required and the likely benefits in terms of the development that the individual will receive. Ask them to nominate people whom they think suitable. The benefits of this approach are that:

- You are engaging and partnering with the business from the outset.
- You send a clear message about targeting resources to meet business needs.
- The quality of the proposed candidates should be high, as you have benefited from an initial level of screening.
- The business heads are already invested in the process.
- The potential applicant will feel valued and complimented by being nominated.

There are potential downsides though. Using nomination by managers may have equality and diversity implications and could be more likely to be challenged by unions. Also, one coach lead said ruefully that she found that managers were less skilled at identifying suitable people than she had hoped, even though she had specified the attributes that she was looking for.

Hand picking: Some lead coaches choose to hand pick some or all of their trainee coaches. Depending on what you are looking for, you could decide to approach colleagues who are already experienced in learning and development. It is worth bearing in mind, though, that some people prefer not to be coached by someone from HR or L&D. They can be concerned about confidentiality and feel reluctant to be completely honest in case what they say 'goes somewhere'. It is desirable to have a mix of coaches including some in operational roles who enjoy developing people. You may have crossed paths with employees who have volunteered in the past to be mentors or who have been openly enthused on programmes like Coaching Skills for Managers. If you decide to hand pick, do bear in mind the desirability of having a diverse pool.

Recommendations: Once your coaching pool is up and running, your coaches may well become advocates within the business for coaching and start to recommend others to apply for subsequent cohorts of trainees.

You may also be approached by employees who have already had some coach training in a previous capacity. You have a choice of whether to invite them to join in with your first cohort or simply to ask them to join the community later. One lead coach told me that she had identified several in an initial trawl and asked them to coach a colleague for 45 minutes while she observed. It gave her a good fix on their competence, which turned out to be high.

If you decide not to extend an invitation to all staff, and you are in a unionised environment, it is advisable to engage the business and the unions in your process from the start. You may also need to carry out an equality and diversity impact assessment on your final selection list to reassure the business that there has been no discrimination or unconscious bias.

Your application process

Most organisations have a two-stage process involving a first sift of the completed written applications and then a second stage, involving meeting the applicants either in person or virtually. Try to ensure that unsuccessful applicants receive feedback. This helps the applicants to feel that they have been fully considered against the selection criteria and get some clarity about what they could do to improve their chances if they reapply at a later date.

While face-to-face or virtual competency-based interviews are the most popular next step, some organisations have used variants such as including role-play, or setting up and observing a peer coaching activity to assess their communication skills and potential to develop the competencies you are looking for. Some organisations encourage managers to take part in the interview panel so as to provide visibility and buy-in to the coach selection process.

Identifying the right people to be potential coaches

What are the qualities and skills you are looking for?

An effective internal coach needs a blend of personal qualities, professional skills and organisational awareness if they are to nurture transformative growth in their clients. The following table is based on a number of studies published by the International Coaching Federation, Association for Coaching and CIPD. While your applicants are unlikely to have all of these qualities and skills at the outset, they will need to demonstrate that they have the potential to acquire them.

Table 9.2 A coach's personal qualities, professional skills, organisational awareness

Personal qualities	Professional skills	Organisational awareness
Empathy: Understands the feelings of others; builds trust and rapport by demonstrating genuine care. **Emotional intelligence:** Recognises and manages their emotions and those of others; handles interpersonal	**Active listening:** Fully present; pays attention to the client without interrupting; paraphrases and summarises to ensure understanding. **Effective questioning:** Uses powerful,	**Alignment with organisational goals:** Ensures coaching efforts support broader organisational objectives; balances individual development with organisational priorities.

(Continued)

Table 9.2 (Continued)

Personal qualities	Professional skills	Organisational awareness
relationships judiciously and sensitively. *Authenticity:* Coaches with honesty and integrity; creates a safe space where the client feels valued and respected. *Patience:* Allows the client to process and grow at their own pace; holds silence for space to think. *Curiosity:* Asks thoughtful, open-ended questions; demonstrates genuine interest in the client's goals and challenges. *Self-awareness:* Understands their own strengths, biases, and limitations; continuously reflects on and improves their own coaching practice.	solution-focused questions to unlock insights; encourages deeper reflection and self-discovery. *Feedback:* Provides constructive, actionable, and balanced feedback; ensures feedback is specific, timely, and aligned with the client's goals. *Goal setting:* Helps client set realistic, measurable, and meaningful goals; encourages accountability and commitment to action *Adaptability:* Adjusts coaching style to suit the client's needs and organisational context; helps the client to navigate change and uncertainty with confidence.	*Cultural sensitivity:* Understands and respects the organisation's culture, values and stance on EDI, in order to ensure they are sensitive to and aware of how best to adapt coaching approaches to align with individuals and the cultural context. *Confidentiality and trust:* Maintains discretion and professionalism in all interactions; builds a reputation for integrity within the organisation. *Influence and leadership:* Inspires change without relying on authority, acts as a role model for collaboration, learning and growth. *Stakeholder management:* Engages effectively with leaders, peers and employees; manages expectations and communicates progress clearly.

Case study

Selecting employees for a coach training programme

A UK-based charity, undergoing a major change programme, recognised the need to build a coaching culture in order to enhance employee engagement and organisational performance. They decided to extend their small team of qualified coaches, working in L&D, and train more internal coaches to represent a wider group of employees from across the charity.

The primary goal was to build a diverse group of managers who would coach on top of their day jobs, focusing on supporting clients to develop skills, relationships, confidence and resilience. A secondary goal was to include under-represented groups in the cohort. The selection panel included the coach, the steering committee, the Head of Equality & Diversity and the Head of OD. They defined criteria such as strong interpersonal skills, emotional intelligence, mentoring experience and sufficient time to commit fully to the coaching role.

Application process

The charity used an online, multi-channel approach to identify candidates, including self-nomination, peer recommendations and senior leader endorsements. Out of 1750 employees, 80 applied. These applicants attended a webinar that outlined the role and training requirements. After the webinar, 30 potential applicants withdrew, recognising the scale of the commitment required. The 50 remaining applicants underwent a thorough assessment involving behavioural interviews to assess coaching mindset and interpersonal skills, and role-play scenarios to evaluate their coaching approach and problem-solving in action. This whittled them down to 20 candidates who were selected for training in the ILM Level 5 Certificate in Effective Coaching and Mentoring.

The training

The 10-month training programme included:

- Workshops on coaching frameworks, active listening and goal-setting.
- Practice sessions with feedback from certified coaches.
- Follow-up support through peer coaching forums and access to resources.
  Out of the 20 selected, 19 completed the training successfully.

Lessons learned

1 *Clear criteria:* Defined selection criteria ensured that only suitable candidates were chosen, limiting attrition in the training programme. It was crucial that managers had time to fulfil their coaching duties without compromising their core responsibilities.
2 *Structured process:* The combination of self-nomination, peer recommendations and assessments made the selection process credible and effective.
3 *Clarity on what results were expected:* The charity started with the end in mind and communicated the purpose of the coaching to the organisation to ensure that the selection process was fit for purpose.

Qualifications, accreditations and apprenticeships

Coaching qualifications vs. accreditation

Qualifications

Coaching qualifications are acquired through completing formal coach training programmes designed to develop coaches' skills and knowledge in coaching techniques, psychology and methodologies. The programmes comprise a mixture of theory and practice. Many organisations train their employees to become competent coaches but give them the choice as to whether they complete all the written assignments to gain the qualification. Some decide not to do so, but sometimes the drivers for a formal qualification are the coaches themselves.

Yedreshteyn (2008) explored why some coaches were pushing for a qualification:

> "There are several potential reasons why the internal coaches were interested in having Executive Development create a Certificate programme for them. They said that it would help them gain credibility in the eyes of clients, help them learn more about coaching, help all of the coaches have the same knowledge, but there may also be other reasons. Coaches … may need to be recognised … and having a title of "Certified" Internal Executive Coach may give them the affirmation they are looking for". (p. 101)

There are a number of routes to qualification. You can source training from a specialist provider whose courses offer a qualification or, if you are the lead coach, you can be trained to deliver a qualification programme yourself. ILM Level 5 Certificate in Effective Coaching and Mentoring, for example, provides a national qualification that can be delivered by any provider who is qualified to do so, and it is very popular within the internal coaching world. It is often the minimum qualification required by coaching networks where organisations share their coaches across organisational boundaries. There are many other excellent coaching qualifications offered by a variety of providers including universities, business schools and the Chartered Management Institute (CMI).

In 2024, there were 30–40 ILM coaching and mentoring qualification providers in the UK, offering a variety of ILM-accredited programmes for coaching, including Levels 3, 5 and 7 qualifications. It is essential that programmes such as the ILM's are delivered by practising professional coaches and supervisors who can deal with the inevitable questions and wobbles from the trainee coaches. If you are not running the programme yourself, make sure you talk to the tutor who will be delivering it and not just to a salesperson. Check whether they are really listening to your needs and the purposes for which you are setting up the coaching scheme. Are they prepared to do any fine-tuning to meet your requirements?

Formal coach training might not be sufficient on its own. Adaptive, flexible and context-specific coaching approaches are increasingly valued. The ideal may be a combination of both formal coaching education and personalised, experiential learning provided within the organisation. Chapter 10 explores the options for your providing CPD (continuing professional development) and experiential opportunities like triad work for your coaches, post-qualification.

Coaching accreditation

Accreditation involves the recognition of your coaches' competence and is based on providing evidence that they meet industry standards and observe a code of ethics. It would be quite difficult – though possible – to provide the necessary evidence for accreditation without first acquiring a qualification. There is generally also a requirement for proof of having carried out a minimum number of coaching hours. In the UK, the four main professional bodies that bestow accreditation are the EMCC (European Mentoring & Coaching Council), AC (Association for Coaching), ICF (International Coaching Federation) and APECS (Association for Professional Executive Coaching and Supervision) and there are generally different levels, e.g., Foundation, Practitioner, Senior Practitioner and Master Practitioner.

The benefit of having the members of your coaching pool secure accreditation from a recognised professional coaching body is that it demonstrates their adherence to ethical standards and professional practice, in turn enhancing the credibility of your coaching service. Certainly, accreditation is often regarded as an important marker of competence when organisations are recruiting external coaches. However, the requirement to demonstrate a minimum number of coaching hours can make it difficult for many internal coaches to get beyond the foundation level and, if you want your coaches to go through that process after they have trained and acquired the necessary hours of experience, then you may need to offer them some support. Don't underestimate the time and effort that it will take for each of your coaches to do the necessary work to prove that they meet the standards. It can be quite arduous.

If you are very keen that your coaches are accredited, you can make life easier for them by sourcing training that is either closely aligned with the accreditation requirements of one of the professional bodies or directly leads to accreditation as part of the training (it will take longer, as a result). The ICF, AC and EMCC all take a competence/evidence-based portfolio approach to accreditation, which involves candidates' skills being validated against competencies.

There are also numerous academic providers such as the Academy of Executive Coaching, Henley Business School, Hult International Business School (formerly Ashridge) and universities such as Oxford Brookes, Sheffield Hallam, Warwick and Chester that have their coaching programmes accredited and aligned with one or more of the professional bodies' requirements, ensuring that they meet high standards.

You may also want to think about paying for your coaches' membership of one of the professional bodies, giving them access to CPD opportunities including webinars on the latest thinking.

Apprenticeships

Employers in England who have an annual pay bill of more than £3 million pay the apprenticeship levy and, since 2020, have been able to use the Apprenticeship Scheme to fund the training of their coaches. The way it works is that the sum raised by the levy is stored in a fund which employers can access to help pay for apprenticeship training.

In May 2020, the Coaching Professional apprenticeship was approved by the Institute for Apprenticeships and Technical Education (IFATE) who set the curriculum and outlined the knowledge, skills and duties required. This was endorsed by all three major professional bodies (ICF, EMCC and AC) as well as over 100 employer representatives. Training organisations embarked on designing coaching programmes to deliver the curriculum and, from a standing start, the coaching professional apprenticeship scheme has gained considerable traction as shown in Table 9.3.

BPP Education Group – comprising BPP, Estio Training, Firebrand Training and Buttercups Training – is the UK's largest apprenticeship and training provider delivering apprenticeship training to over 31,000 learners each year.

In November 2020, BPP in partnership with Grant Thornton launched their Coaching Professional apprenticeship, which takes 15 months to complete. A 12-month practical period is followed by a three-month 'gateway' where apprentices prepare for their final assessments. These external assessments consist of three elements: a 40-question multiple-choice test, observation of two x one-hour coaching sessions followed by questioning and a one-hour interview supported by a portfolio.

In 2021, BPP received EMCC Global's EQA (European Quality Award) for the programme. To date, over 350 graduates have become members of EMCC UK and have also been supported to achieve their EMCC Global EIA (European Individual Award).

Apprentices work through a series of modules, developing their coaching knowledge, skills and behaviours. Areas of focus include reflective practice, ethics, communication, contracting, emotional intelligence, stakeholder engagement, organisational culture and evaluating coaching. Coaching theories and models

Table 9.3 Coaching professional apprenticeship statistics 2022–2024

	2022/2023	2023/2024
National numbers enrolling (England)	2104	2995
National Qualification Achievement Rate (England)	61.4%	64.4%

include GROW, Nancy Kline's thinking environment, Gestalt, Cognitive Behavioural Coaching, Solutions Focused coaching and NLP.

All apprentices are assigned a BPP Performance Coach who supports them throughout the programme. Performance Coaches provide support with course content, feedback on assessments and coaching practice and supervisory support. All learners access a series of two-hour live webinars and three x two-day coaching workshops where they are immersed in a practical skills environment, receiving feedback on their coaching practice from peers and tutors.

The BPP team of professionally qualified coaches also recognises the contribution they can make to the wider coaching profession with colleagues contributing to the work of professional bodies through governance roles, supporting coaching schemes which promote the CSR agenda, and engaging in research and collaborative activities. Findings and outputs are shared through a variety of coaching networks.

Initially, BPP noticed that many of the apprentices were working in HR/OD/L&D roles within their organisation so they encouraged a more diverse approach to the development of internal coaches across organisations. Apprentices have now joined the programme from a wide range of professional roles and departments.

The line manager of an apprentice is involved in the process, attending quarterly reviews and providing support and feedback to the apprentice. Where line managers are not familiar with coaching, BPP offers a specific induction session at the start of the programme, explaining how they can support their direct reports embarking on the coaching apprenticeship and maximise the value of coaching within the organisation.

BPP are experiencing an increase in the numbers enrolling onto the programme, which mirrors the national trend, and their students have achieved positive success indicators with a first-time pass rate of over 90% and a 73% achievement rate (QAR) in 2023/2024. At a coaching skills level, over 50% of graduates have achieved a distinction for their practical coaching assessment.

Alice's story

Coach training through the apprenticeship scheme

Alice discovered coaching while working in the recruitment team at a British university. L&D had booked an external coach to support a leadership programme and, when a participant dropped out, Alice volunteered for a 90-minute session. During the session, she had a lightbulb moment and realised that her role was too process-driven for her and didn't have nearly enough people content. When a role in OD came up, she successfully applied for it.

Serendipitously, BPP was running a pilot of the 'Coaching Professional Level 5 Apprenticeship' with a group of universities. Alice applied to be part of her university's cadre of four participants on the pilot and won a place.

Alice loved the programme. She hadn't necessarily intended to become an internal coach, she simply wanted to use a coaching approach in her new OD role. The programme – lasting 15 months – offered supervision with a BPP supervisor every six weeks. He would send her questions to reflect on in advance, after which the sessions evolved into discussing challenges around clients and assignments.

Alice also utilised a number of other sources of support:

- Monthly catch-ups with her line manager to discuss how it was going. In practice, she needed to drive that process, either tacking a discussion onto her regular 1-1s or scheduling a separate meeting.
- Morning Kanban meetings with her OD colleagues (who, together with her boss, were helpful with suggestions of people whom she might coach as part of the required fifty hours of coaching practice).
- Monthly meetings with her three colleagues who were also on the programme (organised by BPP).
- A WhatsApp group of all 20 participants on the pilot across several universities. This turned into a monthly meeting. Alice found the discussions about assignments and book recommendations really helpful (though daunting at first).

The programme assessment involved putting together a portfolio with a number of elements including a reflective journal, a coaching log and a learning log with an end-point interview to discuss it.

The programme was not without its challenges, namely making time (particularly when written assignments were due) and also, at times, wrestling with a critical internal voice. Alice had thought that she would be really structured in her learning, but it felt more chaotic than she had anticipated. She also found that real-life sessions with clients didn't follow the neat models that she had watched on videos.

But Alice was clear about the benefits. She felt that she had gained in overall confidence and quickly started using her new skills in her day job. She trained to be an action learning set facilitator for the university's management programme and then successfully applied for a new role to set up a coaching and mentoring network at the university. She became an internal coach herself and between 2023 and 2025 she helped the network grow from six coaches to 35. Her next challenge is to provide supervision for the coaches.

Training content and skills development

Many organisations will already have a trusted training provider that offers coach training, but it is worth shopping around to see what is available that will meet your specific needs. Do you want a particular qualification, for example, or to take advantage of the apprenticeship scheme? If you are keen that the training is delivered in person, it may be better value if you can find a local company (though a lot of coach training is now delivered virtually).

You will want the training that your coaches receive to reflect your coaching strategy and purpose. The following are some of the issues to think about. The answers will help you to put together your requirements for training providers.

Training content

What basic skills and knowledge do you want your coaches to have? Most coach training will help your trainees to understand the difference between coaching, mentoring, counselling and consulting. They will explore and practise the basic coaching skills of rapport building, active listening, powerful questioning, goal setting and giving feedback. Finally, they will absorb ideas around the 'self as coach'. In this way they will develop high levels of self-awareness so that they are in a better position to distinguish their own 'stuff' from their clients'. They are likely to be introduced to one or more coaching models such as GROW (Whitmore, 2002), CLEAR (Hawkins & Smith, 2006) or OSCAR (Gilbert & Whittleworth, 2002) and some basic psychological concepts such as motivational factors, needs-driven behaviour and limiting beliefs.

You will need to think about the depth and breadth of training that your coaches will need. Are they mainly going to be coaching your middle managers, or do you plan to deploy them to support senior managers participating in, say, leadership programmes? And will any of them need specialist training, for example in career coaching? You may want them to be introduced to theories like psychological-mindedness, how to recognise unconscious bias, either in themselves or their clients, or adult learning theory (Knowles, 1990).

They may also need to be trained in some tools commonly used in your organisation, e.g., a 360-degree feedback or personality profiling instrument such as Myers-Briggs, DISC, Insights Discovery or the 'Big Five'/OCEAN. If you have a coach management system, they will need training in how to use it.

Finally, check that the trainer provides supervision for the trainees during the training and consider whether it might provide useful continuity for the same supervisor to carry on doing so post-qualification.

Training in addressing ethical dilemmas

Training to understand how ethical dilemmas arise and how to address them is crucial for internal coaches because it helps them navigate complex situations where personal, organisational and professional boundaries intersect. Incorporating this into the training ensures that coaches can start building their ethical maturity. Here are some examples of ethical dilemmas that could usefully be included in training to support your developing coaches.

1 *Maintaining confidentiality:* A client confides in the coach about bullying behaviour they witnessed in the workplace. Employees are under an obligation to report such incidents but the client doesn't want to. The coach must decide whether to maintain confidentiality or report the issue to higher management.
2 *Dual relationships and conflicts of interest:* A manager seeks coaching from a coach who is senior to them in the company. Midway through the assignment, the coach becomes involved in a grievance procedure affecting the client and worries about bias. Proper training prepares coaches to navigate these conflicts by setting clear boundaries and understanding when to refer clients to another coach.
3 *Power dynamics:* An internal coach who is a senior executive may unintentionally exert influence over a junior client's choices or career trajectory, potentially prompting decisions that are not in their best interest. Training can help coaches recognise these dynamics and maintain a coaching relationship that prioritises the client's autonomy and wellbeing.
4 *Respecting autonomy vs. organisational needs:* A client may be considering a career path that doesn't meet the company's current needs or strategic direction. The coach faces the ethical challenge of supporting the individual's goals without pressuring them to choose a path that solely serves the organisation's interests. Ethical training helps coaches balance these competing interests.
5 *Boundary setting and professionalism:* An internal coach develops a close friendship with a client, which undermines the effectiveness of the coaching process. The coach unintentionally becomes overly empathetic and fails to challenge the client's assumptions adequately. Ethical training helps coaches to maintain professionalism and avoid personal biases from influencing their work.

By being aware of the importance of developing your coaches' ethical maturity, you can ensure that your training provider includes content in the training that encourages coaches to notice and manage challenging situations as they arise. They should be able to handle sensitive issues with confidence and know where to seek guidance, if necessary, to ensure that they act in the best interests of both the individual and the organisation.

Skills development

A focus on skills-based training is essential for trainees to learn how to conduct effective coaching sessions, using their interpersonal skills, emotional intelligence, warmth and unconditional positive regard to support clients to grow and achieve their goals.

Coaching practice

Irrespective of what content you choose for the training, you will want your coaches to have plenty of coaching practice to develop their competence and confidence to work with clients and manage stakeholders in the coaching process. Practice is normally done in two ways. The first is triad work during training modules (coach, client and observer) with the trainees taking it in turns to play each role, using real issues and giving structured feedback to each other. The second is selecting clients to coach. The trainees will practise their skills and receive evidence-based feedback to help them improve their competence and confidence. It is important that your trainees' clients are made fully aware that the trainees are learning to be professional coaches.

Some trainers offer coaching demonstrations during the training, with time out for questions and discussion mid-demonstration. These are always very popular with trainees as they can share their thinking and evolving strategies.

Three-way contracting

If you are going to promote three-way contracting as an essential part of your coaching process – and Julia is a great advocate for this – your coaches will need practice in how to do it. The process will hold few fears for trainees who are already trained facilitators, but it can be a daunting prospect for a new coach without a facilitation background. If their new client is a peer, then the client's line manager (the third party at the contracting meeting that kicks off the assignment) will be senior to both of them and a new coach may find this challenging. It is therefore desirable for lead coaches or trainers to spend some time on this. Role-play can work well.

Something else that can be helpful is for a trainee coach to pick someone who is the direct report of another trainee on the programme. As the other trainee coach is the actual line manager in the three-way contracting process, they can offer genuine feedback in a trusting and safe environment. Hence, once qualified, both coaches can reflect on the experience for use in future client work.

Ethics in practice

It is desirable to encourage coaches to practise using an ethical approach in their triad work, e.g., contracting tightly, trying out a sticky issue to develop strategies for what to do when they're not sure of the way forward, discussing what ethical decision-making model they can follow and checking that they know to whom they can talk in confidence if they hit challenges.

It is crucial that your trainee coaches can devote enough time to do the training thoroughly. It must be made clear to them and their line managers what the time commitment will be. Most training will involve considerably more learning hours than simply attending the training modules. Additional essential elements are writing assignments, coaching clients in order to meet qualification requirements, writing up detailed coaching records, undertaking reflective practices (such as keeping a learning journal) and reading books and online materials.

It takes commitment, planning and time management skills as well as determination to keep going when a programme could last from nine months to two years on top of the day job.

A point to note

When coaches finish their training, they can suffer a sense of isolation. It can feel as though that 'wrap-around' support that they experience while training is abruptly withdrawn. The skill is to engage them promptly in a community of coaches with access to continuing support. Chapter 6 includes a case study in building a coaching community, and Chapter 10 is devoted to supervision and CPD, which play a large part in providing your coaches with that sense of continuing support. Particularly important, too, is to get your coaches up and running with a coaching client as soon as possible.

Team coach training

What do organisations need to know when setting up team coaching services and who are the right coaches to deliver this more complex coaching offer? Ideally, trainee team coaches should be competent and experienced coaches already and equipped with a minimum of Level 5 Certificate in Coaching (McGrath, 2024). It is also highly desirable that they have experience of facilitating groups and are familiar with useful tools, approaches and exercises to assist in the design and implementation of team coaching sessions. If you have qualified trainers in L&D who deliver team development events, perhaps you can arrange for them to work in partnership with your team coaches.

Team coaching is a complex and dynamic process which can be exhausting for the coach, as they need to be fully present in moving the process forward in line with the agenda, while noticing the behaviours and emotions being displayed by team members and between team members (not to mention the role of the team leader). As a result, it is very common for team coaches to train and then coach in pairs. You might consider making this your primary model.

Ideally, the training for team coaches would include expanding their repertoire of tools and techniques to apply in a team coaching environment, as well as utilising their one-to-one coaching skills, such as building rapport with individual team members; exploring when to use a facilitative approach with the team and when to use coaching questions to ensure that, during the process, each member of the team has a voice and there is an equal distribution of power; and understanding and developing strategies for addressing a range of challenges and pitfalls. These strategies include:

- Not being dragged into discussions that develop a blame culture.
- Remaining neutral, non-judgemental and objective.
- Being aware of any unconscious biases towards team members.
- Being open to all sides of a story.

- Having the confidence to address unethical or poor behaviour between team members.
- Helping individuals to understand the impact their behaviour may have on other team members.
- Managing the energy in the room.
- Sticking to the agenda.
- Knowing when to go 'off piste' and when to return.

Effective team coaching requires coaches who are comfortable with managing the challenges. Through comprehensive training, your coaches can learn a range of structured approaches and techniques to help them navigate the complexities of group dynamics, while maintaining a positive and productive environment. Team coaching is a growing area and can be a valuable addition to the range of coaching services you can offer to the employees in your organisation.

Matching coaches to clients

It is widely believed by coaches that they should be able to coach pretty much any-one (as long as the client wants to be coached), using their skills of deep listening and rapport building, and that any client's initial preference for, for example, a coach who is 'like them' in terms of personality or familiar with some aspect of their work role, is based on a misunderstanding of what coaching is. That said, clients *do* have preferences and various matching factors can have an impact on whether a coaching relationship will be successful or whether it could run into trouble.

Large organisations with many internal coaches generally use an automated sys-tem for matching coaches and clients – usually called a coach management system (CMS) – either bought in or developed in-house. If you are starting off small, how-ever, so-called 'hand matching' is a simple and effective approach. Both automated and manual systems involve considering a variety of factors to try to ensure that the coach and client are a good fit. One lead coach commented that the move to virtual coaching has been a real boon. She used to have to match based on location. Her 38 coaches are now available to anyone.

Here are some pointers to assist you in the matching process.

- *Professional boundaries:* A strong coaching relationship is built on impartiality. Ensuring that coaches and clients do not have a close personal or professional relationship helps to maintain objectivity. If possible, match your coaches with clients from a completely different part of the organisation.
- *Personalities and communication styles:* Coaches and clients with similar per-sonalities and complementary communication styles tend to get on well and have productive, engaging conversations. Bear in mind, though, that this can also mean that they share the same blind spots.
- *Expertise that meets client needs:* Ideally, a coach will possess the necessary knowledge and experience to support the client's particular focus areas. Whether addressing career transitions, leadership development or onboarding issues, the

right expertise ensures effective support from the coach. Some lead coaches have noticed that the 'asks' from clients have been getting more specific, e.g., wanting a coach who is comfortable with neurodiversity or is an experienced team coach.

- *Cultural awareness and understanding:* Sometimes clients want a coach who has experience of or insights into a particular culture. Maybe they have a similar background or experience. Meeting the client's preferences in this regard can create a more inclusive and empathetic coaching experience that enhances mutual respect and strengthens the overall coaching relationship.
- *Balanced power dynamic:* Coaching works best as a partnership where the client remains in control of their own agenda. A well-matched coaching relationship maintains a healthy balance of guidance and autonomy, empowering clients to take charge of their development while receiving support.

While a coaching pool is still small, the lead coach will know the individual coaches well, together with their strengths, weaknesses and preferences, which enables good matching. But as the pool grows, this knowledge will gradually wane, so it is a good strategy to have clear guidelines and a standardised template for the coaches to develop their own personalised profiles to facilitate good matches. This is even more important for an automated system where the client is choosing a coach from a list.

Developing a coach profile

It is a good plan, towards the end of the training programme, to help your coaches create their own personal profile of who they are and what coaching they want to offer. Profiles should be in a standard format to help you – as lead coach – or potential clients work out who might be a good fit for them. They should offer a detailed representation of the coach's skills, experience, qualifications and personal attributes and should serve as a snapshot of their professional identity and capabilities, to help clients find a coach to meet their needs.

For organisations with a CMS, the profiles of all the internal coaches will be loaded onto the platform so that potential clients can make a shortlist of possible coaches. Some CMSs are sufficiently sophisticated that they can automatically provide clients with a shortlist that reflects their expressed needs.

To access "Constructing a coach profile: A Guide and Template", use the QR Code on page 3.

Helping clients to be clear about what they want

The client, too, needs guidance in expressing what kind of coaching, and coach, they need. It is a good start if they clearly understand what coaching can offer and whether this is the right developmental solution for them. You will need to give consideration as to whether employees can be given access to coaching support without their line manager's consent. Some clients may be seeking coaching solely to explore how to resolve relational tensions between themselves and their manager and would prefer them not to know.

To maximise the likelihood of a successful match between coach and client it can be helpful to provide a set of questions to help the potential client determine what they want from coaching and what they are looking for in a coach to help them achieve their goals. The QR code below links to a template of eight key questions to help the client to articulate what, and whom, they want.

To access "Helping a client decide what they need from a coach: A Template", use the QR Code on page 3.

The chemistry session

If you – as lead coach – are personally managing the matching process, then having the client's requirements and your coaches' profiles should put you in a good place for making a successful match. The next step will either be to allocate a coach to the client or else to provide the client with access to some coach profiles. If you have a CMS, the process will be client-led and they will select a shortlist of coaches from the index of coach profiles on the CMS.

The next stage is for them to arrange an informal chat with one or all of the shortlisted coaches to decide who will be the best fit to meet their needs, goals, preferences and expectations. This informal chat is often called the chemistry session (now sometimes known as the compatibility meeting). This is not a coaching session but aims to explore if they are the right fit for each other on a personal level, whether the coach is the right person to help the client meet their particular goals, if the line manager will be involved in the process and, if so, how and finally practical considerations, e.g., frequency of sessions, duration, face-to-face or virtual, preferred communication channels and so forth.

The coach may also cover some of the basic contracting around confidentiality and boundaries to help set expectations. Agreement to proceed is a mutual process, and it is the right of both client and coach to choose whether to go ahead or not. The first formal meeting will cover the contracting process in more depth, after which the coaching assignment begins.

Summary

Identifying, selecting, training and matching coaches to clients are essential elements in any internal coaching process. Choosing good people and training them well will determine your coaching service's success. The credibility of your coaches will depend on their capability, which will be a reflection of their talent and training. That training is likely to be your biggest financial investment, so you will want to make sure that it fits the bill. However, the training is only the beginning of your investment in your coaches. The next chapter explores the importance of supervision and continuing professional development to sustain your coaches in their ongoing development as they mature and grow into excellent coaches.

Table 9.4 Questions to reflect on

Defining the application and selection process

- What specific selection criteria will ensure that you select the right people to be coaches?
- Have you agreed as an organisation what the coaches will be committing to e.g., the number of clients that they will be expected to take on, both as regards their training and coaching once they have qualified?
- Have you defined what is the most effective selection process that is both fair and equitable to ensure that you choose the right people who will become credible coaches?

Identifying the right people to be potential coaches

- What qualities and attributes are you looking for, so that applicants can be clear about whether they have the right competencies to be coaches?
- Are you designing your communications to reach out to all worthy applicants in all areas and levels in the business, to ensure that you have a wide pool of coaches to support all employees, including minority groups?
- How will you make sure that applicants have the ability and capacity to manage the duality of roles during training and when they start practising as a coach?

Qualifications, accreditations and apprenticeships

- What budget needs to be in place and approved to ensure you have the right funding for the training and support of your coaches?
- What is the best route to ensure that the training is meeting your organisation's expectations around budget, quality and timescales?
- Have you decided if your coaches will need accreditation?

Training content and approaches

- What are your criteria to ensure you select the right training provider to deliver what you need in terms of content, approach and support?
- How will you know that the training provision has the right balance between theoretical underpinning, practice sessions and supervision?

Matching clients to coaches

- What detailed guidance and processes do you need to put in place to ensure you achieve the right match between clients and coaches?
- Are you going for a manual system or do you have the resources to develop or source appropriate coach management software to assist your matching process?

Chapter 10

Supervision and continuing professional development

What this chapter is about

Learning to be an effective coach takes training, practice and support in the form of supervision and continuing professional development (CPD). There is no 'quick fix'. Some trainee coaches have many transferable skills and aptitudes from former work roles and life experience and hit the ground running. Others need longer to settle into the role. Either way, the initial training – however sophisticated – will not be enough to support the continuing development of your coaches. A programme of supervision and CPD is essential for developing their skills, maintaining ethical standards, providing opportunities for them to reflect on and learn from their practice, giving them exposure to different approaches and staying current on practice within the profession. As Hawkins and Schwenk (2006) put it:

"If you don't provide supervision for internal coaches ... the sustainability and return on investment of your coaching initiative is in jeopardy". (p. 17)

This chapter explores:

- What supervision is and what it is for
- The three different functions
- Benefits of supervision
- The pros and cons of one-to-one, group and peer supervision
- Using external or internal supervisors
- Frequency of supervision
- Common issues when supervising internal coaches
- Identifying suitable supervision
- Supervision of team coaches
- Alternatives to supervision
- Continuing professional development

DOI: 10.4324/9781003519911-12

What is coach supervision and what is it for?

There are many definitions of supervision. We like the one that appears in the Global Code of Ethics:

> "A safe space for reflective dialogue with a practising supervisor, supporting the supervisee's practice, development and well-being".

In essence, the purpose is to help the coach to do their job better. You could describe it as your coaches' scaffolding, providing them with support, stretch and sustenance (Barton, 2024a).

For some, the term 'supervision' has uncomfortable overtones of policing or controlling, so they use different vocabulary (supervision groups may be called 'shared learning groups' or 'reflective practice groups') but the debate about finding alternative terminology – widespread in the 2000s – seems to have died away and the terms 'coach supervisor' and 'coach supervision' are accepted.

So, are organisations actually providing supervision for their internal coaches? It is a sad phenomenon that some organisations still insist on their external coaches receiving supervision while failing to offer similar support and quality assurance for their own internal coaches, but the picture has nonetheless vastly improved over the past 20 years. Hawkins and Schwenk's (2006) research showed that while 88% of organisations using internal coaches believed that they should have supervision, only 23% actually provided it. Roll forward to Hawkins and Turner's (2017) research and this figure had risen to 40%. Jepson (2016) found that 62% of internal coaches had their supervision paid for by their organisation and Katharine's and Julia's survey of 137 internal coaches in early 2024 found that 63% were being offered supervision. So while still not universal, supervision for internal coaches is now an established part of the internal coaching landscape.

The three different functions of supervision

Hawkins and Smith (2013) built on work that had gone before, e.g., Proctor (1986) and Kadushin (1992), by identifying three distinct functions of coach supervision, which they called:

1 The *Developmental* function. This is concerned with the development of the coach's skills, knowledge, understanding and personal attributes so that they become an increasingly competent practitioner.
2 The *Resourcing* function. This is about providing a supportive space for the coach to process their experiences when working with clients.
3 The *Qualitative* function. This is where the supervisor helps to ensure that the quality of the coach's practices and standards is professional and ethical.

The developmental function

This aspect of the supervisor's role involves developing the coach's knowledge and skills by encouraging reflection, helping them to explore their practice through discussion of their client work, and providing information, ideas, tips and techniques. The supervisor may give the coach direct feedback, introduce them to a relevant theory or model, or invite them to role-play. The aim is for the coach to become an increasingly competent practitioner. Butwell's (2006) research noted that all the coaches in her small-scale study of a supervision group highlighted skills acquisition as being a key benefit.

Hawkins (2011) agreed that supervision should address building the coach's capacity and pointed out that:

> "In our training of several hundred coach supervisors, we have found that generally they are less skilled at attending to the supervisee's capacity than they are at attending to the current client work". (p. 286)

When supervising internal coaches, this is particularly important because they will usually have fewer clients than external coaches do, which translates into fewer issues springing directly from client work. Indeed, they sometimes have no clients at all for a period, so sessions are best focused on building their capacity and keeping their skills fresh.

Supervisors talk about how supervision sessions tend to change in style and content as coaches become more experienced. When they begin, new coaches tend to want a lot of input and ideas and can get hung up on techniques. As they get more experienced, they may be more interested in talking about underlying themes, about themselves as coaches, and about patterns that they have noticed across their practice. Supervision is not just about discussing client issues. It can also be purely reflective. Two generative questions that some supervisors ask are "Which of your clients do you enjoy working with most/least and why?" and "With which clients do you feel you do your best/worst work and why?"

The resourcing function

Supervisors play a vital role in providing psychological support to coaches who may have doubts and insecurities around their competence, particularly if they have no clients for a period, or may be psychologically taking on board the concerns and worries of their clients. As a chaplain in a Portsmouth hospital was quoted as saying on Desert Island Discs by Donna Ockenden (2025): "You cannot carry everyone's suitcase of grief around with you".

Clients often cry. They may be relieved to have finally acknowledged their situation and are responding to feeling really 'heard'. They may be accessing a painful time in their past when reflecting on current feelings or experiencing overwhelm in a very demanding job. If a coach has a series of sessions with clients who are distressed, it can take its toll. Rosefield (2024) conducted research with coaches to understand their personal experiences of burnout and 'compassion fatigue'. She speculated that factors included the nature of the work, the personality and/or coping style of the coach, and the broader environment. As she said, coaching is inherently demanding, often exposing coaches to high levels of emotional intensity or emotional labour. One lead coach, who was moving on from the role, told Katharine that – with hindsight – she would have done much more to help her coaches manage their own resilience.

Rita's story

A lesson in emotional regulation and support

Rita worked as an internal coach within a pressurised healthcare setting. Her coaching relationship with Naomi, a senior manager, started by chance when Naomi opened up about feeling overwhelmed and Rita offered her a safe space to talk. Rita's approach was holistic, leaning on positive psychology techniques which worked well in her coaching practice. Rita knew Naomi and believed that she would respond well and quickly to coaching.

Their second session together took place outdoors, which resulted in a plan for Naomi to spend more time in nature. They arranged a third session but, before this could happen, Naomi was signed off work with stress. Despite this she was keen to continue with the coaching.

Rita was unprepared for the differences she observed when they met again. Naomi was anxious, fidgety, talking rapidly and disjointedly and not making eye contact. She had also visibly lost weight. Rita suggested a grounding breathing exercise, but Naomi couldn't focus. She said that her thoughts were consuming her, and she could not switch off. Her heart was 'pounding out of her chest' and she didn't know how to 'keep it in'.

Rita discovered that Naomi wasn't eating or sleeping well and had lost any interest in socialising. She had been prescribed anti-anxiety medication by her GP which had helped a little. Rita felt real concern for her wellbeing and specifically asked Naomi whether she had had any thoughts of taking her own life. She immediately answered yes. That yes was supposed to be a no, and Rita could feel her own heart pounding now. She could hear her internal voice screaming 'stop, this is not coaching…'. Two paradoxical thoughts arrived together: 'I can't do this' and 'Keep talking, you can do this'.

Rita acted on pure intuition and dropped the thought: 'I can't do this'. She knew that her sole job was to keep Naomi safe and to pay attention to all the cues she was being given. Naomi herself knew she needed to be in hospital and together, calmly, they agreed a plan to get her what she needed.

Naomi was admitted into hospital and after two weeks contacted Rita to let her know she was okay. She eventually went on to make a full recovery, returning to work part-time.

Rita's learning

Two lessons have stayed with Rita:

1 *Use supervision for wellbeing:* Rita realised that until then she had limited supervision to talking about specific challenges with clients. She hadn't talked about her own feelings, her triggers or her fears. Discussing Naomi's impact on her in a safe supervision session was essential to allow her to let go of, and process, her own emotions. She also now checks in with herself after a session and keeps supervision as a regular activity rather than accessing it ad hoc.
2 *Build in self-care:* Rita knew how to look after herself, but was often too busy to act on this. She is now intentional about engaging in regular activities that keep her well.

The qualitative function

This facet of the supervisor's role requires the supervisor to uphold the standards of the profession, model good practice, and assure the quality, professionalism and integrity of the coach's practice. Chapter 5 puts considerable emphasis on the role of supervision in helping coaches resolve dilemmas ethically. As Carroll and Shaw (2013) put it:

"There comes a time when the voices of others enter the dialogue and weave their influence ... Different perspectives can provide wider vision and help us to make mature choices". (pp. 353–354)

From the perspective of the employer, the 'qualitative' function of supervision provides a degree of quality assurance. The supervisor is there to talk through any aspect of your coaches' practice that could put the client or organisation at risk or to offer guidance as to how they might practise more safely. Most coaches very much value the reassurance that they are operating ethically and professionally.

However, there is evidence to suggest that supervisors tend to be much more enthusiastic about their developmental role (Lewis, 2024) and that there can be a lack of consistency (Turner & Passmore, 2018) in how they evaluate the application of codes of ethics. As lead coach, think carefully about what you want from your coach supervisors. Do you want them to feed back to you generic issues where there appears to be a knowledge gap or a need for some refresher CPD? You could ask for a regular report from your supervisor or request regular meetings with them to check that all is well and ask if any themes have emerged.

Contracts often don't specify any expectations around feedback on performance issues. Supervisors tend to regard their supervisory conversations with internal coaches as a confidential space where the responsibility for making any changes rests squarely with the coach. It is worth thinking about whether the supervision process is providing you with the reassurance you need.

Finally, Patterson (2011) talks about the *four* tasks of coaching supervision:

1   Assuring professionalism, integrity and ethical practice of the supervisee.
2   The personal and professional learning and development of the supervisee.
3   The rest, refuelling and restoration of the supervisee.
4   Celebrating and honouring the work of the supervisee. (p. 123)

The constraints of confidentiality mean that coaching can be a lonely business, and the supervisor is in an ideal position to affirm a coach's work, so we appreciate the addition of 'celebrating and honouring the work of the supervisee'.

Benefits of supervision

Practitioners agree that supervision has many benefits (Clutterbuck et al., 2016; Robson, 2016). Wingrove et al. (2020) demonstrated that internal coaches felt particularly positive about group supervision, appreciating the opportunity to check and improve their level of competence in comparison to their peers, and to achieve a sense of community. Similarly, Zimmermann et al. (2023) noted that group supervision mitigated the isolation that coaches can experience.

Some examples of feedback from internal coaches attending Julia's supervision groups.

- We get into some really deep, emotional issues that are good to share and we gain perspective and insight from others.
- It's so important to reflect and share experiences, insight and learning – and essential when working with such high emotional challenges that have a big impact on us as coaches.
- Helpful as a group to have reassurance that this is not about us, but about the client agenda so 'get over yourself'! Just to be with the client and listen is enough.
- Great space to learn, grow, be challenged, be supported and share our experiences.

The benefits can be perceived differently by different stakeholders. Hawkins and Schwenk (2006) pointed out that while "coaches are interested in making themselves more effective", those organising coaching services "put more emphasis on quality assurance" such as:

"protecting the client; minimising the organisational risk of unethical or unprofessional practice; ensuring the coaching is focused on work objectives and within the boundaries of the coach's capability [and] … raising coaching standards by continually improving quality and effectiveness". (p. 7)

The pros and cons of one-to-one, group and peer supervision

One-to-one, group and peer supervision offer different experiences. How do you decide what to offer? Hawkins and Schwenk (2006) point out that each variety of supervision has its limitations:

- Individual supervision can lead to dependency.
- Group supervision can be overtaken by the dynamics of the group and leave insufficient time for each individual.
- Peer supervision can become collusive. (p. 15)

Any of these approaches can be held either face-to-face or virtually. Here is a summary of some of the benefits and challenges.

Table 10.1 Benefits and challenges of supervision approaches

One-to-one supervision: supervisor and coach

Benefits	Challenges
• Provides more opportunity for the coach to expose their concerns and vulnerability • Allows the coach more time for personal contribution and reflection • Enables supervisor to explore insights and outcomes from one session to the next	• Very intense process for coach • Can be cost-prohibitive creating longer periods between supervision sessions

Group supervision: supervisor and a group of coaches

Benefits	Challenges
• Provides opportunity for the coach to gain support from fellow coaches • Increases richness of shared insight and learning from other coaches' experiences • Enables supervisor to meet CPD needs • More cost-effective • Offers opportunity to gather organisational learning	• Coaches may feel less inclined to share personal dilemmas and own vulnerability for fear of being judged by peers • May reduce the likelihood of more introverted coaches contributing to the group process

One-to-one peer supervision

Benefits	Challenges
• Provides a more relaxed environment as coaches are likely already to have an established relationship • Allows each coach time to share concerns and share reflections • No cost (other than taking time away from work)	• Reduces richness of insight and learning from supervisor's insight • Process may be less robust or structured • Peers may collude more readily without external challenge to their assumptions

(Continued)

Table 10.1 (Continued)

Peer group supervision

Benefits	Challenges
• Sharing of concerns and gaining support from fellow coaches • Increases richness of shared insight and learning from other coach's experiences • No cost (other than taking time away from work)	• More opportunity for collusion between peers than face a difficult dilemma • May be less objective challenge from peers than a supervisor may give • Extrovert coaches may have a louder voice and reduce likelihood of introvert coaches contributing to a group process

One-to-one supervision

In one-to-one supervision, the coach has the supervisor's undivided attention. Many coaches say that they prefer one-to-one supervision as it is possible to dig much deeper. There is privacy to role play or get into personal material – such as deep-seated patterns that are getting in the way – that might feel unsafe to share in a group session. One internal coach summarised the benefits for her as being easy to organise (only two diaries), offering complete confidentiality and all the time was dedicated to her.

Group supervision

Groups tend to have five to eight coaches and meet at regular intervals. Some groups run for a whole day, others for half a day (or two to three hours). Coaches bring issues to the group – run by a qualified coach supervisor – about their own development as a coach or client-related matters for discussion and learning. The ideal is to have a stable membership, as trust within group supervision takes time to develop (de Haan, 2017; Hodge, 2014), but organisations report that, for practical reasons, this can be very hard to achieve.

Key benefits of group supervision include the richness of the learning as there is "more than one supervisor in the room" since the coaches partly supervise each other, the sense of community and connectedness with other coaches and, for internal coaches, being supervised with other coaches working in the same system can be really helpful because they are dealing with the needs and expectations of the same group of stakeholders. Additional benefits for the organisation are the potential for harvesting organisational learning (extracting themes that emerge from coaching across the organisation), building a community of practice and helping to break down silos as coaches from different parts of the business get to know each other.

However, even if a supervisor is excellent at trying to engage everyone, group supervision can allow individuals to coast, particularly now that most supervision is delivered virtually. The coaster may be learning from others' contributions but their lack of input reduces the overall value for the group. At the other end of the spectrum, most groups do not have time for every coach to present an issue.

Virtual supervision

Virtual group supervision is a practical and cost-effective option, but it requires different strategies to maintain engagement, manage the technology and develop trusting connections. In Julia's experience there are both advantages and challenges to this approach.

Benefits

- Participants can join from anywhere, making it far more flexible to access and schedule sessions.
- There is a richness in discussion and diverse perspectives as there tends to be participation from a broader range of coaches.
- Organisations don't have to factor in travel expenses or booking of rooms.
- If hosted by the organisation, coaches have the facility to share documents and whiteboards.

Challenges

- Weak broadband connections can cause audio and video lag, disrupting the flow of the conversations.
- Coaches can get distracted by multitasking or by interruptions from pets!
- It can be harder to interpret body language, which may impact communication – especially missing non-verbal cues.
- Ensuring equal participation can be more difficult for the supervisor in a virtual landscape.
- Extended online sessions can be mentally draining for both the supervisor and the coaches. In a three-hour virtual group supervision session, regular five-minute breaks are essential to avoid screen fatigue.

Peer supervision

Coaches can supervise each other in pairs or groups. To work well, the coaches in the group need to be fairly experienced, properly trained in how to use a specific model of supervision and comfortable with having their practice discussed.

Training in peer supervision offers learning about basic group dynamics. Examples include noticing who is leading the group (even though it has no designated leader), how to give someone feedback in front of others, how to recontract in the moment and so forth. Such programmes may offer live demonstrations, practice in triads and training in accessing one's 'internal supervisor', i.e., getting in touch with one's cognitive, intuitive and somatic responses. Peer supervision groups have to work out how they are going to deal with confidentiality issues, how to challenge each other appropriately, how to avoid colluding and how to invite colleagues into better, or more ethical, practice without shaming them. Advocates say that, as long as a proper process is followed, it can work very well. Without that 'it can wobble' and turn into co-coaching or 'something cosier'.

Final thoughts: the process that best meet your coaches' needs may be to alternate group and one-to-one supervision, getting the best of both worlds.

Peer coaching with supervisor observation

A variant on group supervision, that still involves a trained supervisor, is peer coaching with supervisor observation. In this process, the supervisor observes and provides feedback to peer coaches who coach each other. The supervisor acts as a facilitator and guide, ensuring that the peer coaching process remains constructive and focused on professional growth. The supervisor's responsibility is to observe the dynamics between the peer coaches, paying attention to how they communicate, support one another and manage challenges. The supervisor's feedback encourages reflection, highlighting both effective coaching strategies and areas for improvement. The supervisor ensures that the feedback provided is clear, actionable and non-judgmental, helping coaches both to refine their techniques and deepen their understanding of coaching principles. After a period, the coaches may be able to meet unsupervised and self-manage the process.

Using external or internal supervisors

As lead coach you will need to decide how to source supervision for your coaches. Will you bring in external supervisors or train one or more of your most experienced internal coaches in supervision? Or perhaps you, as lead coach, are already qualified, or plan to qualify, as a supervisor yourself.

There are some distinct pros and cons to using internal or external supervisors. They mirror the arguments for using internal or external coaches.

Benefits of using external supervisors

- An enhanced sense of confidentiality as the supervisor is unlikely to know the person about whom the coach is talking.
- They offer a different kind of challenge, as they will not have the same blind spots. Internal supervisors may make assumptions about the organisational culture, while externals are freer to ask a question that opens things up.
- They can bring in fresh ideas, different perspectives and new models.

Disadvantages of using external supervisors

- The costs are likely to be higher.
- Call-off contracts where coaches can seek ad hoc supervision, as and when they need it, may be seen as a less cost-effective unless the service is fully utilised by coaches.
- They do not always understand the organisational agenda and the culture, so time is taken up explaining it (though probably diminishing over time).
- They can introduce a power imbalance, particularly with an inexperienced coach.

Benefits of training internal supervisors

Internal supervisors offer excellent value for money and are more likely to be able to make themselves available to coaches for a quick discussion of, say, an ethical dilemma. They also understand the system, the internal politics and the functional specialisms (quite complicated in some organisations).

Which of your coaches might be suitable to train as supervisors? Moyes (2009) asked the question: "Do good coaches automatically become good supervisors?" (p.168). Drawing on therapeutic literature she cited Borders (1992) who concluded that: "a pivotal skill in this role transition is the cognitive shift from thinking like a counsellor to thinking like a supervisor". As lead coach you need to make a judgement as to which of your coaches is most likely to be able to make this cognitive shift, who shows readiness for being trained to use a supervision framework competently and who has the aptitude to deliver the three functions of supervision.

Rachel's story illustrates the personal and organisational benefits of her training to be a supervisor.

Rachel's story

The value of a supervision qualification

A large National Health Service Trust had an established internal coaching pool of around 50 coaches and provided both one-to-one and group supervision for them.

The Trust decided to invest in training some of the more experienced coaches to be internal supervisors, considering that this would represent better value for money than employing external supervisors. All but one of the coaches trained to ILM7 standard – completing all the practical work – but without taking the extra step of obtaining the formal ILM7 supervision qualification, i.e., completing written assignments. One of the coaches, Rachel, decided to obtain the qualification. These are her reflections.

Challenges

1 *Funding:* The qualification was not cheap, so Rachel had to negotiate the funding for it. She did some extra work in return for the organisation paying for her qualification.
2 *Time:* On top of a busy day job it was hard for Rachel to make time for the assignments.
3 *Two-tier supervision:* There was a concern that supervision by the other supervisors might be seen by the coaches as 'second class' compared with Rachel's. To minimise this possibility, the Trust arranged supervision for all the internal supervisors – with or without the formal qualification and also held an annual CPD session for them.

Benefits experienced

1 *Confidence:* Completing her supervision qualification had a very positive impact on Rachel's confidence – she felt that she had really professionalised her practice.
2 *Effectiveness as a supervisor:* Rachel absorbed a lot from completing the qualification. In particular, she appreciated the value of learning reflective practice (drawing on the work of Gillie E J Bolton) and being introduced to a structured 'Supervision skills self-assessment' process, adapted from Hawkins & Shohet (see QR code below), which she incorporated into her own practice. She updated the self-assessment regularly. It provided an opportunity to reflect on her supervision practice, for further exploration with her supervisor.
3 *Feedback from her 1:1 supervisees:* Prompted by completing the qualification, Rachel developed a feedback form which she sent to her supervisees annually (see QR code on the next page). This helped her to reflect on and develop her practice, helped her supervisees to reflect on their supervision needs and helped the organisation: one supervisee noted that she would benefit from short *ad hoc* supervision sessions for any 'sticky' issues. As a result, the standard coaching supervision contract was adjusted to include the offer of *ad hoc* twenty-minute sessions, on request.
4 *Feedback from her group supervisees:* Rachel instituted monthly group supervision drop-in sessions for the coaches – co-run with the other supervisors – then introduced an annual evaluation using an online survey. The Trust benefited from feedback about the effectiveness of the drop-in sessions (QR code on the next page for an example), identification of organisational themes and suggestions for future CPD topics.

To access the documents (listed below) that Rachel developed, use the QR Code on page 3:

"Supervision Skills Self-assessment: A Template"
"Coaching Supervision Evaluation: A Template"
"Summary of Evaluation Feedback: An example"

Challenges in using internal supervisors

Three concerns expressed within the coach supervision world about the use of internal supervisors are firstly that they are hooked into the organisational culture and the same systemic dynamics as their supervisees, which may make it more difficult for them to challenge assumptions, or even to see the need to challenge them, because they share them. Also, the supervisors' pre-existing relationships with coaching colleagues may make it less easy for those colleagues to give them honest feedback about the quality of the supervision. And finally, there is an inherent conflict for the internal supervisor between the needs of the coaches and those of the organisation. This can be delicate, particularly where the supervisor is also the lead coach with managerial responsibilities for assuring the quality of the internal coaching pool.

Thomson (2011) says some interesting things relevant to the last point. He highlights the inherent conflict between the supervisor's role in enhancing a coach's learning in a non-directive, client-centred, unconditional, non-judgemental way while at the same time "holding a responsibility to ensure the quality of a coach's work and to monitor the coach's compliance with a relevant code of practice", arguing that "their acceptance necessarily becomes judgemental and their positive regard becomes conditional" (p. 107).

None of these points outweighs the benefits of training internal supervisors, but it is desirable that you give thought to how to manage the risks.

Frequency of supervision

The conventional wisdom is that supervision should be regular and achieve the best possible balance between the coaches' needs and the resources available. Underlying this is an assumption that the more supervision organisations can provide, the better for the coaches. The missing piece in this equation is whether the coaches engage with it, so it is worth considering this first.

Most coaches express a positive attitude to supervision, but this doesn't necessarily translate into doing it (Zimmermann et al., 2023). Generally, where organisations provide supervision for their internal coaches, they make it voluntary. The outcome, often, is that only around half (or less) attend supervision regularly. There are many reasons for this. The coaches may not appreciate its value. Or they may fear being shamed or negatively perceived by others (De Haan, 2012). Or they may be "nervous about spending too much time on something that … might be seen by their line manager as a 'luxury'" (Butwell, 2006. p. 51) or "see supervision as only necessary in a crisis … rather than a necessary form of ongoing learning, reflection and quality control" (Maxwell, 2011, p. 191).

Several lead coaches who participated in Katharine's original research (St John-Brooks, 2010) said that, with hindsight, they wished they had been firmer about insisting that coaches attended supervision sessions. Others said that they were changing policy to making supervision a 'condition of practice' to encourage better attendance.

So, how frequent should it be? Judith Barton, Director of Coaching & Mentoring at British School of Coaching suggests a number of criteria for coaches to consider (Barton, 2024a; Barton, 2024b):

- How many coaching hours do you actually deliver?
- What sort of reflector are you? Do you already do a lot of thinking about your practice, e.g., while you're walking? Perhaps you journal or are a follower of the Morning Pages concept by Julia Cameron?
- Where are you in your practice? How mature are you as a coach?
- What type of coaching do you do? Some would argue that if you're working in an emotional field much of the time then you may well need more hours than if you're more attuned to goal/task-driven type coaching.
- What client feedback are you getting? If you are being posed some challenges, then you're going to need more support.

Her rule of thumb is that coaches who deliver over 10 hours of coaching a week should receive supervision every four weeks. For those who coach for five to ten hours, push it to five or six weeks. For coaching less than five hours a week, attend supervision every two months, and for one to two hours a week – once a quarter.

All the professional bodies recommend regular supervision, e.g., the EMCC recommends one hour to every thirty-five hours of coaching (minimum quarterly) but, for internal coaches, a ratio often has little meaning as a benchmark. If a coach has one client and sees them for one 90-minute session each month for six months, then takes on another client for six months, that is only 18 hours of coaching in a year. That is why Barton's formulation above may be more useful than the EMCC's (or those of the other professional bodies). Many lead coaches now prefer to fix a particular interval, say, a maximum of two to three months between supervision sessions, irrespective of how many hours their coaches are coaching. It helps, particularly when the coaches are quite inexperienced, on the grounds of keeping the momentum up and keeping the coaches learning.

In Katharine and Julia's survey of 137 coaches in early 2024, 39% were offered supervision once a quarter, 13% every two months and 10% once a month (with the rest offered once or twice yearly or no supervision at all). Lead coaches can only work with the resources they have.

There can be an issue around accessing supervision from external supervisors between formal sessions. External supervisors often offer unpaid *ad hoc* help when coaches have ethical dilemmas to resolve quickly. However, this is taking advantage of their goodwill and, ideally, organisations should negotiate a contract with the supervisor that includes 'emergency' consultations of this kind. Internal supervisors tend to regard *ad hoc* supervision sessions as very much part of their role.

If resources are tight, you might consider an approach developed by Crosse (2024), based on research into the different strategies coaches use to support their development. It offers a simple structure for alternating between facilitated and self-managed group supervision. The idea is to hold a professionally led session every 6–8 weeks, with peer-led reflective sessions in between. It works best with a stable group that is familiar with the supervisor's approach. The bonus for organisations is that it can reduce costs without compromising developmental value.

The important thing is prompting the coaches to take the time for reflecting regularly on their practice. There are other ways too to support your coaches' reflections, including CPD. These alternative approaches are covered later on in this chapter.

Common issues when supervising internal coaches

The nature of supervising internal coaches is different from supervising external coaches for two main reasons: internal coaches do much less coaching plus they tend to bring to supervision more issues around confidentiality, holding boundaries and role conflicts (St John-Brooks, 2019).

Supervisors of both internal and external coaches have noted that their internal coaches' clients tend to bring a more 'issue-based' agenda, i.e., day-to-day work problems. The coaches can feel that they are being forced into the role of mentors or helping the client with matters that are properly the responsibility of their line managers. Internal coaches also seem to experience more cancellations, so they have to rely on their personal influencing skills to keep things on track. It is really important that your coaches contract clearly with their clients around the issue of cancellations and emphasise the mutual commitment to investing time in the process.

Coaches often have anxieties around involving the client's line manager at the beginning and end points (see Chapter 9 for guidance on handling three-way contracting meetings). They can experience difficulties with the logistics of organising the meeting, particularly if the client and their line manager work on different sites and they want it to be face-to-face. They can also feel nervous about handling the conversation and the supervisor can sometimes help them to rehearse. One particular worry raised is around having credibility with the client's line manager, particularly if they are senior to the coach.

Since job-plus coaches are unlikely to have more than three coaching clients at any one time, and may well have only one (or none), they generally have fewer client issues to bring to supervision. The focus may often be more on skills development and the session have more of a CPD feel about it. Partly as a consequence of having fewer 'flying hours', the coaches can also have more issues around lack of confidence and resilence.

Internal coaches can bring frustrations about their organisation with them and hold emotions from their clients reinforced by their being part of the same system. This can present a challenge for the supervisor. As one said: 'You don't want them to moan throughout the session. On the other hand, they are carrying the frustrations of their clients too and if this parallel process is not surfaced then it can get in the way'.

Identifying suitable supervision

Models of supervision

There are many different theories drawn from a variety of fields that can inform supervisory practice: gestalt, positive psychology, systemic, psychodynamic, cognitive/behavioural and neuro-linguistic programming (NLP) are examples of the approaches underlying the practice of many supervisors.

One of the most popular models is Bath Consultancy Group's Seven-eyed Process Model (Hawkins & Smith, 2006), which was adapted from a therapeutic model of supervision to meet the needs of coaches. Munro-Turner (2011) identified limitations in the seven-eyed model and made modifications, resulting in the '3 worlds 4 territories' (3W4T) model of supervision. The similarity between the two models is that they both take a systemic approach, considering multiple levels of influence, including the coach, client and wider context.

The difference lies in their structure and focus:

- Hawkins' seven-eyed model explores supervision through seven 'eyes' or lenses, emphasising relational, systemic and reflective aspects of the coaching process.
- The 3W4T Model translates supervision into three interconnected 'worlds' (the client's world, the coaching session, and the supervision session). Within these worlds, the supervisor can attend to four territories of experience for each of the players involved (themselves, the coach and the coaching client). The four territories are Insight, Readiness, Authentic Vision and Skilful Action.

While both models enhance reflective practice and effectiveness, Hawkins' model is more detailed in relational dynamics, whereas the 3W4T model provides a structured contextual framework.

When you approach a supervisor it is worth discussing with them what approach they use with their clients.

Sourcing an external supervisor

15–20 years ago, finding a supervisor could be hard, but no longer. Many organisations source supervision from the provider that trained their coaches. Others, however, believe that it is important to bring in different perspectives through both their supervision and the CPD they arrange, so that their coaches are exposed to a variety of approaches. To that end, they purposely procure supervisors from a different source. It is important to check out that your supervisor is well-trained and qualified and can provide references from satisfied client organisations.

The following bodies, amongst others, can help you locate someone with the necessary expertise:

- European Mentoring & Coaching Council (EMCC)
- International Coaching Federation (ICF)
- Association for Coaching (AC)
- Coaching Supervision Academy (CSA)
- Association for Professional Executive Coaching and Supervision (APECS)

Some universities and business schools offering qualifications in coaching and coach supervision may also have directories of accredited supervisors, including those with team coaching experience.

Think about what you want from your supervisors and have an in-depth contracting conversation with them. It would be unwise to hire one simply on the basis of someone's recommendation, only to find out later that they do not cover all the bases that matter to you.

The EMCC's Supervision Competence Framework (EMCC Global, 2019) can be a helpful structure for the contracting conversation. It outlines eight core competencies:

- Manages the supervision contract and process
- Facilitates development
- Provides support
- Promotes professional standards
- Develops self-awareness
- Promotes relationship awareness
- Develops systemic awareness
- Facilitates group supervision

Training an internal supervisor

If you decide to train one or more of your coaches in supervision, many of the institutions that train coaches now also offer coach supervision training. When selecting a training programme, consider factors such as accreditation, curriculum comprehensiveness, delivery format and alignment with your organisation's specific needs. Training your internal supervisor(s) using a programme recognised by reputable bodies can enhance the credibility and effectiveness of your internal coaching service.

Supervision of team coaches

Team coaching is still in its infancy compared with 1:1 coaching, but there are already plenty of organisations deploying internal team coaches. Hodge and Clutterbuck (2019) noted that highly able one-to-one coaches sometimes believe that their skills are directly transferable to team coaching but that this is rarely so because team coaches need to draw on a wide array of knowledge and skills that may come from any of the following disciplines:

> "organisational development, executive coaching, group facilitation, process consulting, adult learning, systems and constellations, and family therapy". (p. 162)

They concluded that most team coaches both want and need supervision with this complex work and are:

> "looking for support and challenge that enables them to gain awareness of what might be happening within the whole client system … They seek insights from the supervisor about how to balance the purpose and tasks of the coaching while managing the psychological aspects of the team dynamics and relationships".

Hodge's (2020) 'map' reveals how complex the relationship management can be and Clutterbuck and Graves (2024) point out that team coaching can be challenging

> "with the highs and lows much more extreme and magnified than for 1:1 coaching". (p. 295)

The team coach can inadvertently be drawn into becoming the *de facto* leader or a member of the team. They need to think about both self-care and external support.

It's hard to be a solo team coach. Even with a small team of, say, four people you can't notice everything. One thing that can work well is to twin an experienced team coach with a less experienced one in order to develop them. It can be easier for an internal coach than an external coach to find a pair as there aren't the same cost implications (apart from the opportunity cost) with which external coaches must contend. If your internal team coaches are coaching in pairs, then do try to ensure that they receive supervision on their team coaching together.

Supervisors of team coaches need a lot of knowledge and experience to provide the right support. Clutterbuck and Hodge (2017) suggest that this should include:

- Experience and expertise in both one-to-one and team coaching.
- Strong academic and/or psychological background.
- Professional qualification in supervision (not necessarily coaching supervision).
- Strong grounding in group process and group facilitation.
- Ideally, experience of actually working in and leading a team.
- An understanding of organisational structures including across cultures and remotely.
- An appreciation of the scope of team coaching and how it extends to HR, Finance, IT, L&D, OD and any other corporate functions.

They point out that the complexity of supervising a team coach needs to be reflected in the model of supervision that the supervisor deploys. In addition to the seven relationships recognised in Hawkins' Seven-eyed Supervision model, supervisors of team coaches need to consider at least two other relationships, namely those between the team members and between the team members and the team leader.

Supervision for the supervisors

It is good practice for supervisors themselves to be supervised. Where a supervisor is external it is desirable to check out with them what their own supervision arrangements are during the contracting conversation. If you have decided to train your own internal supervisors, then the responsibility for providing supervisory support for them is yours. In practice, internal supervisors are usually also internal coaches, so a common practice is to source a supervisor who can supervise them on both their coaching and supervision practices, allocating different parts of the session to each.

Alternatives to supervision

Supervision of your coaches by a qualified supervisor is established best practice but if funds will not stretch to that, there are other ways for your coaches to reflect on their practice and develop their skills.

Action learning

Action learning was founded by Reg Revans (1982) in the 1930s. He noticed that his colleagues could support each others' learning, even if they were from different parts of the organisation with diverse issues to resolve. The simple act of articulating their problems, asking each other direct questions, and sharing experiences was invaluable.

Running an action learning set is a structured process, led by a facilitator, usually involving:

1 Check-in – each set member has a few minutes to report any significant developments since they last met (job move, restructured team, new baby).
2 Decision as to running order and how much 'airtime' each set member will have.
3 Articulation by each 'presenter' in turn of their issue, without interruption, specifying the nature of the contribution that they want from the other set members.
4 Questioning of the presenter by other members, to help them to come to a deeper understanding of their issue and their options for resolving it. Set members are discouraged by the facilitator from giving advice, telling stories of how they have dealt with similar issues (unless the presenter has specifically asked for such input), or passing judgement. Members are urged to ask open questions.

5 Support from the members to the presenter to decide what action they should take.
6 Reflection by all set members on what happened and what questions were particularly helpful.

Childs et al. (2011) suggest that the questions set members could ask themselves include whether they helped the presenter to:

• clarify the situation, the options or the way forward
• achieve a deeper insight
• consider new ideas or options
• identify/release hidden emotions that are blocking the process.

Generally, a quarter of an hour or so is allocated at the end of the session to reflect on what went well, what went less well and how the learning could be even better next time. Since the membership of a set stays constant, members build strong relationships and feel able to hold each other to account. The emphasis is on learning and the absence of judgement.

Action learning is peculiarly well-suited to coach supervision because the kinds of questions that set members are encouraged to ask the 'presenter' are coaching style questions, so the process itself is also a mechanism for developing coaching skills. It is also cheap – any trained action learning set facilitator could run it effectively, without needing to be a coach. There are often individuals in L&D departments who are already trained in action learning facilitation.

Childs et al. (2011) suggest the following benefits of supervisory action learning sets:

• Low cost – while they start with a facilitator, to embed the structure of the sessions, the sets can easily become self-managed groups.
• They provide an antidote to the isolation that internal coaches can experience.
• Even inexperienced coaches feel empowered as they learn that they have perspectives that are helpful to others.
• The sets provide an opportunity for the coaches to take risks in a safe environment, experiment and try out different approaches and behaviours.
• All members are actively involved and engaged.
• The process is self-sustaining – group members can continue to meet if funding dries up. (p. 35)

Developing ground rules

For all kinds of group learning, including action learning sets and formal supervision groups, it is important to set some ground rules for how group members will treat each other. The R4C4P4 framework is one helpful approach.

The R4C4P4 framework was developed by Gergen and Gergen (2001) to ensure that the group dynamic is respectful, collaborative and productive.

R4	C4	P4
Respect	Confidentiality	Participation
Responsibility	Commitment	Privacy
Relationship	Communication	Preparation
Results	Challenge	Practicalities

Figure 10.1 The R4C4P4 framework

These principles help to guide group interactions, aiming to foster an open, supportive and working relationship among group members in the following ways.

Respect: It emphasises the importance of mutual respect among group members, creating a safe and supportive environment where internal coaches feel comfortable sharing their experiences, challenges and insights without fear of judgement or criticism.

Collaboration: By fostering a collaborative atmosphere, the framework encourages internal coaches to work together, share best practices and learn from each other's experiences. This collective approach can lead to more effective problem-solving and innovative solutions.

Productivity: It helps maintain a focus on achieving specific goals and outcomes during group supervision sessions, ensuring that the time spent in these sessions is used efficiently and effectively, leading to tangible improvements in coaching practices.

Positive psychology: The framework incorporates principles of positive psychology, which can help internal coaches build on their strengths and develop a growth mindset. This can lead to increased confidence and resilience, both of which are essential for effective coaching.

Reflective practice: It encourages reflective practice, allowing internal coaches to critically examine their own coaching methods and identify areas for improvement. This ongoing process of self-reflection and learning can lead to CPD and enhanced coaching skills.

By integrating these principles, the R4C4P4 framework can help create a supportive and productive environment during action learning group meetings (or, indeed, group supervision sessions).

Mentoring

Some organisations provide new coaches with a mentor, drawn from the internal coaching pool, who already has a few years' experience of coaching in the organisation. The mentor can offer support and, if necessary, advice or suggestions for approaches that might help them, so there can be a supervisory aspect. But they offer the big advantage of being free – other than their time, of course. Often, the lead coach can also make themselves available to support the new coaches.

Co-coaching/peer coaching

Another approach is the idea of a 'coaching buddy', usually someone who was trained in the same cohort, so that the coaches already know each other. These buddy arrangements can be more or less formal and offer the new coaches an opportunity to coach each other and to practise their skills in contracting and providing feedback and challenge. Some buddies arrange regular monthly co-coaching sessions. Others take a more *ad hoc* approach.

Reflective learning

The EMCC definition of supervision starts with "A safe space for reflective dialogue ..." because guided reflective learning is a key aspect of receiving supervision from a professional. In the absence of – or in addition to – formal supervision you could encourage your coaches to keep a reflective journal. Most coach training includes this, so your coaches should already be familiar with the principle. Some coaches write a reflection after every coaching session as a matter of good practice and, in addition, reflect at intervals on their thoughts and feelings, aspirations and worries, as a way of exploring what is going on in their work. It all contributes to the learning cycle of action, reflection, new understanding and new practice.

One easy-to-use approach is the reflective coaching practitioner model (Campone, 2011). She points out that reflective practice:

> "differs from simply 'thinking about what happened' insofar as it is characterised by intention, purpose and structure ... The purpose of reflective practice is to facilitate one's own learning from experience". (p. 15)

Scott (2019) too supports the practice of maintaining a reflective journal and discusses how coaches can use reflection-in-action to develop their coaching craft. His article emphasises the importance of reflection in enhancing coaching skills and suggests that coaches can benefit from both reflecting afterwards and thinking on their feet during sessions to improve their practice.

A reflective journal serves as a tool for coaches to deepen their self-awareness, monitor their growth and enhance their coaching effectiveness. By regularly documenting thoughts, emotions, successes and challenges, coaches can identify patterns in their practice, understand their own reactions to coaching situations and refine their techniques. It allows for critical self-reflection, enabling coaches to learn from both positive and difficult experiences.

In their journal (which can be anonymised to preserve confidentiality) your coaches can explore the following sorts of areas:

- *Client sessions:* Reflect on each coaching session, including the progress made, breakthroughs and any challenges faced.
- *Coaching techniques:* Evaluate the methods and strategies used during the session to see if they were effective or need adjustment.
- *Personal feelings and reactions:* Explore their emotional responses and those of the client in order to review how they may impact the coaching relationship.
- *Client progress:* Note observable changes or improvements in the client's behaviour, mindset, or results and reflect on any client feedback to explore their perspective.
- *Learning and insights:* Identify any new insights or knowledge gained during the session that can inform future practice and reflect on their own strengths as a coach and areas where they could improve.
- *Ethical considerations:* Consider whether their coaching practice aligns with ethical guidelines and professional standards in the Global Code of Ethics.

We provide an example of a template to aid reflective practice by journalling.

To access "Completing a Reflective Journal: A Template", use the QR Code on page 3.

To become an expert reflective practitioner takes practice. Most coach training encourages trainee coaches to reflect on their experiences. If you are thinking that it could be a useful continuing tool for your coaches, you could consider discussing with the trainer what model of reflective learning might best suit your needs.

Continuing professional development (CPD)

The Chartered Institute of Personnel and Development (CIPD) which represents trainers and HR professionals sets out five key principles for CPD:

1 Professional development is a continuing process that applies throughout a practitioner's working life.
2 Individuals are responsible for controlling and managing their own development.
3 Individuals should decide for themselves their learning needs and how to fulfil them.
4 Learning targets should be clearly articulated and should reflect the needs of employers and clients as well as the practitioner's individual goals.
5 Learning is most effective when it is acknowledged as an integral part of work rather than an additional burden.

It can be seen from this that a key principle is self-directed learning. Ideally, your coaches will emerge from their training with a learning and development plan, and it is up to you to encourage them to keep it up-to-date and to use it as the basis for an annual or six-monthly conversation with you about their progress and development needs.

However, as lead coach you will also have a sense of what the whole pool needs on the basis of what you are hearing from the supervisor(s), the coaches themselves and (if applicable) your steering group. There may also be particular approaches to which you would like to expose your coaches or skills you would like them to practise, so there will always be a balance to strike between the needs of individuals and the requirements that the business has of the coaching pool as a whole. For example, you may decide that it would be useful to train your coaches to give managers feedback on a 360 instrument used by your organisation or to offer selected coaches training in a development tool like MBTI, StrengthsFinder or FIRO(B).

What are the benefits of providing CPD?

There are many reasons why you should ensure that your coaches have access to as much CPD as possible:

- Those of your coaches who wish to become accredited members of professional bodies must be able to demonstrate their commitment to CPD. All the professional coaching bodies encourage their members to undertake it.
- It is a way of ensuring that your coaches continually improve, that the quality of what they deliver remains high, and that they extend their portfolio of approaches over time. Since internal coaches generally do much less coaching than externals, they need regular input of CPD and supervision to keep their skills levels up.
- Ideally, coaches should model learning behaviour and demonstrate that continuing learning matters ('practise what we preach').
- Delivering CPD as a joint learning experience for your coaches helps to build your coaching community of practice.

On top of what you provide yourselves, you can encourage your coaches to attend CPD events run by the coaching professional bodies, as they are often open to non-members too. Most of them also offer corporate memberships that provide access for your internal coaches to CPD events.

What are the options for CPD?

There is a range of options for CPD to support your coaches with their ongoing development, as well as staying connected with communities of coaches to enhance their engagement and professional practice.

Skills practice

As already noted, internal coaches can feel a little isolated once they finish their training so it helps to arrange some CPD events to keep them feeling connected and enhance their skills. One approach is to have regular lunchtime sessions – in person or online – when coaches can practise coaching each other in triads (coach, client and observer). They will have become used to this process during their training and it offers them an opportunity to practise contracting, coaching and giving and receiving feedback which is particularly helpful if they do not yet have any clients. In an hour you can fit in 15 minutes of one person coaching another followed by five minutes of feedback from the observer, then the same for the other two in turn.

One of the member benefits offered by the Association for Coaching is their co-coaching groups that are organised on a regional basis in the evenings. Your coaches would simply show up, be invited to join a triad and start coaching. There is usually a small charge for refreshments but the opportunity offered for new coaches to practise in a supportive learning environment is invaluable.

New approaches and techniques

Many organisations try to run at least three sessions a year introducing their coaches to something new. Their original coach training provider is often the first port of call. In Katharine's and Julia's survey of 137 internal coaches in early 2024, participants mentioned the following as CPD topics that had most enhanced their practice: asking good questions, clean language, dealing with ethical dilemmas, psychological approaches, time to think (Nancy Kline's work), using silence, career coaching, team coaching and somatic coaching/breath work.

They also identified the following as the topics about which they would most like to have CPD in the future: wellbeing/resilience/mental toughness, helping clients with their confidence/self-esteem, EDI/Unconscious bias and working with neurodiversity.

Commonly a workshop will include the introduction of a theory, model, or approach and then allow time for the coaches to practise using it. Provision need not be expensive. If someone has written a book on a subject, they are often prepared to come and talk about it for a very small fee or in exchange for your buying some copies of their book to put in your coaching library – or to give to a few of your coaches. Many coaches also access podcasts or TED Talks in their own time.

The following story is an example of where some CPD in a particular approach really enriched a coach's practice.

Catriona's story

Using the Lumination® coaching game

I'm always looking for new ways and fresh ideas to enhance the coaching experience and one simple to use and very powerful tool is the Lumination® coaching game. Its flexibility means it can be successfully used in a 1:1 coaching session with clients, with small groups and to train coaches.

Lumination® is a coaching process, designed as a board game! The premise is that the player/client goes along their path and meets coaching questions, suggestions and guides along the way – all of which offer different insights, perspectives and ideas. It introduces a playful dimension to coaching conversations which can facilitate insightful conversations, as well as supporting relationship-building. There is also something about the use of a physical tool where people are looking at something, holding cards, throwing dice, which can take them out of habituated ways of thinking.

1:1 coaching: I have used the game as it is intended and have also brought the cards into a coaching session and used the great questions. As a coach I find it incredibly useful – it takes the pressure off me as a coach to sustain the process and pose the questions but is flexible enough to give me the opportunity to hold the space for longer, ask supplementary questions and check in on the client's state and feelings.

Small groups: This is my preferred use of the game. Not only does the coaching client/player get support with their goal from the game, but they also get support from fellow players – a little like a supervision group. Multiple perspectives are afforded to all the players and the wisdom of the 'guide' cards inevitably proves to be a game changer. The beauty of the game is that the coaching client/player is still in control: they can decide how deeply (or not) to think and respond, so they feel safe.

Every time I have used the game in a group, the feedback has been similar: "How does the game know to ask me that question?"; "This is so accurate, it's uncanny"; "This has been so powerful" being common themes.

Training/CPD: The game is a great way to introduce people to coaching because it is experiential rather than teaching them 'how' to coach. It helps new coaches gain confidence in using a coaching approach – in particular, by providing them with a way to practise using open questions and move away from giving advice, which can often be a challenge at the beginning – but also works really well with experienced coaches.

Whole day events

It can sometimes be easier for internal coaches to block out a whole day in their diaries for supervision and CPD than ring-fencing several two-hour sessions. Some organisations accordingly organise a whole day event once or twice yearly for CPD in the morning, networking as a community of coaches over the lunch break, and then running supervision groups – or using some other methodology for sharing experience – in the afternoon. These are sometimes styled as a conference and can include a presentation by a senior coaching champion (ideally the CEO or a Director) to show appreciation for what the coaches are doing, talk about the organisation's strategic priorities and explain how the coaching service is helping to support them. Some organisations time these events to coincide with the end of a training programme for a new cohort of coaches so that it can double as a celebration (and the newly qualified coaches may receive a certificate from the awarding body).

There can be great value in including your external coaches too in such events and promoting the sharing of experience between them and your internal coaches.

Resources on the intranet

While all coaches need to practise, many coaches have a learning preference for reading about coaching too. It can be useful to establish a library of coaching books and journals and also to put electronic resources onto the intranet in a space devoted to your internal coaches. If you have invested in a sophisticated coach management system, there is likely to be an area especially reserved for resources. These can take the form of articles, webinars, descriptions of new tools or techniques, questionnaires (e.g., the short, non-proprietary version of Honey & Mumford's Learning Styles questionnaire), tools to help reflection, or videos of coaching demonstrations. Many organisations have a shared drive for the coaching community where anybody can put articles, book reviews, a report on some workshop they have been to or a new tool they have used. It can be very popular with the coaches.

Participating in a community of practice

One way of increasing your coaches' access to CPD opportunities is to set up, or join, a wider community of practice. Here is one story.

Northwest Higher Education Coaches' Network

Community of practice

June 2018 saw the first meeting of the UK's Northwest Higher Education Coaches' Network, a community of coaches dedicated to enhancing practice and raising the profile of coaching amongst academic and professional services colleagues.

Within a few years, the network comprised eleven universities and participants were a mixture of coaching leads, internal coaches and external coaches working in universities. At the beginning, full-day meetings were held twice a year, covering a variety of topics. The Covid pandemic resulted in a shift to quarterly online meetings lasting for around 90 minutes, but the aim was still the same: to provide a space for networking, learning and sharing practice and support with like-minded people.

The format of meetings varied according to the topics and whether there was a speaker or if it was a practice-sharing session. Models, techniques or other kinds of resources would be shared afterwards on the website for those who couldn't attend – sometimes with a mini video of the member introducing the topic. Examples included using emotional intelligence in coaching, team coaching, online coaching platforms, setting up and running an internal coaching pool, mental health and therapeutic coaching, implementing effective coaching processes and coaching and neurodiversity.

Tracy Ellis, Organisational Developer, University of Liverpool founded the network. She, and other members of the network, have reflected on the benefits and challenges involved in setting up and running it.

Benefits

- The community of practice has provided a welcome additional source of CPD, support and resource.
- Coaches benefit from the added impartiality, which allows them to share challenges with peers from other universities.
- Coaches appreciate having some space and time outside their own institution in order to think.
- Coaches welcome hearing about peers' experiences. They feel that they are not alone in facing particular challenges.
- Networking opportunities have resulted in building supportive relationships.

Challenges

- The network depends on people's goodwill – participating in sessions and sharing resources and experience. This tends to involve the same people and it can be a challenge to broaden the volunteer base.
- The ever-increasing trend in universities to do more with less has resulted in fewer people prepared to spend discretionary effort on supporting voluntary initiatives. The lead has noticed a downward trend in this effort and worries about the sustainability of the network.
- It can sometimes be difficult to find speakers who are willing to give their time freely.
- Virtual meetings can lead to participants being more passive than they would be if they were attending an in-person meeting. This can be discouraging for the speaker and those participants who are actively engaged.

The future

It is hoped that the community will continue to grow its membership organically. The challenge will be to keep members engaged at a time of increasing work pressures. If emphasis continues to be placed on the value of networking, peer support and continuing professional development, coaches in Northwest HE institutions will continue to value the opportunities the network brings.

Summary

Coaching supervision and CPD are essential for coaches. They are key to ensuring that the standards and integrity of the internal coaching service are maintained, risks are managed and the coaches continue to grow. Group supervision also provides one route for systemic themes arising from the many coaching conversations to be fed back into the organisation. Despite these benefits, there are still organisations that invest heavily in training their internal coaching resource but fail to ensure that their coaches receive regular supervision and CPD.

As coaching supervision becomes more firmly established and the need for CPD recognised, many organisations are exploring how to deliver it rather than asking why their coaches need it. This chapter has looked at ways of providing it to suit different budgets. Not only do these activities increase individual coaches' capability but they play a key role in the development of coaching within the organisation.

Table 10.2 Questions to reflect on

Purpose of supervision

- What do you need to do to gain organisational support for the funding of supervision?
- How can you engage your coaches in the process of supervision?
- What are the implications of introducing supervision in terms of time demands on your coaches?
- Will you take advantage of the opportunity offered to harvest organisational learning?

Group supervision vs. one-to-one supervision

- What approach to supervision will best suit your organisational needs?
- How will you deal with confidentiality issues in group supervision if coaches have a personal/professional relationship with other group members' clients?
- Have you been explicit in the contracting process around the levels of disclosure when a coach discusses a client issue during 1:1 supervision?
- What frequency of supervision will work best for your organisation?
- How can you ensure coaches with a minimal coaching load get value from supervision?

Internal vs. external supervision

- What factors are relevant to you when assessing the pros and cons of internal vs. external supervisors for coaches?
- Will it be more cost-effective for you to train and use your own internal supervisors?
- What plans do you need in place to ensure there is 'emergency supervision' for any coach who has an ethical dilemma that needs immediate resolution?
- What are your expectations for supervision of your supervisors?

Issues in supervising internal coaches

- How can you ensure your supervision targets the type of issues that internal coaches are likely to experience?
- How do you ensure that any external supervisor appreciates the challenges for your internal coaches and how can they best meet those needs?

(Continued)

Table 10.2 (Continued)

Procuring supervision

- What are you looking for in a supervisor?
- What selection criteria and assessment process do you need to put in place to identify an individual who will meet your needs?

Alternative approaches

- What resources do you have or need to create as viable alternatives to one-to-one or group supervision?
- Are there any current L&D initiatives already in place such as action learning sets or mentoring, which can be adapted as alternatives to supervision with a trained supervisor?
- What could you include in the coach training to give your coaches a model for reflecting on their practice?
- Could co-coaching, coaching circles, or peer supervision give your internal coaches sufficient support as an alternative to supervision by a qualified supervisor?

Continuing professional development (CPD)

- What is your commitment to supporting CPD for your coaches?
- What are your options for providing CPD at low or no cost to the business?
- What options are there to share CPD events with other organisations that have internal coaches?

Chapter 11

Evaluation

What this chapter is about

Evaluating the effectiveness of your coaching service shouldn't be a 'nice to have' or just icing on the cake. It is an essential element in justifying to decision-makers that the investment you have made in your coaches is worthwhile and ensuring the sustainability of coaching in your organisation.

This chapter explores:

- What evaluation is and why it is important
- Deciding what to evaluate
- Using the Kirkpatrick-Phillips evaluation model to refine your approach
- Approaches to gathering data
- Demonstrating return on investment (ROI)

What evaluation is and why it is important

First, let us distinguish between monitoring and evaluation. Most lead coaches seek to monitor activity: keeping track of how many live coaching relationships there are (including how many coaches have no clients), how many individual sessions are taking place and how many assignments there have been over the year. If you have invested in coach management software, this sort of information should be available to you at the click of a mouse. That is monitoring. Evaluation is about outcomes: analysing the impact of those coaching relationships on the individual client and more widely on the team or business. Ideally, you need to keep track of both levels of activity and what impact the coaching is having.

Why is evaluating your coaching service important?

Research undertaken by the CIPD (2010) found that only thirty-six per cent of the participants in their study were evaluating their coaching. They sent out a strong message, saying that for sustained investment, organisations *must* evaluate. One excellent general reason is performance. McBain et al. (2012) found that higher

DOI: 10.4324/9781003519911-13

performing organisations evaluate their leadership development provision to a greater degree than poorer performing ones.

Carter et al. (2005) looked at examples of how organisations have gone about evaluating their coaching and identified three basic categories of evaluation. Organisations were seeking to prove something, improve something or learn something.

Proving something

Lead coaches need evidence that the coaching pool is fulfilling the purpose for which it was set up. It is the only way that you can be sure that your coaches, and the overall coaching service, are doing a good job. There is an expectation that the coaching will be effective. You probably already hear stories from coaching clients or their managers that reinforce that belief but that is not the same thing as solid evidence.

It is desirable to be able to demonstrate to sponsors, funders or your steering group that the organisation's money is being spent to good effect. Even if you were not asked to provide a business case at the outset, you could still be asked for one in the future and it is good to be ready. A steering group would normally expect a regular report with a summary of activity but some evaluation data would be even better, even if it is only at the level of client self-reporting.

Having the metrics can help you to prove that your internal coaching resource provides equal or better value for money than sourcing coaching externally.

Improving something

Lead coaches need to know what is working well and what would make it even better. Evaluating should help you to find out how good your coaches are or if there is any 'refresher' training needed, or if you need to provide a broader range of CPD for your coaches.

Learning something

Lead coaches also need to build up a picture of what issues are coming up in the coaching conversations in case there are some common themes that might benefit from a concerted effort or special initiative across the organisation.

An evaluation undertaken within the NHS (Mortlock & Carter, 2012) used a pre-coaching questionnaire to ask clients about the benefits they expected and what topics they intended to focus on. This data was compared with the results of a post-coaching questionnaire to establish whether the benefits actually materialised. It also provided useful aggregated information on the kinds of issues that the clients said they wanted to work on. Finally, it provided some insight into systemic issues and was used to improve (or make more focused) leadership development interventions.

If you find that a significant volume of the coaching goals chosen by your managers relate to, say, coping with long hours, burn-out, poor work-life balance and stress, then there is likely a systemic issue that needs attention. Post-pandemic, with employees often working from home for part or all of the time, many organisations are reporting that staff are feeling anxious, disengaged, and unconfident about dealing with face-to-face interactions. Analysis – at an aggregate level to maintain confidentiality – of your clients' coaching goals and evaluation of whether they are meeting them can provide you with both valuable organisational intelligence and evidence of the value of the coaching.

The following case study shows how looking closely at the data helped one organisation.

Case study

Using evaluation to inform wellbeing strategy

One international NGO, operating in fragile states around the world, found that their coaches were regularly reporting that their clients, who were often working away from their families for long periods of time, seemed to be hovering on the borderline between stress and real anxiety. It was so much part of the culture to 'grin and bear it' that clients felt that it would be taken as a sign of weakness if they asked for professional help. The lead coach included this evaluation finding in a report to the head of HR. As a result, a pilot project was set up introducing a small, peripatetic counselling team in one region of the world in conjunction with a message from the CEO to say how important it was that staff paid attention to their health and wellbeing. The very positive feedback from the pilot resulted in the introduction of counselling teams in every region around the world.

Why might you not evaluate?

Most organisations do not evaluate the impact of their coaching service, so what are the arguments against? You may have started off small, with two or three internal coaches, and feel that a brief regular check-in with your coaches and their clients is sufficient. One organisation in Snape's (2012) research said:

> "we made a decision not to get too involved in measuring effectiveness because it is so difficult to do - we prefer to spend the money on making our coaches better". (p. 36)

Some lead coaches feel so busy delivering coaching and managing the service that making time for formal evaluation is unrealistic. They feel that they know that the coaching is valuable from oral feedback from the clients and clients' line managers and that is good enough for them. They do not feel the need for quantitative data to tell them what they "already know".

There are risks, though, to disregarding evaluation. What if your coaching champion leaves the organisation or economic conditions demand deep cuts in non-core expenditure? You may be required to demonstrate the value of your coaching service to someone with no experience of coaching and its benefits. Can you immediately answer the question: "What value has your internal coaching scheme been delivering for the organisation?" For the future of the service, if no other, it is desirable to gather some basic metrics even if your sponsor does not currently ask for any. Evaluation need not be complicated or expensive but it does involve expenditure of thought and energy.

Deciding what to evaluate

Let us say that you have decided to evaluate the impact of your coaching service. What next? This is the point where having a strategy and a clear purpose for the coaching (see Chapter 7) is helpful because: 'if you don't know where you're going, how will you know if you've got there?'. In your strategy, you may already have defined some success measures. If so, they will be your starting point but, if you haven't, this is the moment to do some work on them. Are you seeking, by coaching parents who have returned to work after parental leave, to raise retention levels? Are you coaching managers from marginalised groups in order to increase their representation at senior levels? Do you want to see if leadership coaching for middle managers in your talent pool is actually leading to more home-grown senior managers and directors than in previous years? If so, your measures will flow naturally.

Here are some factors to consider from an individual, team and organisational perspective.

Table 11.1 Factors to consider when measuring the effectiveness of your coaching

Individual	Team	Organisation
• Skill development & competency growth	• Improved collaboration & communication	• Alignment with strategic goals and outcomes, e.g., revenue & efficiency
• Increased confidence & self-efficacy	• Enhanced problem-solving & innovation	• Increased employee engagement & retention
• Career progression & role satisfaction	• Higher team performance & productivity	• Stronger coaching culture & leadership pipeline
• Behavioural change & mindset shifts	• Strengthened trust & psychological safety	• ROI on coaching programmes
• Goal achievement & performance metrics	• Greater accountability & shared ownership	• Organisational commitment to wellbeing
• Emotional resilience & stress management	• Better collective wellbeing & work-life balance	• Diversity, equity & inclusion outcomes
• Sense of belonging & inclusion	• EDI awareness & inclusive team dynamics	

It is helpful to establish a baseline so that you can demonstrate what progress you have made. Ideally, you can gather data about what is happening now (e.g., retention rates, promotion rates) in order to measure any changes further down the track. A clear purpose and a baseline are a really helpful start to calculating variations in the metrics at an organisational level.

If you want to take a structured approach, then try to develop some success measures at the outset and evaluate against them, recognising that this may be easier to do for some levels of outcome (organisational) than others (personal). You may be offering personal development coaching to your talent pool and, in real life, an individual's goals can be vague and difficult to measure, e.g., 'get on better with my boss', 'feel more confident' or 'make more of a personal impact'. Also, the purpose of your coaching service may change over time, so you will need to be alert to that and adapt your measures accordingly.

When you are at the thinking stage about what you are going to evaluate and how, it is worth considering who needs the data and why? Are you seeking to persuade someone of something? Or give someone a level of reassurance? The reason for the evaluation will dictate what kind of information you decide to gather and in what form. Your position in the accountability chain will also have a bearing on your approach to evaluation. You may, in effect, tell your sponsor(s) or steering committee what kind of evaluation data you are going to give them, or you may need to mould your approach to suit your sponsor.

One lead coach from a professional services organisation said that the information he collected depended on "how much the sponsor liked data". His first sponsor wanted to hear anecdotes, such as what the partners were saying about the coaches, perceptions of the credibility of the coaches and some quotations from coaching clients of what they had gained from the experience. That was good enough for him. His successor, on the other hand, wanted a spreadsheet with numbers of clients seen, numbers of clients achieving their coaching goals, numbers of clients getting through promotion boards and retention figures. It was 'horses for courses'. A mixture of hard metrics plus qualitative information such as quotations, testimonials or case studies to bring the metrics to life can often hit the spot. Testimonials can usefully serve three purposes:

a Provide authentic, tangible proof of the effectiveness of coaching, making it more appealing to potential clients.
b Highlight specific improvements in employee performance, leadership skills, or workplace morale, thus showcasing measurable benefits.
c Decision-makers are more likely to invest in coaching when they read about employees' positive experiences and success stories.

Knowing at an early stage what kind of evaluation you are planning is important if it involves input from your coaches and their clients. If you want the clients, say, to complete a post-coaching questionnaire – probably sent out from the centre – you need to tell your coaches and they need to tell their clients, during their contracting conversation, what data will be collected, how it will be shared and used, and to whom any results will be reported (McDowall & Lai, 2024). You may be wanting clients to complete a pre-coaching questionnaire too about what benefits they expect and what goals they want to pursue so that you can compare that with the results of a post-coaching questionnaire. If so, you will need to alert your coaches to that process and maybe offer guidance about the best way of making goals SMART, with measurable outcomes, if that is what you want.

None of this is to say that you cannot introduce evaluation months or years after your coaching pool has been set up. It is just easier to embed at the outset. In the following story, a very simple evaluation approach was introduced, six years after the inception of the coaching scheme.

Harriet's story

Collecting the minimum, but still valuable, data

Harriet took over an internal coaching pool, numbering 40 internal coaches, in a large legal firm in 2023. The coaches in the pool had an excellent reputation, and it had been well run by her 'hands-on' predecessor, who had set it up in 2017. She had no team to support her, and her predecessor had failed to convince her boss to invest in an electronic coach management system, so all the matching of coaches and clients was done by her and recorded on a spreadsheet. The monitoring was done monthly by contacting each coach individually by email – a very time-consuming process – but there was no evaluation data. Harriet had big plans for the pool, including more supervision and CPD for the coaches, expanding the pool and building them into a proper coaching community.

Harriet's previous job had been in a firm that took evaluation of the coaching service seriously, so she was keen to do some data gathering but had very little time to devote to it. She decided to start by collecting, quarterly, the absolute minimum, i.e.,

- How many coaches were active during the quarter
- How many coaching relationships were active at the end of the quarter
- How many hours each coach had delivered during the quarter
- What proportion of the coaches had no clients during the quarter

To capture the impact, a post-coaching questionnaire was sent to every client at the end of an assignment, requesting a score on a five-point Likert scale against three statements:

- The coaching was a beneficial use of my time.
  (1 Strongly Agree, 2 Agree, 3 Undecided, 4 Disagree, 5 Strongly Disagree)

- I made satisfactory progress on my coaching goals.
  (1 Strongly Agree, 2 Agree, 3 Undecided, 4 Disagree, 5 Strongly Disagree)
- I would recommend coaching to a colleague.
  (1 Strongly Agree, 2 Agree, 3 Undecided, 4 Disagree, 5 Strongly Disagree)

Harriet limited the questions to three because she had very limited time for analysis but the data that she gathered was so positive – consistently over 90% of '1' scores across all three statements – that she successfully persuaded her line manager to invest in a coach management system thus freeing up her time for more ambitious work expanding and developing the pool.

Using the Kirkpatrick-Phillips evaluation model to refine your approach

Coaching is all about facilitating learning for the client and the most widely used model to evaluate learning interventions is Kirkpatrick's (1994). Phillips (1996) expanded Kirkpatrick's model of the four levels of evaluation to include a fifth stage of Return on Investment (ROI). We have adapted these five stages to focus on the impact of coaching.

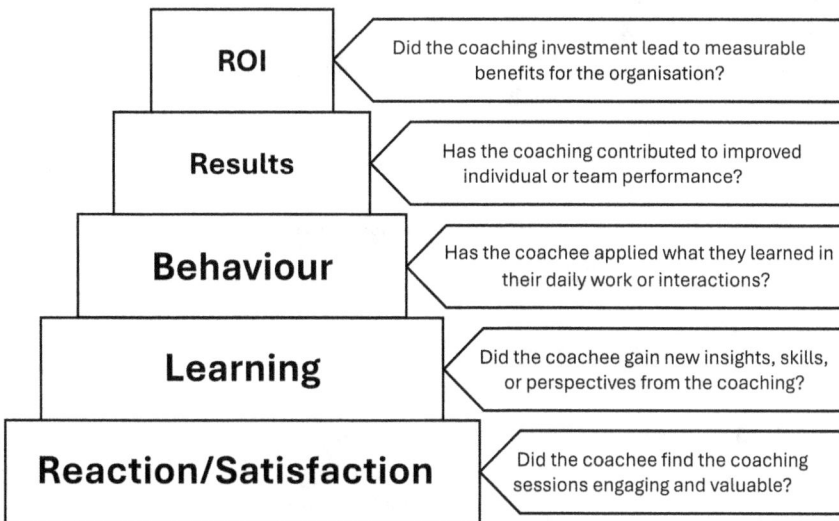

ROI — Did the coaching investment lead to measurable benefits for the organisation?

Results — Has the coaching contributed to improved individual or team performance?

Behaviour — Has the coachee applied what they learned in their daily work or interactions?

Learning — Did the coachee gain new insights, skills, or perspectives from the coaching?

Reaction/Satisfaction — Did the coachee find the coaching sessions engaging and valuable?

Figure 11.1 Kirkpatrick-Phillips model adapted to evaluate internal coaching programmes.

The Kirkpatrick-Phillips model proposes evaluation at five different levels: Reaction (Level 1), Learning (Level 2), Behaviour (Level 3), Results (Level 4) and Return on Investment (ROI) (Level 5).

Level 1: reaction

This level measures what the client's response is to the coaching. What did they think and feel about it? Key questions could include:

- Was the coaching process engaging and valuable?
- Did clients feel supported and comfortable with their coach?
- Did they achieve their objectives?
- Did their coach accommodate their personal learning style?
- What worked well and what worked less well for them?

Feedback is generally collected through a questionnaire or interview immediately after the coaching to assess satisfaction.

Level 2: learning

This level evaluates the skills, knowledge or personal insights gained through coaching. It could focus on improved leadership abilities or communication skills; increased self-awareness, emotional intelligence or problem-solving capabilities; new approaches to handling challenges or decision-making; improved ability to manage change, time, stress or complex situations; higher levels of self-confidence or better working relationships.

Assessments could include reflective journals, self-assessments, 360-degree feedback or input from the coach. Most commonly, clients are asked to complete a questionnaire asking what they have learned.

The following case study describes a process using a questionnaire for completion by clients to get Level 1 feedback followed by a further questionnaire to try to gain some Level 2 feedback. The piece includes an additional, interesting idea of asking both coaches and clients what had happened to them since the coaching.

Case study

Evaluation by questionnaire

In 2020, a Government agency with 1,400 employees launched an internal coaching service. By 2023, the number of active coaches, trained to ILM5 level, had settled at around 20 and the agency had invested in a coach management platform. Every coach built a personal profile and potential clients could browse the profiles, insert their coaching goals and select their own coach.

The platform automatically sent an evaluation form to the client after the final coaching session, then another three months later. These were the questions on the two forms.

Level 1: *Reaction* First evaluation form

- The frequency of meetings was satisfactory (on a scale from 1 to 10).
- How effective were these sessions in terms of supporting the achievement of your goals? Please rate the quality (on a scale from 1 to 10).
- Reflecting on your recent coaching experience, were your initial goals met? If you responded 'Yes', to what extent were they met? If you responded 'No' or 'Partially', what do you believe contributed to this?
- Reflecting on your experience, would you recommend coaching to colleagues?
- Would your goals have been met if you had not accessed a coach?
- What one word would you use to describe your coaching experience?

Level 2: *Learning* Second evaluation form

- Looking back, what impact has the coaching had on you and the contribution you make to the agency?
- When you reflect on your overall contribution to the agency since accessing the coaching, have you noticed anything different? Can you provide any examples?
- If you had not accessed a coach, what would have happened?
- Have you regularly discussed your progress with your manager?
- Do you consider the coaching a worthwhile investment of your time?

Completion rate of the initial evaluation form over the first two years was 72% and the results provided strong evidence for the positive impact of the coaching. Few clients, however, responded to the questionnaire sent three months later despite reminders. Those that did, reported increased confidence, securing a promotion and having a better understanding of what they could achieve.

In April 2024, the lead coach decided to conduct some 'destination tracking', i.e., exploring what had changed for both coaches and clients who had been in coaching relationships over the previous three years.

She discovered that over half the coaches had been promoted. They said that their experience of being a coach had contributed to their promotion as they felt more confident and handled themselves differently in the interview. In addition, nearly a quarter of the coaching clients had been promoted. They felt the coaching had contributed to their promotion saying that the coach had empowered them to seek out opportunities, they had gained in confidence and they had learnt techniques to manage the stress of the interview.

Learning

The lead coach felt that the post assignment questionnaire provided useful data to evidence the value of the coaching but the jury was still out on the value of sending the second questionnaire. The destination tracking data, while time-consuming to collect and analyse, felt really worthwhile.

Level 3: behaviour

This level measures the extent to which the clients apply what they have learned so that their behaviour visibly shifts. Examples of behavioural changes could be improved performance or leadership on specific tasks or projects; enhanced ability to manage teams, resolve conflicts, or handle stress; adoption of new strategies for time management or improved communication style or working relationships.

A 'before and after' 360 feedback report is used in some leadership development programmes to try to capture such changes. The 'after' 360 questionnaire is often administered three to six months after the coaching has finished. In many coaching programmes, feedback from the line manager provides the main evidence for behaviour change.

If there are no changes in behaviour, this does not necessarily mean that no learning has taken place. It could mean that the individual has chosen not to apply it yet, or the context has made it difficult for them to apply it.

Level 4: results

This level focuses on the organisational impact of the coaching programme (you could choose to look at the impact on a unit/division rather than the whole organisation). It evaluates whether the coaching has led to measurable outcomes aligned with organisational goals, such as increased employee engagement or morale, higher team productivity or improved collaboration or improved retention rates for high-potential employees.

As with level 3, level 4 assumes a causal link between the coaching and any perceived changes in the client plus a causal link between the client's impact and any perceived change in the organisation. Often, the question being asked is 'What impact on the business has a cohort of people (who were all being coached) achieved?' These outcomes can be measured using key performance indicators, employee surveys and HR metrics. The next two case studies both involve utilising data already being gathered by the organisation.

Case study

Evaluation using existing HR metrics (1)

In 2022, a large accountancy firm, which had trained 150 internal coaches over a ten-year period, decided to conduct a systematic evaluation of the coaching delivered. It became apparent that relevant data already existed across various HR systems.

The evaluation used the existing HR data and compared it with information collected on coaching relationships. An analysis was conducted comparing a variety of outcomes for employees who had completed coaching (400 employees over a 3-year period) with those who hadn't (4600 employees). The study looked at three aspects:

- Performance (using employees' annual performance ratings).
- Promotion rates.
- Attrition/retention rates.

All three measures showed better outcomes for the employees who had been coached. They were:

- 40% more likely to achieve a higher performance rating.
- Just over 50% more likely to be promoted.
- And retention had marginally improved.

Case study

Evaluation using existing HR metrics (2)

For many years, a multinational telecoms company conducted six monthly employee engagement surveys, sent to all staff, involving 60 statements to gauge staff engagement and wellbeing. Examples were: "When decisions are made in my team, we think carefully about the impact they will have on our customers" and "I feel comfortable voicing challenges to our current ways of thinking, even when bringing up tough issues".

In 2022, during a period of significant change within the company, they began providing coaching to their senior leaders, consisting of six 1:1

sessions. In order to evaluate the coaching's impact, results from the Employee Engagement surveys for a sample of 61 leaders who had received coaching were compared with those for 56 managers who did not receive coaching. Considerable thought was put into selecting the control group of 'like-for-like' managers (e.g., same country, same level in the hierarchy). Members of both the 'coached' and 'not-coached' groups had to have been working in the company for at least two years to provide a baseline of data.

Six to 12 months after the coaching had been completed, an analysis was conducted to see what had changed for both the coached and not-coached groups. The questions focused on team member engagement, purpose and observations of managers taking action. The results were very positive. Coaching was found to have a significant impact on the teams of the managers who received it. Despite its being a period when the organisation was transforming, coached managers increased their team engagement scores, while managers who were not coached experienced a decline in their teams' engagement results. Notably, team members of coached managers reported a 9% increase in their 'manager action-taking' in the engagement results, while teams with managers who did not receive coaching saw a 9% decrease in action-taking by their managers. This 18% gap between the two groups was statistically significant. Team Purpose and Engagement saw similar trends. Also, coached managers felt that their job competence had improved by an average of 31% (their managers perceived an 11% increase).

Notably, 16.7% of the coached managers were promoted or progressed vs. a global all-employee average of 11.3% – a significant increase.

Learning

The lead coach had observed that leaders can experience 'assessment fatigue' from being expected to complete surveys for many different purposes. Being able to use existing data was very positive. She felt that it was particularly valuable to have conducted the evaluation when there was a lot of change in the company – when you might have expected leaders to be under a lot of pressure or feeling unsettled. Another thing that she was pleased about was putting thought into who to include in the control group. It gave the company real confidence in the reliability of the results.

Level 5: return on investment (ROI)

In principle, the ROI level calculates the financial value of the coaching programme. This involves comparing the costs of the coaching initiative (e.g., coach training and time investment) with measurable benefits, such as cost savings from improved efficiency or reduced turnover, increased revenue from better decision-making or innovation and avoidance of costs associated with poor leadership or disengaged employees.

For example, if a coaching programme helped reduce staff turnover by 10%, the savings from avoiding recruitment and onboarding costs could be factored into the ROI calculation. Nevertheless, this is much easier said than done! Heroic assumptions have to be made about causation to put a financial number on something like 'increased revenue from better decision-making'. There has always been a dearth of research into successful return on investment calculations for coaching programmes and, nowadays, ROI is more often translated into non-financial returns like improved wellbeing or staff engagement. These can be measured through a variety of HR surveys (e.g., an employee engagement survey) conducted annually in many organisations, which can be disaggregated to unit or divisional level. As Passmore and Shi (2023) say, when posing ten questions that organisations should ask of external coaching providers:

> "[Evaluation] should move beyond client satisfaction scores and include organisation metrics reflecting the nature of the coaching programmes, such as wellbeing, leadership development or performance metrics".

The final section in this chapter discusses ROI in more depth.

Approaches to gathering data

Assembling data to provide evidence for the five Kirkpatrick-Phillips levels involves three broad approaches:

1 Collecting information from the coaching client
2 Widening the scope to ask others to provide feedback
3 Gathering evidence at a divisional or organisational level.

Collecting information from the coaching client

In practice, evaluation is generally confined to this first level (McDowall & Lai, 2024). Most commonly, organisations ask clients to complete a survey at the end of the assignment and coach management systems often automatically send these out. However, completing the questionnaire can slip to the bottom of the client's priorities once the coaching is finished. With this in mind, some lead coaches either interview the client themselves, taking them through a series of questions, or ask the coach to do so in the final session and then feed the answers back into the system.

Drawbacks to asking the coach to do this are that clients often find it hard to be objective or completely honest when they are in the presence of the coach, particularly when the fact that it is the final session may involve emotion. In a successful coaching assignment, the coach and client will have built a close relationship, so it is natural for the client to want to be complimentary.

They may find it easier to be objective if completing a questionnaire by themselves or talking to the lead coach.

It can be helpful to point out in the preamble to any questionnaire that the questions are largely being asked in the cause of learning, so that the programme can be improved and the coaches can develop.

Questionnaires seeking to capture Kirkpatrick-Phillips's Levels One and Two information (the client's reaction and what they think they have learned) are particularly common, but it only takes a few more questions to try to capture data about behaviours (Level Three) and contribution to the organisation (Level Four). The following sorts of questions can do the job:

1 What were your goals?
2 What did you learn during the coaching?
3 What are you doing differently as a result?
4 What are the key benefits that you have gained? For example, do you have any greater awareness of how you come across to people? Are you approaching anything differently from how you did before?
5 What benefits has the organisation gained? For example, is there any improvement in your effectiveness or delivery of challenging targets that you can attribute to the coaching?
6 How has the coaching contributed to the broader work of your team or the organisation?

To access "Evaluation template: An example", use the QR Code on page 3.

An approach that yields more data, but is much more demanding of the client, is to ask them at the beginning of the assignment to consider and complete a form that covers such things as:

• These are my coaching goals.
• This is how they will link to my business objectives.
• These are my success measures.
• This is how my changes in behaviour will be measured.
• These are the potential business benefits.
• These are the potential benefits to my personal development.

At the end of the coaching assignment, the client can then self-score against their pre-coaching criteria, and these scores can be fed into the system to provide data which can be aggregated. To assess the impact of the coaching even better, you could ask the question: "What percentage of the change would you attribute to the coaching?"

However, even at this level of sophistication, there are clearly limitations to a process confined to 'self-report' scoring. Not only is it hard for the client to be objective about some things but they may be natural optimists or pessimists, or feel an obligation to demonstrate that they benefited from the organisation's investment in them. This may result in bias (and you may have noticed, in the case study earlier on in this chapter, the difference in the 'self-rated' scores compared with those made by the client's line manager).

Goals

Goal setting certainly lends itself to an evaluative approach but goals are not every-thing. Megginson (2008) writes rather poignantly of the chief executive of an NHS trust saying to his coach:

> "I don't have to set targets in these meetings, do I? It will be such a boon just to look at what is happening at work and have some time to think about it. Is that okay?" (p. 2)

In the increasingly demanding work environment, coaching sessions may be the only time when clients can get away from targets and goals and be able to reflect on what they are doing. Do not assume, therefore, that every coaching assignment must be goal-oriented. It would be a pity if a desire to evaluate were to be translated automatically into a goals-driven approach.

Timing

The full value of coaching may not become apparent for some months. Any attitude shift, for example, will take a while to settle and for the full impact to materialise. To reflect this, some organisations ask the client to complete a questionnaire im-mediately after the coaching programme and then again six to nine months later to capture whether the change has been maintained.

Widening the scope to ask others to provide feedback

Requesting feedback from third parties, in particular from the client's line man-ager, provides another layer to any evaluation. The questions above, about goals linked to business objectives, success measures, behaviour changes and busi-ness benefits, would benefit from being discussed and agreed with the client's line manager in any initial three-way meeting. They can provide the basis for feedback at the end of the coaching from the client's line manager and a joint scoring of the client's progress at any concluding three-way meeting. Another, less time-consuming, approach is simply to send the closing questionnaire to both the client and the line manager. There will then be two different sets of scores rather than agreed scores – interesting in their own right – though it might mean that a useful opportunity for direct feedback from the line manager to the client is lost.

Involving third parties is particularly helpful for measuring changes in behav-iour (Kirkpatrick-Phillips Level 3). And do not forget the coach. Even if they work in a different part of the organisation and never see the client performing in a work setting, they may well have observed differences in the course of an assignment, particularly if one of the goals has been around personal impact.

Seeing a shy client approach for a final session making strong eye contact, smiling confidently, and shaking hands firmly was one of Katharine's happiest coaching moments!

The following case study shows the value of including third-party input when evaluating behaviour change. It was carried out by a researcher using sophisticated statistical techniques, but the principle holds good for less complex evaluations. Two interesting outcomes were, first, that the sponsors gave lower scores to the perceived behaviour changes than the participants did, thus underlining the usefulness of third-party input and, secondly, that involving sponsors in this particular evaluation resulted in increased engagement in the coaching process by the clients.

Case study

Third-party input into evaluation

A pilot coaching programme was set up in twenty-four local councils across the North West and Eastern regions of England to determine whether coaching might contribute to improvements in strategic thinking, and to corporate leadership, among senior HR professionals. A comprehensive approach to evaluation included an end-of-programme impact questionnaire for participants, their coaches, and their organisation sponsors (typically the CEO) that sought information relating to the perceived and actual impact of the coaching along three key dimensions: personal effectiveness, HR function leadership, and strategic thinking and corporate leadership.

They used a Likert scale questionnaire to score behavioural changes and the results included:

- Along all impact dimensions, and for all items, "positive responses were found for all the evaluation groups". So there was agreement that changes in behaviour had taken place.
- Participants consistently rated the extent of change much higher than their sponsors did on fifteen of the nineteen assessment items. Sponsors did rate the impact of the coaching positively along all of the items, but to a lesser extent than the participants.
- Participants whose sponsors took the trouble to complete the evaluation were more engaged in the process than those whose sponsors did not. The implication for coaching was that "we can be confident that engagement on all sides, not merely from participant and coach, is vital to the overall success of the programme".

This case study is an abridged version of one that appeared in Carter, Wolfe and Kerrin (2005), by kind permission of the authors.

360-degree feedback

Another way of involving colleagues is using a 360-degree feedback instrument. Katharine once coached several cohorts of participants on a government leadership development programme where the clients and their colleagues (line managers, peers and staff) completed a 360-degree feedback questionnaire both before and after the programme. The results of the pre-programme feedback played an important role in helping the clients to identify what issues to work on, and the post-programme feedback gave them a fix on what progress they had made. Even though, inevitably, there were changes in personnel – the client sometimes moved roles or a significant proportion of their 'raters' did - the clients nevertheless found that it made a very useful input to their development. It was also a good way of bringing additional voices into the coaching room.

Data collected at organisational level

Information gathered at an organisational or divisional level can play more than one role in evaluation. Sometimes it can be used to shed light on the impact that coaching may have had on an individual leader's management of their team. Or, if the entire leadership cadre in the organisation or a particular division's leadership team receives coaching, then more effective leadership can show up in the perceived leadership scores in an organisational climate survey. You might reasonably ask: "But how do you know if any increased scores can be attributed to the coaching?" Organisations tend to be more relaxed about causal links than an academic researcher might be. One HR Director said, "It's generally agreed that any changes in how leaders are viewed, if they have received coaching in between, can be partly attributed to the coaching".

Carter and Peterson (2010) suggest using metrics that your organisation already gathers (an approach used in two of the case studies earlier in this chapter). Consider what surveys are conducted and what statistics are habitually collected. Can they be adapted for your purposes, could they be broken down to a level that could be useful to you or could you add a few helpful questions to the next iteration of a survey? Metrics that may be readily available and can be useful include employee turnover, productivity, morale, sickness absence, promotion rates for women and ethnic minority staff, customer satisfaction, staff complaints, retention figures, applications for internal vacancies and performance ratings.

An alternative is to conduct a specific piece of research to test out whether the coaching has had an impact at the organisational level. For example, if your coaching programme has been targeting an organisational problem around poor performance review meetings by senior managers (by coaching them to, for example, hold difficult conversations and give more thoughtful developmental feedback) then you could do some research into the quality of the paperwork produced before and after the coaching and/or monitor the number of appeals made by staff disagreeing with their performance reports, if such a process exists in your organisation. If you conduct a regular staff survey, an alternative approach with this same example could be to add some new questions or use a one-off 'pulse survey' to check things out. You could include a question about staff's views of the quality of appraisal meetings and see if scores rise after the coaching. Or specifically target coaching on managers in one division of the organisation and see if the scores in that division rise.

Something mentioned by Yedreshteyn (2008) is the importance, when evaluating the overall service, of requesting feedback from clients who drop out of the process. Post-coaching questionnaires are often only filled in by clients who complete all the sessions, so the voices of those who dropped out can be unintentionally excluded.

A very effective, though time-consuming, way of evaluating the impact of a coaching intervention is to undertake a comparison between a group of clients who have received coaching and another group who have not. The case study below is another example that uses a control group.

Case study

Evaluating coaching for employee wellbeing

In March 2020, Alison Carter from the Institute of Employment Studies (IES) was invited to evaluate the impact of a virtual personalised coaching service in primary care across England. Coaching was being introduced to support the wellbeing of front-line primary care workers as they responded to the pandemic and its aftermath.

Over the period April 2020 to July 2021, an evaluation was carried out through a survey deployed on three occasions: before and immediately after coaching plus a follow-up some months later. Thirty interviews were also undertaken.

Changes in perceived wellbeing and resilience were measured using the short Warwick-Edinburgh Mental Wellbeing Scale (SWEMWBS) and brief resilience coping scale (BRCS), respectively. For analysis, a matched sample approach was selected, identifying individuals whose results could be compared at different time points. This is different from simply taking aggregate analysis at time points that may not be of the same individuals. All three surveys were completed by 261 people who had been coached and 195 who had not.

The findings provided compelling evidence for the effectiveness of the coaching in improving employee wellbeing. Specific findings were:

- Following coaching, there was a significant increase in staff wellbeing and resilience. By contrast, staff who were not coached experienced a deterioration in both.

- Although wellbeing scores declined between post-coaching and follow-up, scores at follow-up remained higher than they had been prior to the coaching.
- Just one 45-minute coaching session resulted in wellbeing and resilience improvements (although multiple sessions gave rise to greater improvements).
- The more employees' wellbeing increased, the less likely they were to have an intention of leaving the organisation.

The results informed tweaks to the programme including encouraging people to book more than one session. Results were also presented as part of a successful business case for continued funding and the programme won a health sector award for 'Best Workforce Initiative 2021'.

The coaching programme ultimately ran from April 2020 to March 2024 with 8,914 staff coached including general practitioners, dentists, pharmacists, optometrists, and their colleagues at all levels. Periodic survey analysis continued at six-monthly intervals to monitor if the coaching was continuing to deliver results for new clients. Findings showed the coaching was equally as effective at improving wellbeing and resilience regardless of when the coaching began.

One of the challenges in designing the evaluation approach was thinking from the outset about what the audience for the results would find credible. In this case it was decided to include a comparison group (of staff not coached) to provide senior leaders with confidence that the improvements found in the data were not the result of other factors.

Demonstrating return on investment (ROI)

When seeking justification for investing money in a project, budget holders often look for a calculation of the expected ROI. The standard method for calculating it is subtracting the estimated costs of the coaching from the estimated value of the benefits/outcomes of the coaching and then expressing the difference as a percentage of the costs.

Costs

For an internal coaching service, the costs could include the salaries of the administrators, training the coaches, providing external supervision (or training up internal supervisors), sourcing CPD and visiting speakers, developing, buying or leasing a coach management system and small items like refreshments for coaching events.

Carter (2013) reported that when she undertook notional cost exercises for client organisations, and asked lead coaches to work out a figure for the cost per coaching engagement, very different numbers were produced depending on whom she asked and what they perceived as a cost. Two regional lead coaches from the same organisation both included supervision and CPD costs but one also worked out the opportunity cost of the coaches' time spent coaching rather than delivering on the day job (using average salary costs for a 'typical coach'). Should you also include the opportunity costs of the coach taking time to prepare for sessions and to reflect afterwards? Or neither? And what about the time taken for CPD and supervision?

Something worth bearing in mind is the negative impact on an ROI calculation of having spare capacity, i.e., trained coaches with no clients. The costs involved in training and supporting them have to be spread across the whole scheme even though there are no matching benefits, which underlines the importance of keeping your coaches active.

One tip from a lead coach is to capture and track every single cost associated with the coaching service from day one. If you are working full-time managing the coaching, then are you going to include your own salary in the calculation? Costs like travel expenses for visiting speakers, refreshments for coaching events and salary costs would normally come out of different budgets so make sure that you track them all. Jo Holliday, ROI evaluation specialist at abdi ltd., pointed out that a negative return is common in the first year of rolling out programmes. This is because evaluation measures are based on the first year after the programme, with no time for benefits to mitigate your initial outlay (Soulsby, 2012).

Benefits

Putting a financial value on the benefits of coaching poses considerable difficulties. If someone gains confidence and gets the promotion they deserve, what is the monetary value to the organisation? If someone starts delegating better and working ten-hour days rather than twelve-hour days, thus seeing more of her husband and children, feeling less stressed and shouting less at her staff (who are feeling happier too and more fulfilled because their work is more interesting), what monetary value should be attached? What if that more effective delegation results in some of her staff being busier and more stressed themselves and they decide to leave? What is the value then?

It can be hard to prove that causal link between the impact of coaching on an individual and financial results for the business. Sarah Jones, Group Head of Leadership Development at Standard Chartered (quoted in Hawkins & Schwenk, 2006) clearly had no such doubts when she commented:

> "We are keen to ensure that employees receive individual attention and development. This results in higher staff engagement and we see the results in stronger business performance and lower employee turnover". (p. 18)

It can be difficult, however, to establish precise business benefits which can be directly attributed to the coaching of an individual client.

When internal coaches work in the public sector, with no bottom line, it is even more difficult to ascribe a monetary value to the benefits. What if a senior civil servant in the diplomatic service is being coached around her relationship-building and negotiation skills, which results in a successful diplomatic alliance being formed with likely long-term political and economic benefits? The civil servant may ascribe thirty per cent of the result to the impact on her of the coaching, but thirty per cent of what?

A less complex approach to proving financial value, with fewer imponderables, is to work out a notional figure for the cost per internal coaching session, taking into account all the costs outlined above, then to compare it with the cost per session charged by external coaches. In a snapshot survey in 2021, average external executive coaching rates in the UK came in at around £265 per hour (Passmore, 2021), which can act as a useful comparator.

In 2012, the BBC worked out that their internal coaching sessions cost £50 per hour (Macann, 2012), after taking into account two full-time staff managing the coaching programme, the costs of in-house training, CPD and accreditation costs (they did not include opportunity costs). The internal coaching service had delivered, at that time, 600 programmes of ten hours of coaching. They took the lowest fee charged on the external coach list, multiplied it by 600 programmes of ten hours, and reported back the sizeable difference. If you try something similar, remember that there are central costs involved in the assessment, selection, administration, invoicing, and so forth of external coaches that could reasonably be taken into account too – not just their fees.

An alternative approach to ROI

The original concept of ROI was concerned purely with financial returns, but as Grant et al. (2010) pointed out, financial metrics are typically not the direct focus of coaching interventions. Evaluations of coaching nowadays concentrate more on other sorts of measurable returns to demonstrate impact. Grant (2012) argued that ROI is an unreliable measure of coaching outcomes anyway and that we do coaching a disservice by overly focusing on the financial outcomes. In addition, the concept of a third 'generation' of workplace coaching (Grant, 2017) puts the wellbeing of employees much more in the spotlight.

Evidence of positive impact on organisational priorities can instead come from metrics showing improvements in factors such as employee engagement, happiness scores, customer service feedback and organisational reputation amongst its competitors.

The bottom line is that coaching can help employees to be happier, more fulfilled and more productive; customers, clients and patients to receive better service, value and experiences; and the organisation to develop and thrive. The task is to find appropriate measures to prove it.

Both Grant (2012) and Hicks et al. (2012) have looked at wellbeing and staff engagement as alternative measures. Grant suggests focusing on them on the grounds that "organisations function better with mentally healthy employees who are engaged in their work activities". Hicks et al. cite a meta-analysis of Gallup studies by Harter et al. (2003) that showed that the:

"presence of positive workplace perceptions and feelings are associated with higher business-unit customer loyalty, higher profitability, higher productivity and lower rates of turnover". (p. 3)

Their own research revealed that coaching had a positive impact on both the way that the coaching clients worked and their feelings towards work and, specifically, that:

"coaching increased overall well-being scores both at work and in general by improving coachees' ability to feel relaxed, to feel useful and to think clearly. At work, the coaching also helped coachees to improve their ability to deal with problems well and to feel closer to other people". (p. 31)

How might you go about measuring non-financial benefits delivered by your coaching service? The case studies earlier in this chapter provide examples of measuring improvements in strategic thinking and corporate leadership, improvements in wellbeing and resilience, higher promotion rates and reduced attrition.

Only you know what you want to measure, based on your coaching strategy and the purpose for which the coaching service was set up, plus what metrics your organisation already collects regularly or that you might be able to compile without too much expenditure of time and energy.

There are many well-validated instruments that can be used to assess wellbeing, resilience, employee engagement and employee satisfaction and loyalty. Most are free but you may need to obtain permission to use them. They include:

Wellbeing

- Short Warwick-Edinburgh Mental Wellbeing Scale (SWEMWBS) (Tennant et al., 2007)
- Positive and Negative Affect Scale (PANAS) (Watson et al., 1988)
- Depression, Anxiety, and Stress Scales (Lovibond & Lovibond, 1995)

Resilience

- Brief Resilience Coping Scale (BRCS) (Sinclair & Wallston, 2004)

Staff engagement

- IES Employee Engagement Scale (Robinson et al., 2004)
- 12-item Gallup Q12 (Harter et al., 2003)
- Utrecht Work Engagement Scale (Schaufeli et al., 2006)

Employee satisfaction and loyalty

- Employee Net Promoter Score, or eNPS (Reichheld, 2006)

You might be thinking "where would I find the time and resource to use instruments such as these and analyse the results?" We have included them because while some of you will be fighting a battle to keep coaching alive in your organisation using minimal resources, others may have a well-established pool with good support and might see some benefit in trying your hand at some evaluation. Some organisations have successfully identified a local university offering a coaching Masters and asked if one of their students might be interested in conducting an evaluation for their research project. It is a route worth exploring.

Evaluation of team coaching

Clutterbuck and Graves (2024) describe team coaching as:

> "the newest member of the coaching family [which is] growing up fast but there remains plenty to learn about the process" (p. 296)

and point out that no study has yet looked at the costs and benefits of team coaching, compared with 1:1 coaching for each member of the team. They also describe current evaluation processes as 'embryonic' and 'anecdotal'. So far, practices involve rerunning surveys and questionnaires that have been used at the start of the assignment to demonstrate progress, feedback from team members and the intuition of team coaches based on specific moments or 'shifts' during sessions (Graves, 2021).

Some final tips:

- Be clear about what the purpose of your coaching is.
- Keep data collection as simple as you can.
- Consider your audience for the results you select and what data will be most relevant for them.
- Compare results from coached staff with a group of non-coached staff, if you can.
- A focus on impact gives you the evidence needed to write a successful business case for continued funding.
- Engage your coaches in support of your data gathering (and the reason for it) and keep them informed.
- Be transparent and seek consent from the clients before coaching begins.

Summary

This chapter signposted early CIPD research pointing out that while the use of coaching was steadily increasing, organisations were missing the opportunity to evaluate, thus failing to capture its value. It is essential to be able to demonstrate that coaching has lasting benefits because any successful internal coaching resource requires ongoing investment.

Applying the Kirkpatrick-Phillips model to internal coaching provides a structured way to assess the value of coaching at multiple levels. It ensures organisations move beyond subjective feedback and demonstrate the tangible benefits of coaching programmes and how they are strategically aligned with business objectives.

This chapter suggests a number of ways to collect data, evaluate the process and provide feedback about your internal coaching programme. Being able to articulate the tangible benefits and value that your internal coaching contributes, to those in the business who determine organisational priorities and control budgets, can be key to the sustainability of your internal coaching programme.

Table 11.2 Questions to reflect on

Why evaluate?

- What are the key reasons for evaluating coaching in your organisation?
- Can you use your steering group to help engage directors in supporting data collection and cascading learning from your evaluations?
- What do you need to prove?
- What do you want to improve?
- What would you like to learn?

What will you evaluate?

- How does the strategic purpose of your internal coaching service inform what you need to evaluate?
- What data do you need to collect?
- Which approach and methods will help you get the data you need?
- What needs to be covered in guidance for coaches, clients and line managers to explain their role in providing feedback?

Kirkpatrick/Phillips's five levels of evaluation

- Reaction: How will you capture data to find out whether coachees found the coaching sessions engaging and valuable?
- Learning: How will you capture data to find out whether coachees gained new insights, skills, or perspectives from the coaching?
- Behaviour: How will you capture data to find out whether coachees applied what they learned in their daily work or interactions?
- Results: How will you capture data to find out if the coaching contributed to improved individual or team performance?
- ROI: How will you capture data to find out if the coaching investment led to measurable benefits for the organisation?

Approaches to gathering data: Focusing on the client

- How do you collect honest and accurate feedback from recipients of your coaching service?
- What do you need to consider in terms of maintaining client confidentiality?
- How can you encourage clients to give honest feedback in situations where they like their coach but did not get a lot of value from the coaching relationship?
- If designing a questionnaire, what questions could you add to capture data about behaviours (Level 3) and contribution to the organisation (Level 4)?
- Would introducing a pre- and post-coaching questionnaire add value?
- When do you want clients to complete post-coaching evaluation? How can you balance the need to give clients time with the decreased likelihood of getting questionnaires returned as time passes?

(Continued)

Table 11.2 (Continued)

Approaches to gathering data: Feedback from colleagues and data at an organisational level

- Could you use three-way meetings with the client's line manager at the start and end of the coaching programme as the basis for evaluating progress?
- What information might you gather at an organisational or divisional level to inform your evaluation?
- Does your organisation regularly gather any metrics that could be useful in evaluating the coaching service? Could you use any existing surveys or add a few questions to, for example, an annual staff engagement survey?
- Could you conduct or commission a specific piece of research to test out whether the coaching has had an impact at an organisational level in order to demonstrate ROI?

Evaluating the coaching service

- How might you evaluate the overall coaching service?
- When evaluating the overall service, how could you collect information from clients who drop out during the coaching process and do not complete the post-coaching review?

Return on investment

- How would you estimate the cost of coaching? Would you include the opportunity cost of the coach's time? If relevant budgets are held by different departments, to whom would you speak to obtain accurate figures?
- How would you estimate the value of coaching outcomes? Whom would you need to engage in a discussion to get the business perspective?
- What alternatives to financial ROI might you consider? Could you link your evaluation to key organisational objectives, for example, increasing staff engagement or improving wellbeing?
- How could you resource the evaluation cheaply? Could you find a coaching Masters student to conduct it for you as part of their research project?

References

Advisory, Conciliation and Arbitration Service (ACAS). (2017). Published guidance on addressing unconscious bias in the workplace. https://www.acas.org.uk/improving-equality-diversity-and-inclusion/unconscious-bias

Allan, J., Passmore, J., & Mortimer, L. (2011). Coaching Ethics: Developing a model to enhance coaching practice. In: J. Passmore (Ed.), *Supervision in Coaching: Supervision, Ethics and Continuous Professional Development* (pp. 161–172). London: Kogan Page.

Athanasopoulou, A., & Dopson, S. (2018). A systematic review of executive coaching outcomes: Is it the journey or the destination that matters the most? *The Leadership Quarterly, 29*(1), 70–88.

Bajpai, B. (2024). Coaching in the digital age: Exploring digitalisation's impact on executive coaching: A theoretical framework and proposed agenda shift. *International Journal of Evidence Based Coaching and Mentoring, S18*, 3–15. doi:10.24384/z9r0-sj31

Barton, J. (2024a). *Guide to Supervision, episode 1.* https://www.britishschoolofcoaching.com/guide-to-supervision-ep-1/

Barton, J. (2024b). *Guide to Supervision, episode 2.* https://www.britishschoolofcoaching.com/guide-to-supervision-ep-2/

Biquet, M. (2021). *Ethical Dilemmas in Coaching Today: Coaching Professional Dilemmas Survey.* Accessible at: www.researchgate.net/publication/385806083_ETHICAL_DILEMMAS_IN_COACHING_TODAY_Coaching_professional_dilemmas_survey

Borders, D. (1992). Learning to think like a supervisor. *The Clinical Supervisor, 10*(2), 135–148.

Brook, J. (2015). 'Common Barriers to Coaching Culture', Strengthscope, 26 November. Available at: https://www.strengthscope.com/blog/common-barriers-coaching-culture-overcome

Brown, B. (2017). *Braving the Wilderness: The Quest for True Belonging and the Courage to Stand Alone.* New York: Random House.

Butwell, J. (2006). Group supervision for coaches: Is it worthwhile? A study of the process in a major professional organisation. *International Journal of Evidence Based Coaching and Mentoring, 4*, 43–53.

Campone, F. (2011). The reflective coaching practitioner model. In: J. Passmore (Ed.), *Supervision in Coaching: Supervision, Ethics and Continuous Professional Development* (pp. 11–29). London: Kogan Page.

Carroll, M., & Shaw, E. (2013). *Ethical Maturity in the Helping Professions: Making Difficult Life and Work Decisions.* London: Jessica Kingsley Publishers.

Carter, A. (2005). *Providing Coaching Internally: A Literature Review.* HR Network Paper MP43. Brighton: Institute of Employment Studies.

Carter, A. (2009). "Your best bet". *Coaching at Work, 4*(6), 46. www.coaching-at-work.com.

Carter, A. (2013). Conversation with Katharine St John-Brooks on 29 January 2013.

Carter, A., & Peterson, D. (2010). Evaluating coaching programmes. In: J. Passmore (Ed.), *Excellence in Coaching: The Industry Guide,* 2nd edition (pp. 228–239). London: Kogan Page.

Carter, A., Wolfe, H., & Kerrin, M. (2005). Employers and coaching evaluation. *International Journal of Coaching in Organizations, 3*(4), 63–72.

Charan, R., Drotter, S., & Noel, J., 2011. *The Leadership Pipeline: How to Build the Leadership-Powered Company.* 2nd edition. San Francisco: Jossey-Bass.

Childs, R., Woods, M., Willcock, D., & Man, A. (2011). Action learning supervision for coaches. In: J. Passmore (Ed.), *Supervision in Coaching: Supervision, Ethics and Continuous Professional Development* (pp. 31–43). London: Kogan Page.

CIPD. (2008). *Learning and Development Survey Report 2008.* London: Chartered Institute of Personnel and Development. Available at: https://trainingzone.co.uk/highlights-of-the-cipd-learning-and-development-survey-2008/

CIPD. (2010). Real-world coaching evaluation: A Guide for Practitioners. https://www.google.com/search?sca_esv=14d9d936db00f47b&q=Chartered+Institute+of+Personnel+and+Development+(CIPD)+2010+publication,+%22Real-world+Coaching+Evaluation:+A+Guide+for+Practitioners,%22&spell=1&sa=X&ved=2ahUKEwjinurLzLGMAxXCTaQEHejLLa0QBSgAegQICRAB&biw=1600&bih=739&dpr=2

CIPD. (2023). *'The Importance of a Coaching Framework'.* London: Chartered Institute of Personnel and Development. Available at: https://www.cipd.co.uk/knowledge/strategy/learning-development/coaching-framework

Clarkson, P. (1997). *The Bystander: An End to Innocence in Human Relationships.* London: Whurr Publications.

Clutterbuck, D., & Graves, G. (2024). Team coaching. In: Elaine Cox, Tatiana Bachkirova, & David Clutterbuck (Eds.), *The Complete Handbook of Coaching,* 4th edition. London: Sage.

Clutterbuck, D., & Hodge, A. (2017). *Team Coaching Supervision Survey.* Available at: https://alisonhodge.com/wp-content/uploads/2020/03/team-coaching-supervision-survey-2017.pdf

Clutterbuck, D., & Megginson, D. (2006). *Making Coaching Work: Creating a Coaching Culture.* London: Kogan Page

Clutterbuck, D., Whitaker, C., & Lucas, M. (2016). *Coaching Supervision: A Practical Guide for Supervisees.* London: Routledge.

CoachSource. (2018). *Executive Coaching Research Study 2018.* CoachSource. https://www.emccglobal.org/wp-content/uploads/2018/04/2018-Brian-Underhill-min.pdf

Connor, M., & Pokora, J. (2012). *Coaching and Mentoring at Work: Developing Effective Practice,* 2nd edition. Maidenhead: Open University Press.

Crenshaw, K. (1989). Demarginalizing the intersection of race and sex: A Black feminist critique of antidiscrimination doctrine, feminist theory, and antiracist politics. *University of Chicago Legal Forum, 1989*(1), 139–167.

Crosse, E. (2024). Executive coaches' views on continuous coach development: A Q methodological study. *International Journal of Evidence Based Coaching and Mentoring, 22*(2), 98–114.

Data Protection Act 2018. Available at: www.gov.uk/data-protection [Accessed 9 February 2025].

De Haan, E. (2008). *Relational Coaching: Journeys Towards Mastering One-to-One Learning.* Chichester: Wiley.

De Haan, E. (2012). *Supervision in Action: A Relational Approach to Coaching and Consulting Supervision.* Maidenhead: McGraw-Hill Education.

De Haan, E. (2017). Large-scale survey of trust and safety in coaching supervision: Some evidence that we are doing it right. *International Coaching Psychology Review, 12*(1), 37–48.

De Haan, E., & Nilsson, V. (2023). What can we know about the effectiveness of coaching: A meta analysis based only on randomised controlled trials. *Academy of Management Learning & Education*. https://doi.org/10.5465/amle.2022.0107

De Vries, K. (2019). Moving from frozen code to live vibrant relationship: Towards a philosophy of ethical coaching supervision. In: J. Birch & P. Welch (Eds.), *Coaching Supervision, Advancing Practice, Changing Landscapes*. London: Routledge.

Diller, S., & Passmore, J. (2023). Digital coaching: A qualitative inductive approach. *Frontiers in Psychology, 14*, 1148243. doi:10.3389/fpsyg.2023.1148243

Doyle, N. (2024). *Neurotypes Venn Diagram: Based on the DANDA Chart Work of Mary Colley*. Available at: https://geniuswithin.org/what-is-neurodiversity/

Doyle, N., & Bradley, E. (2023). Disability coaching in a pandemic. *Journal of Work-Applied Management, 15*(1), 135–147. doi:10.1108/JWAM-07-2022-0042

Duff, M., & Passmore, J. (2010). Coaching ethics: A decision-making model. *International Coaching Psychology Review, 5*, 140–151.

EMCC Global. (2019). *Supervision Information Document*. https://www.emccglobal.org/wp-content/uploads/2022/01/EMCC-competences-supervision-EN.pdf [Accessed 22 February 2025].

Fatien Diochon, P., & Nizet, J. (2019). Ethics as a fabric: An emotional, reflexive, sensemaking process. *Business Ethics Quarterly, 29*(4), 461–489.

Feltman, C. (2008). *The Thin Book of Trust: An Essential Primer for Building Trust at Work*. Bend, OR: Thin Book Publishing.

Fletcher, A., & Macann, E. (2011). Balancing act. *Coaching at Work, 6*(1), 30–33.

French, J. R. P. Jr., & Raven, B. (1959). The bases of social power. In: D. Cartwright (Ed.), *Studies in Social Power* (pp. 150–167). Michigan: Univer.

Frisch, M. (2001). The emerging role of the internal coach. *Consulting Psychology Journal: Practice and Research, 53*, 240–250.

Frisch, M. (2005). Extending the reach of executive coaching: The internal coach. *Human Resource Planning, 28*, 23.

Gergen, J. L., & Gergen, M. M. (2001). The R4C4P4 approach to developing ground rules for group supervision. In: M. McMahon & W. Patton (Eds.), *Supervision in the Helping Professions: A Practical Approach* (pp. 147–162). Frenchs Forest, NSW: Pearson Education Australia.

Gettman, H. J., Edinger, S. K., & Wouters, K. (2019). Assessing contracting and the coaching relationship: Necessary infrastructure? *International Journal of Evidence Based Coaching and Mentoring, 17*(1), 46–62.

Gilbert, A., & Whittleworth, K. (2002). *The OSCAR Coaching Model: Simplifying Workplace Coaching*. Monmouth, UK: Worth Consulting Ltd.

Global Code of Ethics. (2021). Retrieved 1 March 2025. www.globalcodeofethics.org

Gormley, H., & van Nieuwerburgh, C. (2014). Developing coaching cultures: A review of the literature. *Coaching: An International Journal of Theory, Research and Practice, 7*(2), 90–101.

Grant, A. M. (2012). ROI is a poor measure of coaching success: Towards a more holistic approach using a well-being and engagement framework. *Coaching: An International Journal of Theory, Research and Practice, 5*(2), 74–85.

Grant, A. M. (2017). The third 'generation' of workplace coaching: Creating a culture of quality conversations. *Coaching: An International Journal of Theory, Research and Practice, 10*(1), 37–53. doi:10.1080/17521882.2016.1266005

Grant, A. M., Passmore, J., Cavanagh, M., & Parker, H. (2010). The state of play in coaching today: A comprehensive review of the field. *International Review of Industrial and Organizational Psychology, 25*. doi:10.1002/9780470661628

Graßmann, C., Scholmerich, F., & Schermuly, C. C. (2020). The relationship between working alliance and client outcomes in coaching: A meta-analysis. *Human Relations, 73*(1), 35–58.

Graves, G. (2021). What do the experiences of team coaches tell us about the essential elements of team coaching? *International Journal of Evidence Based Coaching and Mentoring*, S15, 229–245.

Gray, D. E., Garvey, B., & Lane, D. A. (2016). *A Critical Introduction to Coaching and Mentoring*. London: Sage Publications.

Grover, S., & Furnham, A. (2016). Coaching as a developmental intervention in organisations: A systematic review of its effectiveness and the mechanisms underlying it. *PLoS One, 11*(7), e0159137. doi:10.1371/journal.pone.0159137

Haden, S. (2013). *It's Not About the Coach: Getting the Most from Coaching in Business, Life and Sport*. Winchester, UK: Business Books.

Harter, J. K., Schmidt, F. L., & Keyes, C. L. M. (2003). Well-being in the workplace and its relationship to business outcomes: A review of the Gallup studies. In: C. L. M. Keyes and J. Haidt (Eds.), *Flourishing: Positive Psychology and the Life Well-lived* (pp. 205–224). Washington, DC: American Psychological Association.

Hawkins, P. (2011). Building emotional, ethical and cognitive capacity in coaches – A developmental model of supervision. In: J. Passmore (Ed.), *Supervision in Coaching: Supervision, Ethics and Continuous Professional Development* (pp. 285–307). London: Kogan Page.

Hawkins, P. (2012). *Creating a Coaching Culture*. Maidenhead: Open University Press.

Hawkins, P., & Schwenk, G. (2006). *Coaching Supervision: Maximising the Potential of Coaching*. London: Chartered Institute of Personnel and Development.

Hawkins, P., & Smith, N. (2006). *Coaching, Mentoring and Organizational Consultancy: Supervision and Development*. Maidenhead: McGraw-Hill.

Hawkins, P., & Smith, P. (2013). *Coaching, Mentoring and Organizational Consultancy: Supervision and Development*. Maidenhead: Open University Press/McGraw Hill.

Hawkins, P., & Turner, E. (2017). The rise of coaching supervision 2006–2014. *Coaching: An International Journal of Theory, Research and Practice*, 1–13. doi:10.1080/17521882.2016.1266002

Hawkins, P., & Turner, E. (2020). *Systemic Coaching: Delivering Value Beyond the Individual*. Abingdon: Routledge.

Hicks, B., Carter, A., & Sinclair, A. (2012). *Impact of Coaching: An empirical longitudinal study into coachee well-being, engagement and job satisfaction following a coaching engagement at work*. IES Research Network Research Report, Institute for Employment Studies.

Hodge, A., & Clutterbuck, D. (2019). Guidelines for team coach supervision. In: Jo Birch & Peter Welch (Eds.), *Coaching Supervision: Advancing Practice, Changing Landscapes* (pp. 161–175). Abingdon: Routledge.

Hodge, A. A. (2014). *An action research inquiry into what goes on in coaching supervision to the end of enhancing the coaching profession*. (Unpublished doctoral dissertation). UK: Middlesex University.

Hodge, A. A. (2020). *Mapping the complex territory of team coaching and supervision*. Blog. https://alisonhodge.com/wp-content/uploads/2020/08/mapping-team-coaching-august-20.pdf

Hunt, J., & Weintraub, J. (2006). *Coaching on the Inside: The Internal Coach*. Taken from www.babsoninsight.com

Institute of Leadership & Management (ILM). (2019). *Creating a Coaching Culture*. Available at: https://leadership.global/resourceLibrary/creating-a-coaching-culture-2011.html?utm_

Institute of Leadership & Management (ILM). (2024). 'The critical role of coaching skills in modern organisations', *ILM News and Blog*, 30 September. Available at: https://www.i-l-m.com/news-and-events/news-and-blog/the-critical-role-of-coaching-skills-in-modern-organisations

International Coaching Federation (ICF). (2021). *Covid-19 and the coaching industry.* Retrieved 17 February 2025 from https://coachingfederation.org/app/uploads/2020/09/FINAL_ICF_GCS2020_COVIDStudy.pdf

International Coaching Federation (ICF). (2023). *Insights and Considerations for Ethics.* Available at: https://coachingfederation.org/insights-considerations-for-ethics

Iordanou, I., & Hawley, R. (2020). Ethics in coaching. In J. Passmore (Ed.), *The Coaches' Handbook: The Complete Practitioner Guide for Professional Coaches* (pp. 333–343). Abingdon: Routledge.

Iordanou, I., Hawley, R., & Iordanou, C. (2017). *Values and Ethics in Coaching.* London: Sage.

Isaacson, S. (2021). *How to Thrive as a Coach in a Digital World: Coaching With Technology.* London: McGraw Hill/Open University Press.

Jarosz, J. (2021). The impact of coaching on well-being and performance of managers and their teams during pandemic. *International Journal of Evidence Based Coaching and Mentoring, 19*(1), 4–27.

Jarosz, J. (2023). The cube of coaching effectiveness. *International Journal of Evidence Based Coaching and Mentoring, 21*(1), 31–49. doi:10.24384/gkny-df71

Jarvis, J., Lane, D., & Fillery-Travis, A. (2006). *The Case for Coaching: Making Evidence Based Decisions.* London: CIPD.

Jepson, Z. (2016). An investigation and analysis of the continuous professional development and coaching supervision needs of newly qualified and experienced coaches: A small-scale practitioner-based study. *Coaching: An International Journal of Theory, Research and Practice, 9*(2), 129–142. doi:10.1080/17521882.2016.1210186

Jones, R. J., Woods, S. A., & Guillaume, Y. R. F. (2016). The effectiveness of workplace coaching: A meta-analysis of learning and performance outcomes from coaching. *Journal of Occupational and Organizational Psychology, 89*(2), 249–277. doi:10.1111/joop.12119

Jordan, M., & Henderson, A. (2024). How do internal executive coaches make sense of organisational role boundaries? An interpretative phenomenological analysis study. *International Journal of Evidence Based Coaching and Mentoring, 22*(1), 234–249. doi:10.24384/90k3-5m55

Kadushin, A. (1992). What's wrong, what's right with social work supervision. *The Clinical Supervisor, 10*(1), 3–19.

Kahneman, D. (2011). *Thinking, Fast and Slow.* New York: Farrar, Straus and Giroux.

Kidder, R. (2009). *How Good People Make Tough Choices: Resolving the Dilemmas of Ethical Living.* New York: Harper.

Kirkpatrick, D. L. (1994). *Evaluating Training Programs: The Four Levels.* San Francisco, CA: Berrett-Koehler.

Knowles, M. (1990). *The Adult Learner: A Neglected Species.* Houston: Gulf Publishing Company.

Lane, D. A., & Corrie, S. (2006). *The Modern Scientist-Practitioner: A Guide to Practice in Psychology.* Routledge: London.

Lawley, J., & Tompkins, P. (2000). *Metaphors in Mind: Transformation Through Symbolic Modelling.* London: The Developing Company Press.

Leedham, M. (2005). The coaching scorecard: A holistic approach to evaluating the benefits of business coaching. *International Journal of Evidence Based Coaching and Mentoring, 3*(2), 30–44.

Levenson, A. R., McDermott, M., & Clarke, S. (2004). What coaching can do for your organization … and what it can't. *Centre for Effective Organizations, Marshall School of Business, CEO Publication,* G-04-20 (472). Available at: https://ceo.usc.edu/wp-content/uploads/2004/12/2004_20-g04_20-What_Coaching_Can_Do.pdf?utm_

Lewis, J. J. (2024). Conceptualising how coaching supervisors meet their supervisees' needs: Towards a coaching supervision intervention framework. *International Journal of Evidence Based Coaching and Mentoring, 22*(2), 220–239. doi:10.24384/3wdr-6p52

Long, K. (2012). Building internal supervision capability in organisations. *The OCM Coach and Mentor Journal, 12,* 2–6.

Lovibond, S. H., & Lovibond, P. F. (1995). *Manual for the Depression Anxiety Stress Scales.* Sydney: Psychology Foundation of Australia.

Macann, E. (2012). Reflected glory. *Coaching at Work, 7*(2), 15–17.

Mackintosh, A. (2003). Why the internal company coach has to be strong! *The Coaching and Mentoring Network Resource Centre.* Downloaded from www.coachingnetwork. org.uk

Maclean, A. (2024). Change agent or neutral bystander? An exploration of how the coaching practices of internal coaches in Higher Education Institutions support organisational change. *International Journal of Evidence Based Coaching and Mentoring, 22*(S18), 16–31. https://radar.brookes.ac.uk/radar/items/5fba75af-2d18-4a48-806c-b08f236cc678/1/

Mahon, A. (2002). *Moral Leadership in Business: Towards a New Economy of Virtue.* Frankfurt: Peter Lang.

Maxwell, A. (2011). Supervising the internal coach. In: T. Bachkirova, P. Jackson & D. Clutterbuck. (Eds.), *Coaching & Mentoring Supervision* (pp. 183–185). Maidenhead: Open University Press/McGraw-Hill.

Maxwell, A. (2013). *Conversation With Katharine. St John-Brooks.*

McBain, R., Ghobadian, A., Switzer, J., Wilton, P., Woodman, P., & Pearson, G. (2012). *The Business Benefits of Management and Leadership Development.* London: CMI/Penna.

McDowall, A., & Lai, Y.-L. (2024). Evidence, measurement and evaluation in coaching. In: Elaine Cox, Tatiana Bachkirova, & David Clutterbuck (Eds.), *The Complete Handbook of Coaching,* 4th edition. London: Sage.

McGrath, C. (2024). *In conversation with Julia Duncan, co-author.*

Megginson, D. (2008). Is goal setting the only way to coach? *In view: The Journal from the NHS Institute for senior leaders.* A Special Supplement, April 2008.

Michalik, N. M., & Schermuly, C. C. (2024). Online, offline, or both? The importance of coaching format for side effects in business coaching. *Journal of Managerial Psychology, 39*(6), 775–794. doi:10.1108/JMP-01-2023-0068

Mortlock, S., & Carter, A. (2012). Quality assured. *Coaching at Work, 7*(6), 34–37.

Moyes, B. (2009). Literature review of coaching supervision. *International Coaching Psychology Review, 4,* 160–171.

Mukherjee, S. (2012). Does coaching transform coaches? A case study of internal coaching. *International Journal of Evidence Based Coaching and Mentoring, 10,* 76–87.

Munro-Turner, M. (2011). The three worlds four territories model of supervision. In: T. Bachkirova, P. Jackson, & D. Clutterbuck (Eds.), *Coaching and Mentoring Supervision: Theory and Practice.* Maidenhead: McGraw-Hill/Open University Press.

Myers, I. B., McCaulley, M. H., Quenk, N. L., & Hammer, A. L. (1998). *MBTI Manual: A Guide to the Development and Use of the Myers-Briggs Type Indicator,* 3rd edition. Palo Alto, CA: Consulting Psychologists Press.

Newell, D. (2024). Is your investment in coaching and mentoring fit for purpose? *People Management, May 2024.* www.peoplemanagement.co.uk/article/1871370/investment-coaching-mentoring-fit-purpose

Norman, C. (2024). *Cultivating Coachability: How to Leverage Coaching Readiness so Thinkers can Optimise Value.* Bristol: Right Book Press.

Ockenden, D. (2025). Desert Island Discs, BBC Radio 4, broadcast on 23 March 2025.

Passmore, J. (2009). Coaching ethics: Making ethical decisions – Novices and experts. *The Coaching Psychologist, 5*(1), 6–10.

Passmore, J. (2021). *Future Trends in Coaching – Executive Report.* Henley-on-Thames: Henley Business School and EMCC International.

Passmore, J., & Crabbe, K. (2023). Building a coaching culture: The LEAD framework. *The Coaching Psychologist, 19*(2), 13–23.

Passmore, J., & Shi, Y. D. (2023). What criteria should we use when selecting a coaching provider? In J. Passmore, & S. Isaacson (Eds.), *The Coaching Buyer's Handbook*. London: Libri Publishing.

Passmore, J., & Turner, E. (2018). Reflections on integrity – The APPEAR model. *Coaching at Work*. February 2018. Retrieved on 9 January 2025 from www.coaching-at-work/2018/02/23/reflections-on-integrity-the-appear-model

Patterson, E. (2011). Presence in coaching supervision. In: J. Passmore (Ed.), *Supervision in Coaching: Supervision, Ethics and Continuous Professional Development* (pp. 117–137). London: Kogan Page.

Pedrick, C., & Baldelli, L. (2023). *The Human Behind the Coach*. Great Britain: Practical Inspiration Publishing.

Peltier, B. (2001). *The Psychology of Executive Coaching: Theory and Application*. New York: Brunner-Routledge.

Phillips, J. J. (1997). *Return on Investment in Training and Performance Improvement Programs*. Houston, TX: Gulf Publishing Company.

Plotkina, L., & Sri Ramalu, S. (2024). Unearthing AI coaching chatbots capabilities for professional coaching: A systematic literature review. *Journal of Management Development, 43*(6), 833–848.

Proctor, B. (1986). Supervision: A co-operative exercise in accountability. In: A. Marken & M. Payne (Eds.), *Enabling and Ensuring: Supervision in Practice*. Leicester: National Youth Bureau and Council for Education and Training in Youth and Community Work.

Rawls, J. (1971). *A Theory of Justice*. Cambridge, MA: Harvard University Press.

Rees, C. S., Breen, L. J., Cusack, L., & Hegney, D. (2015). Understanding individual resilience in the workplace: The international collaboration of workforce resilience model. *Frontiers in Psychology 6*, 73. doi:10.3389/fpsyg.2015.00073

Reichheld, F. F. (2006). *The Ultimate Question: Driving Good Profits and True Growth*. Boston, MA: Harvard Business School Press.

Revans, R. W. (1982). *The Origin and Growth of Action Learning*. Brickley, UK: Chartwell-Bratt.

Robinson, D., Perryman, S., & Hayday, S. (2004). *The Drivers of Employee Engagement. IES Report 408*. Brighton: Institute for Employment Studies.

Robson, M. (2016). An ethnographic study of the introduction of internal supervisors to an internal coaching scheme. *International Journal of Evidence Based Coaching and Mentoring 14*(2), 106–122. https://radar.brookes.ac.uk/radar/items/127de0ba-0c3f-435e-a45a-170fbd7f1804/1/

Robson, M. (2020). *Being an internal coach: A study of the experience and its impact on those who took on the role*. Doctoral thesis, York St John University. Downloaded from: http://ray.yorksj.ac.uk/id/eprint/5382/

Rogers, K. M. (2011). Legal considerations in coaching. In: J. Passmore (Ed.), *Supervision in Coaching: Supervision, Ethics and Continuous Professional Development* (pp. 175–189). London: Kogan Page.

Rosefield, M. (2024). Burnout and compassion fatigue in coaches: A case for coach-care. *The Coaching Psychologist, 20*(1). doi:10.53841/bpstcp.2024.20.1.28

Schalk, M., & Landeta, J. (2017). Internal versus external executive coaching. *Coaching: An International Journal of Theory, Research and Practice, 10*(2), 127–143. https://www.tandfonline.com/doi/abs/10.1080/17521882.2017.1310120

Schaufeli, W. B., Bakker, A. B., & Salanova, M. (2006). The measurement of work engagement with a short questionnaire: A cross-national study. *Educational and Psychological Measurement, 66*, 701–716.

Scott, M. (2019). Thinking on your feet: How coaches can use reflection-in-action to develop their coaching craft. *Applied Coaching Research Journal, 4*, 40–47.

Selwyn, (2007). The Use of Computer Technology in University Teaching and Learning: A Critical Perspective *Journal of computer assisted learning.* Wiley Online Library.

Shockley, K. M., Gabriel, A. S., Robertson, D., Rosen, C. C., Chawla, N., Ganster, M. L., & Ezerins, M. E. (2021). The fatiguing effects of camera use in virtual meetings: A within-person field experiment. *Journal of Applied Psychology, 106*(8), 1137–1155. doi:10.1037/apl0000948

Sinclair, V. G., & Wallston, K. A. (2004). The development and psychometric evaluation of the brief resilient coping scale. *Assessment, 11*(1), 94–101. www.ncbi.nlm.nih.gov/pubmed/14994958

Snape, S. (2012). *An evaluation of internal coaching in the UK.* Unpublished Master's dissertation. Henley Business School: Reading University.

Solzhenitsyn, A. (1973). *Gulag Archipelago 1918–1956.* New York: Harper & Row.

Soulsby, R. (2012). Interventions must increase credibility through evidence-based results. *Coaching at Work, 7*(6), 8.

Southwell, C. (2022). *Coaching, Managing, or Mentoring? What's the difference?* Blog. Let's Talk Talent. https://letstalktalent.co.uk/blog/coaching-managing-mentoring-whats-the-difference/

Starr, J. (2011). *The Coaching Manual: The Definitive Guide to the Process, Principles and Skills of Personal Coaching,* 4th edition. Harlow: Pearson.

Steare, R. (2009). *Ethicability (n): How to Decide What's Right and Find the Courage to Do It.* Great Britain: Roger Steare Consulting Ltd.

Steinberg, B. (2020). *Are You Ready to Be Coached?.* Brighton, Massachusetts: Harvard Business School Publishing. Accessed at https://hbsp.harvard.edu/product/H05YF3-PDF-ENG on 1 March 2025.

St John-Brooks, K. (2010). What are the ethical challenges involved in being an internal coach? *International Journal of Mentoring & Coaching, VIII*(I), 50–66.

St John-Brooks, K. (2019). Supervision for internal coaches. In: Jo Birch & Peter Welch (Eds.), *Coaching Supervision: Advancing Practice, Changing Landscapes* (pp. 147–160). Abingdon: Routledge.

St John-Brooks, K., & Isaacson, S. (2024). Internal coaching. In: Elaine Cox, Tatiana Bachkirova, & David Clutterbuck (Eds.), *The Complete Handbook of Coaching,* 4th edition (pp. 300–315). London: Sage.

Stokes, P. (2007). *The Skilled Coachee.* Paper delivered at 14th EMCC Conference in Stockholm, 2007.

Stokes, P., Hill, A., & Kelly, K. (2023). Exploring ethical codes. In: W.-A. Smith, J. Passmore, E. Turner, Y.-L. Lai, & D. Clutterbuck (Eds.), *The Ethical Coaches' Handbook: A Guide to Developing Ethical Maturity in Practice.* London: Routledge. Available at: https://www.taylorfrancis.com/chapters/edit/10.4324/9781003277729-4/exploring-ethical-codes-paul-stokes-angela-hill-kristin-kelly

Tennant, R., Hiller, L., Fishwick, R., Platt, S., Joseph, S., Weich, S., & Stewart-Brown, S. (2007). The Warwick-Edinburgh Mental Well-Being Scale (WEMWBS): Development and UK Validation. *Health and Quality of Life Outcomes, 5,* 63.

Thomson, B. (2011). Non-directive supervision in coaching. In: J. Passmore (Ed.), *Supervision in Coaching: Supervision, Ethics and Continuous Professional Development* (pp. 99–116). London: Kogan Page.

Ting, S., & Scisco, P. (2006). *The CCL Handbook of Coaching: A Guide for the Leader Coach.* San Francisco, CA: Jossey-Bass.

Turner, E. (2012). Confidentiality and CPD opportunities top internal coaches' wish lists. *Coaching at Work, 7*(4), 8.

Turner, E., & Passmore, J. (2018). Ethical dilemmas and tricky decisions: A global perspective of coaching supervisors' practices in coach ethical decision-making. *International Journal of Evidence Based Coaching and Mentoring, 16*(1), 126–142. doi:10.24384/000473

Varkonyi-Sepp, J. (2013). Report: Special Group in Coaching Psychology 8th Annual Conference. *International Coaching Psychology Review, 8*(1), 104–108.

Wasylyshyn, K. (2003). Executive coaching: An outcome study. *Consulting Psychology Journal: Practice & Research, 55,* 94–106.

Watson, D., Clark, L. A., & Tellegen, A. (1988). Development and validation of brief measures of positive and negative affect: The PANAS scales. *Journal of Personality & Social Psychology, 54,* 1063–1070.

Whitmore, J. (1992). *Coaching for Performance: A Practical Guide to Growing Your Own Skills.* London: Nicholas Brealey Publishing.

Whitmore, J. (2002). *Coaching for Performance: The Principles and Practice of Coaching and Leadership; GROW Model,* 3rd edition. London: Nicholas Brealey Publishing.

Williams, P., & Anderson, S. (2006). *Law & Ethics in Coaching* (p. 93). New Jersey: Wiley.

Wilson, C., & McMahon, G. (2006). What's the difference? *Training Journal, September,* 54–57.

Wingrove, A., Lai, Y.-L., Palmer, S., & Williams, S. (2020). Self-determination theory: A theoretical framework for group supervision with internal coaches. *International Journal of Evidence Based Coaching and Mentoring, 18*(2), 183–196. doi:10.24384/jxxd-st61

Wrynne, C. (2011). *How Might the Experience of Internal Coaching Differ From the Experience of External Coaching?* Unpublished Master's dissertation. London South Bank University.

Yedreshteyn, S. (2008). A qualitative investigation of the implementation of an internal executive coaching program in a global corporation, grounded in organizational psychology theory. *Dissertation Abstracts International, 69*(7), 4471B.

Zeus, P., & Skiffington, S. (2002). *The Coaching at Work Toolkit: A Complete Guide to Techniques and Practices.* London: Nicholas Brealey Publishing.

Zimmermann, J., Kotte, S., Diermann, I., & Moller, H. (2023). Supervision of workplace coaching and factors impacting upon it: Insights and open questions from the German-speaking countries. *International Journal of Evidence Based Coaching and Mentoring, 21*(2), 250–267.

Index

For Product Safety Concerns and Information please contact our EU
representative GPSR@taylorandfrancis.com
Taylor & Francis Verlag GmbH, Kaufingerstraße 24, 80331 München, Germany

9 781032 858036